GENEALOGICAL EVIDENCE

[Revised Edition]

A GUIDE TO THE STANDARD OF PROOF RELATING TO PEDIGREES, ANCESTRY, HEIRSHIP AND FAMILY HISTORY

by

NOEL C. STEVENSON, J.D.

Member of The State Bar of California

Fellow of The American Society of Genealogists

First Edition Copyright © 1979 by Noel C. Stevenson

Revised Edition Copyright © 1989 by Noel C. Stevenson

ISBN: 0-89412-159.6 (Soft Cover)

ISBN: 0-89412-160.X (Library Bound)

AEGEAN PARK PRESS

P.O. Box 2837

Laguna Hills, California 92654

(714) 586-8811

Manufactured in The United States of America

INTRODUCTION

For many years there has been a critical necessity for a body of rules for judging the reliability of facts relevant to genealogy, history, and biography. To date, though several attempts have been made in this direction, none have been really satisfactory. Some have not been complete, some have inaccuracies, and others are simply not understandable. Genealogists, historians, and biographers must of necessity resort to the same original recorded sources, whether official or private; and in the past it seems that each of these professionals has adopted his own set of rules for accepting or rejecting evidence or information. This is another way of saying that there are some who believe that the rules of evidence in our legal system and in effect in our court proceedings are too technical and are not completely practical for genealogical, historical, and biographical research. This belief is not valid. Rules of evidence as applied in court proceedings, whether before a judge or jury, are strained to the limit in order to seek truth and to promote justice. This is best expressed by Chief Justice Story in his opinion in the case of Chirac vs. Reinecker (1892) 2 Peters 613, 621:

> It is well known that in cases of pedigree, the rules of law have been relaxed in respect to evidence to an extent far beyond what has been applied to other cases. This relaxation is founded upon principles of public convenience and necessity.

Modernly, judges presiding at trials involving heirship, paternity, and genealogy will often "bend over backwards" to admit evidence or facts when such evidence or facts will contribute to truth and justice. In order to aid the genealogist, as well as the historian and biographer, therefore, the rules of evidence as they relate to genealogy have been explained and simplified in this book for easy understanding. All persons concerned with genealogy must know something regarding the law as it applies to evidence concerning pedigrees, ancestry, heirship, and family history. Likewise, lawyers when representing clients in such matters must be capable of presenting evidence, if necessary, in court proceedings. That is, lawyers must have knowledge of cases, precedents, and authorities for evidence that they may wish to present in proceedings that might, for example, concern heirship, paternity, ancestry, etc. Thus, this book has been written not only for the genealogist, but also for the lawyer.

The decision regarding a dedication for this book is difficult. So many persons have encouraged and aided me during the many years required for the research and writing of the text that it is difficult to dedicate the book to any one person. For instance, I thought of Baron Gilbert, author of one of the first treatises on the law of evidence. Then I realized this would not be fair to my original mentor and friend, the late Donald Lines Jacobus, who during many years encouraged and advised me. So, too, I cannot overlook thanking Milton Rubincam who is responsible for the impetus which caused this book to be written and is the proximate cause for the commencement of this book's research which began in 1944. I am, of course, deeply indebted to the Fellows of The American Society of Genealogists, for their encouragement and suggestions, but limitation of space prevents naming all of them.

However, there are those quoted herein or who have encouraged me or have sent valuable information and suggestions and are entitled to thanks and special credit, namely, John I. Coddington, F.A.S.G., Meredith B. Colket, F.A.S.G., Winston De Ville, F.A.S.G., Winifred Holman Dodge, F.A.S.G., Clarice Fisher, Harry Hollingsworth, C.G., Dr. George E. McCracken, F.A.S.G., E. Kay Kirkham, C.G., Joy W. Moulton, C.G., Nancy L. Parker, C.G., Harold Schwartz, M.D., Walter Lee Sheppard, Jr., F.A.S.G., Robert M. Sherman, F.A.S.G., Kip Sperry, A.G., Betty Wardle, Elizabeth Pearson White, F.A.S.G., and last but not least my patient wife Mary Galton Stevenson without whose aid and inspiration this book would never have been completed. Also the courtesy and cooperation of the staff of the Los Angeles County Law Library has been an invaluable contribution.

I would be remiss if I did not mention Wayne Barker of the Aegean Park Press for his patience and untiring labor incidental to the publication of the volume and thanks to Jane P. McManus, CPS, for typing the manuscript.

NOEL C. STEVENSON

TABLE OF CONTENTS

PART I

GENEALOGICAL HAZARDS, RISKS AND REMEDIES

PART II

RIGHT OF ACCESS TO OFFICIAL AND PUBLIC RECORDS

PART III

PRINCIPAL UNOFFICIAL RECORDS

PART IV

SIMPLIFIED RULES OF EVIDENCE

PART V

GENEALOGICAL — LEGAL TERMINOLOGY

PART I

GENEALOGICAL HAZARDS, RISKS AND REMEDIES

CHAPTER 1

PATERNITY, MATERNITY, LEGITIMACY
AND ILLEGITIMACY

*Truth, like all other good things, may be loved unwisely — may be
pursued too keenly — may cost too much.*[1]

Knight-Bruce, Vice Chancellor

Ego Wilhelmus Cognomine Bastardus.[2]

William the Conqueror

Illegitimacy has never been an uncommon circumstance at any period of
man's history, and the evidence of the parish registers show that sexual morality
in England has not varied much in quality since registers were instituted. All
sorts of terms are used to indicate this condition, but the word "bastard" is not
used so often as its various synonyms; this is as it should be, as the word (of
doubtful etymology) is more properly applied to the "bye blows" of the great than
to the produce of proletarian promiscuity.[3]

William the First was proud to say "I am William the bastard," and the
numerous people around today who claim to be descended from him aren't
bothered at all that they are descended from an illegitimate son. But if a recent
scandal blots the family reputation of the genealogical enthusiast, what genealogist wants to be the bearer of bad news and tell the client his parents or
grandparents were illegitimate? That is when the truth "may cost too much."

What is difficult for a genealogist to explain to a client is the meaning of a
"biological pedigree," which simply means that it is not possible to trace one's
ancestry to an absolute certainty or conclusively. It is doubtful that many (if any)
genealogists discuss this subject with their clients. It is easier to tell the client
that the genealogist will "prove" his/her pedigree by consulting the most reliable
records available, or that the pedigree will be established by "a preponderance or

1

greater weight of the evidence." But that is not conclusive proof.

For societal reasons, the law demands that all children have a father as illegitimacy causes legal complications and is an expense to the government and taxpayers in addition to being an embarrassment to the person and family involved.

THE "FOUR SEAS" RULE

The history of society's concern that all children born to a married couple be legitimate was early expressed by the maxim that if the husband was within the four seas of England (*intra quatuor maria*) which included the Atlantic, the Irish Sea, St. George's Channel, the North Sea, the German Ocean, and the English Channel, the child born by the wife was the legitimate issue of the husband.

This rule has been modified to the extent that if the husband was absent for a period of time that it would be impossible for him to be the father, and this nonaccess could be proven, or if he was proven impotent, then the child would be adjudged illegitimate.

In some jurisdictions this modified rule still exists. For example, Section 621 of the California Evidence Code states that "Notwithstanding any other provision of law, the issue of a wife cohabiting with her husband, who is not impotent, is *conclusively presumed* to be legitimate." [Emphasis added]

In fact, "So strong is the legal presumption of legitimacy, that, in the case of a white woman having a mulatto child, although the husband is also white and the supposed paramour [of the wife] is black, the child is to be presumed legitimate if there was any opportunity for [the husband's] intercourse."[4]

Montesquieu alluding to the presumption of legitimacy said that ". . . the wickedness of mankind makes it necessary for the laws to suppose them better than they really are. Thus we judge that every child conceived in wedlock is legitimate, the law having a confidence in the mother as if she were chastity itself."[5]

The presumption of legitimacy cannot be rebutted by proof of the wife's adultery while cohabiting with her husband.[6]

PATERNITY AND AGE

It would be unusual, but not impossible, for a male under the age of sixteen years to sire a child. Theoretically there is no reason why a man cannot sire children at any age. However, it is advisable to be cautious before accepting a man of great advanced age as the father. It is possible that the father is a younger man by the same name, as a search of all records available may disclose.

There are, however, exceptional cases which negate the caution that males of "great advanced age" are incapable of siring children as mentioned in the preceding paragraph. W. Barton Leach of Harvard Law School refers to these exceptional examples as "The Fertile Octogenarian Cases," because of "The most famous of all cases, stemming from *Jee v. Audley* which holds that in determining [certainty of procreation under the rule against perpetuities], a male is conclusively presumed to be capable of having further children regardless of age or physical condition."[7] Factually this may seem descriptive of the octogenarians' "dream world," but legally due to the conclusive presumption that a husband who is not impotent with access to a wife of child-bearing age would be conclusively presumed to be the father of the wife's child regardless of race, color, religion, or previous condition of servitude — which refers to conditions prior to emancipation from the domination of the husband.

THE STATUS OF THE AVERAGE ILLEGITIMATE

Sir William Blackstone summarized the rights (or lack of them) of illegitimate children thusly, "I proceed next to the rights and incapacities which appertain to a bastard. The rights are very few, being only such as he can acquire, for he can inherit nothing, being looked upon as the son of nobody; and sometimes called *filius nullius*, sometimes *filius populi*. Yet he may gain a sirname [sic] by reputation, though he have none by inheritance."[8]

This is of no assistance to a genealogist. If he selects the maiden name of his mother and there is no evidence in the records of the putative father, and he selects a name at random, this unfortunate ancestor has created a genuine cul de sac.

However, there is a presumption that a man who marries the mother of a child born out of wedlock is the father.[9]

Birth of a Child After Termination of Marriage:

There is a statutory presumption that all children born within the usual period of gestation after wedlock are legitimate and that the legitimacy of a child thus born is the child of the husband and is legitimate.[10]

An actual case illustrates this problem; except for the use of fictitious names, the facts are those before the court. Mr. and Mrs. Doe divorced. After the divorce, Mrs. Doe married Mr. Roe, and after this second marriage, a child was born. Mrs. Roe registered her prior husband, John Doe, as the father of the child. John Doe objected. This is an example which illustrates that the facts stated in a birth certificate may be in error. The mother of the child ought to know the identity of the father, but it is possible she did not know. There is the possibility that Mr. Roe (the new husband) was the father, and there was evidence that some other man was the father of the child. The evidence was so conflicting that the only solution would be blood type tests which were not available at the time of this genealogical mixup, and scientific blood type testing is not always conclusive anyway.[11]

Artificial Insemination:

Although this method of inducing pregnancy is not of modern origin, the system now is more scientific. There is the possibility, although remote, that the biological pedigree has been fractured and that the recognized father was not the biological father at all. But trust the law to come to the assistance of society for the solution of all problems:

> "A child born to a woman as a result of conception through artificial insemination to which her husband has consented in writing, is legitimate if the birth occurs during the marriage or within 300 days after the marriage has been dissolved."[12]

The trouble with this legal provision, modernly and anciently, is that the husband either is not informed, or if he did consent in writing it would be a miracle if the document was found. If found, the name of the biological father is not disclosed.

3

There was an ancient remedy for solving the problem of an alleged pregnancy following termination of a marriage. If a woman after the death of her husband claimed to be pregnant, existing heirs could institute a proceeding entitled a *"Writ De Ventre Inspiciendo."* The widow was required to appear before a jury of matrons who inquired into all the facts of the case. If the jury found that she was pregnant or if they were doubtful, she was placed in custody so that no women or other persons who might be suspected of acting falsely should approach her. No women were permitted to visit her until after she delivered — a precaution to prevent the possibility of a spurious child being substituted or introduced. If after the expiration of forty weeks subsequent to her husband's death, she had not delivered a child, or if she proved not to be pregnant, she was punished by a fine and imprisonment for having unjustly prevented the rightful heir or heirs from inheriting the property of the decedent's estate.[13]

A more complicated biological problem arises when a widow remarries within fifteen days or a month after the death of the husband or within such time that it would be impossible for the child to have been begotten by the second husband. In that case the child should be adjudged the issue of the first husband, notwithstanding it was born during the marriage of the widow and the second husband. Justice Willoughby said "That he had once heard of a case of that kind in which it was ruled that the child might choose which husband he pleased for his father."[14] This solution may be a happy one for the court and the child, but not for genealogists.

The disclosure of illegitimacy in genealogies and family histories do not enhance the popularity of a genealogist. The records of these unfortunate facts are withheld and are not discovered except when original records are searched. That the parish registers are filled with many instances of illegitimacy, the record searcher or genealogist soon learns when perusing the registers over lengthy periods of time. The complications for genealogists increase when it becomes apparent that the problem is massive.

A search of parish registers in London and elsewhere is convincing that this is true, as some examples will disclose:

14 Dec. 1706, Mary supposed daughter of Joseph Pitchford and Ann Warwich. (baptized) (St. Giles in the Fields)[15]

28 May 1590, John, the son of a strumpet born at Ockleys, baptized. (Kington, Worcester)

1 Jan. 1560, Bridget and Elizabeth, the daughters of adultery, baptized. (Chesham)

20 Dec. 1702, Sarah, illeg. child of Hugh Isack's widow by anonymous father, baptized. (Selattyn)[16]

When the facts are insufficient (as some of the above examples are), the optimistic genealogist will hope that in some other parish record source or in some record office elsewhere the required evidence to solve the problem will be discovered.

THE ADULTERINE BASTARD PROBLEM

The euphemistic terminology for the above title is "extra marital children," which should be used if one is sensitive to the legal phraseology. This type of illegitimacy presents a unique, difficult, and complicated problem for genealogists, as there is no adequate solution for determining biological paternity. Genealogists are generally concerned with what occurred in past centuries. In spite of modern scientific tests such as blood typing, polygraph or lie detector testing, or the so-called "truth serums," none of which are 100 percent conclusive, a putative father may be excluded if his blood type is such that he could not be the father of the child. However, courts will not exclude the husband of the mother of the child if he had access to her and is not impotent. Courts do not require conclusive proof of paternity as will be explained herein.

The type of adulterine bastard problem which will cause genealogists the most headaches is the child sired by a man who is not the mother's husband. Due to the conclusive presumption that a child born to a married woman, whose husband has access to her and was not impotent, is the child of the husband. That ruins the possibility of tracing the biological pedigree of the child. There is agitation to change this conclusive presumption of paternity, but genealogists are usually concerned with the past and changing the law will be of no assistance in solving the pedigree problems of previous generations.

There are court decisions which include facts disclosing true biological pedigrees, but the courts ignore this evidence and follow the technical conclusive rule of the law rather than bastardize children.

Societal law, not biological ancestry, must be served. That this is a fact is demonstrated in a dissenting opinion by the late Robert H. Jackson, when he was an associate justice of the United States Supreme Court. Justice Jackson said that one of the intensely practical considerations in support of the Court's majority decision was that:

". . . if the Court does not recognize divorces such as these it will. . . bastardize children of the divorcees. . . . In any event I had supposed that our judicial responsibility is for the regularity of the law, not for the regularity of pedigrees."[17]

Some examples:

William, son of Lord Talbot, per Dutchess of Beaufort, ut asseritur, born Nov. 1st, 1743, bapt. Mar. 24, 1743/4.[18]

In the parish of Halam, Nottinghamshire, between 1774 and 1808, out of 204 baptisms 28 were bastards. That averages one out of seven illegitimates.[19]

There are some impressive records due to the activities of some English kings. Charles II was credited with twelve illegitimate children, but his record is exceeded by Henry I with nineteen "love children."

There are several scholarly articles which discuss statistical and practical possibility of biologically false pedigrees.[20] Every person interested in genealogical research and family history should read the results of the research of these authors.

Conclusion:

Rather than impose a personal and undoubtedly a legalistic opinion on this subject, quotations from outstanding authorities in the genealogical and legal profession are included as a summary of the paternity problem.

Mr. Justice Heath, 1797

"The legitimacy of children depends upon the conduct and behaviour of their parents. The only irresistible proof of legitimacy is, that they have been so treated by their parents. However, there is in the history of mankind proofs to the contrary; that persons have been so wicked, that when they have had no issue of their own, they have adopted others to answer some sinister purpose, but the conduct of parents affords such strong presumptions, that unless their conduct be clearly proved, it ought to prevail; it is that which least can deceive."[21]

Donald Lines Jacobus, F.A.S.G., October, 1961

". . . even proved pedigrees, so far as male lines are concerned, are accepted on faith; faith in the marital fidelity of the wives in the pedigree. It is a factor not often thought of, but worth considering. There must be a percentage of error, however slight, due to this cause. For many reasons, I would guess the percentage to be quite low in colonial days. People lived in small communities and to a large extent everyone knew all about everybody else's business. There was gossip and some of the early court records are full of suits for slander, occasionally involving the morality of a married woman. The divorce rate was low, however, and if we could compile statistics, say for a ten-year period, of the number of births in a certain community and of the number of local husbands who divorced their wives for infidelity during that decade, then we should have some basis for estimating a percentage of children who did not belong to their putative fathers. Even then there would be a rather wide margin of error, since we could not prove that some of the wives were falsely accused, we could not tell how many of the children of a guilty wife were not by her husband, nor could we tell how many husbands were ignorant of a wife's infidelity or merely complacent. Merely to voice an unproved belief, I think that through the colonial period the percentage of children who did not belong to their putative fathers would be quite low."[22]

H. Minot Pitman, LL.B., F.A.S.G., 1961

"What is absolute and irrefutable proof anyway? We assume that a child born in wedlock is a legitimate child, but everyone knows that birth in wedlock does not constitute biological proof of paternity. Is there any class of records that cannot be questioned and that are always absolutely right? I know of none. The vital records of a town or health department of a city or state are usually accepted as satisfactory proof, but they are not always correct. This may be due to errors of recording on the part of the clerk, or to false statements, intentional or not, of the relative furnishing the information."[23]

Donald Lines Jacobus, M.A., F.A.S.G., 1963

"Adulterine bastardy is hard to prove if it was the mother who was adulterous. Unless there was a divorce action with good evidence presented, the child would be presumptively legitimate. A friend of mine had (supposedly) two children, actually neither of them his; he was potent, but infertile. He was still living with his wife when he died . . . and of course the children are accepted as his. I am afraid that genealogy isn't much of a science. Some lines which are 'historically' correct may not be so biologically. . . . Such cases must be fairly numerous, taking the population as a whole. . . . I have my tongue in my cheek when dealing with long lines — 15 or 20 generations."[24]

MATERNITY

Fortunately, maternity isn't the problem paternity presents. It is usually common knowledge as to the identity of the mother, if the birth was witnessed by a physician, a midwife, the husband, a neighbor, or relatives. There were no doubt some instances of baby switching, and in some instances these were intentional. The unintentional substitution of babies is more likely to occur in modern hospitals than births which occurred in the home of the mother. The problem is obviously minimal, but the possibility should not be ignored by genealogists. Also there is the type of fraud which has and does occur occasionally when a mother claims her daughter's illegitimate child as hers.

AGE AND MATERNITY

The child-bearing period is a problem to be carefully considered. There is a question which is often critical in regard to the age of a young mother. A Peruvian case history is unusual.

On May 14, 1939, at the Maternity Hospital in Lima, Peru, a Caesarean section was performed on a young girl, and she was delivered of a six and one-half pound baby. According to an official birth certificate the mother was born on September 23, 1933. Her parents insisted that the correct date was September 24, 1934. Doctors who examined the girl to determine her age on the basis of physical development came to various conclusions ranging between five and nine years. The case is fully discussed in a report presented to the Academy of Medicine at Lima and published in *La Reform.1 Medica*, No. 306, Lima, Peru, May 1, 1939.[25]

In regard to the upper age limit, there is a reliable record in England of a mother bearing a child when she was almost 54 years of age, and an unproven claim of a woman in the U.S. who believed she was 59 when the child was born. If a record discloses the mother was 45 or older at the time of the birth of the child, additional research to ascertain if there is a mistake in the age is advisable. No doubt there are births of children to women over 45 years of age, but these events are exceptions to the general rule.

SPACING OF CHILDREN

During colonial times and later, the number of years between births of children was shorter during the first years of marriage and longer as the parents aged. At first the spacing might be less than two years, and then every two years, and then one child every three years. If there is a gap during the early years of marriage of four or five years, it is advisable to search the records for a missing child in whatever records are available, and the child may be disclosed in the last will and testament of the father or mother.

Presumably if a girl married at age eighteen and bore a child every two years, theoretically she would bear sixteen children, if the last child was born when she was age fifty. This would be a rare example, unless there were twins or triplets born to the active couple.

Matthew and Rhoda Blakeslee of New Haven, Connecticut, set a record when their fifteenth child which they named "Careful" was born on 4 May 1764.[26] They were married when Rhoda was one month under age 16; their first child was born nine months and 16 days later. Their last child "Careful" was born about 27 years later when Rhoda was approximately 44 years of age. They did not produce any multiple births, therefore, Matthew and Rhoda's record is one child born on an average of less than two years apart.

A remarkable record for child-bearing is disclosed by the parish registers of Monks Kirby, Warwickshire, which disclosed that when Elizabeth Mott died in 1720, she had been married forty-four years and was the mother of forty-two children. The epitaph on her tombstone reads:

> A loving wife, a tender mother
> Scarce left behind her such another.[27]

PROOF OF MATERNITY

As indicated, there is no problem establishing the identity of the mother of a child by those present *at the time the child is delivered*, if there are witnesses present. But an identification problem does arise at a later date. Assume a hypothetical case of identity when the child has arrived at the age of twenty-one. Assume additionally that this is at a time when fingerprints, footprints, and blood types were not used for identification, but the child was delivered by a physician. The mother is now deceased, but the physician is living. Assume also that the child whom we shall name "John Jones," has filed a petition to establish his identity in the proper court and his counsel has subpoenaed the physician to testify. After the usual preliminaries incidental to testifying, oath, name, profession, address, etc., the hypothetical testimony begins.

Q. Dr. Smith are you a licensed physician?
A. Yes I am.
Q. On or about November 3, 1851, did you deliver a male child to a Mrs. Sarah Jones?
A. I have examined my records and they disclosed that I delivered a male child to a Mrs. Sarah Jones.
Q. Was anything done or said at that time?
A. Yes, the child was christened "John," by a clergyman, which fact I noted in my record of his birth.
Q. Do you see this "John Jones" in this courtroom?
A. No, I would be unable to identify him after twenty-one years.

[Up to this point, John Jones is out of luck, but his counsel is extremely competent.]

Q. Do you have the medical records you mentioned with you?
A. Yes, I do.
Q. When did you record the information regarding John Jones?
A. Within one hour after the delivery of the child.
Q. Did you examine the child to ascertain if he was a normal child without any abnormalities?
A. Yes, and there were no congenital defects detectable.

Q. Please examine your records and tell the court what else, if anything, you wrote concerning this child.

A. I am reading now from the entry dated November 3rd, 1851, in regard to John Jones. In addition weight, height, and the usual medical data I always recorded is this entry: "Visible on the left buttock, is a star-shaped birthmark, reddish-brown in color." Due to the fact that I have never seen a birthmark of this shape before, I drew a sketch of it in my record book.

This is a happy ending for John Jones; the physician's record book is admitted into evidence. Dr. Smith examines Jones (outside the presence of the courtroom), compares his medical sketch with the birthmark on Jones' buttock, returns to the courtroom and testifies that in his opinion the baby he delivered on November 3, 1851, is the same person in the courtroom named John Jones. There is a possibility of another person with the same type of birthmark, but it is one chance in millions. The court grants Jones' petition (or the jury returns a verdict in his favor, if it was a jury trial) because due to the testimony of Dr. Smith, Jones established his case by a preponderance or greater weight of the evidence.

Conclusion:

The maternity of a child is rarely questioned.

Notes and References

1. *Pearse v. Pearse* (1846) 1 DeGe & Smale Reports 12, 28.
2. Bradbrook, William, M.R.C.S., *The Parish Register*, London 1910, p. 34.
3. Ibid.
4. *Piers v. Piers* (1849) 13 Jurist, 569, 572.
5. *3 Ruling Case Law* 726, 1914, 1929.
6. *Sullivan v. Kelly* (1861) 85 Massachusetts Court Reports 148.
7. *Jee v. Audley* (1787) 29 English Reports, 1186 cited by W. Barton Leach in "Perpetuities in Perspective: Ending the Rules Reign of Terror," 65 Harvard Law Review, 721, 732-734.
8. Blackstone's Commentaries, Vol. 1, p. 459.
9. 10 Corpus Juris Secundum 17, West Publishing Company, St. Paul.
10. Ibid, p. 25.
11. [Title of court decision withheld.]
12. Section 216, California Civil Code (1969).
13. Nicolas, Sir Harris, A Treatise on the Law of Adulterine Bastardy. . ., London 1836, pp. 34-35.
14. Ibid.
15. St. Giles in the Fields, Parish Register, London.

16. Bradbrook, William, M.R.C.S., *The Parish Register*, London 1910, pp. 35-36.

17. *Williams v. North Carolina* (1942) 317 United States Supreme Court Reports 287, 324.

18. Ibid, n. 16, p. 35.

19. Tate, W.E., F.R.H.S., *The Parish Chest*, Cambridge University Press, 1946, p. 296.

20. Gebhard, Paul H.; Pomeroy, Wardell B.; Martin, Clyde E.; and Christenson, Cornelia V., of the Institute for Sex Research, Inc., founded by Alfred C. Kinsey, Indiana University, Bloomington [1958]. Chapter 4 is the result of a survey regarding Extra-Marital Conception, pp. 83, et seq.
    Roderick, Thomas H., Ph.D., Roscoe B. Jackson Memorial Laboratory, Bar Harbor, Maine, "Estimations of the Percentage of Genetically False Pedigrees," *The American Genealogist*, Vol. 37, October 1961, pp. 241-243.
    Terasaki, Paul I, et al: "Twins with Two Different Fathers Identified By HLA," *The New England Journal of Medicine*, September 14, 1978, pp. 590-592. [HLA is an acronym for Human Leukocyte Antigen, a scientific test which may include or exclude a reputed father of a child or children.] Dr. Terasaki is a professor of surgery at the School of Medicine, University of California at Los Angeles. Dr. Terasaki has also written an article on this subject which was published in the *Journal of Family Law*, Vol. 16, pp. 543-55, 1977-78.

21. Nicolas, Sir Harris, *A Treatise on Adulterine Bastardy*, . . . London 1836, p. 141, quoting Mr. Justice Heath's opinion in *Day v. Day*, 3rd edition, p. 318.

22. Jacobus, Donald Lines, *The American Genealogist*, Vol. 37, October 1961, p. 245.

23. Pitman, H. Minot, LL.B., F.A.S.G., "Genealogical Proof," *The American Genealogist*, Vol. 37, October 1961, p. 193.

24. Letter signed by Donald Lines Jacobus (partially quoted) to the author, dated June 5, 1964.

25. Leach, W. Barton, "Perpetuities in Perspective: Ending the Rules Reign of Terror," 65 Harvard Law Review 721, 732-34, note 25, March 1952.

26. New Haven Connecticut, Vital Records, *New Haven Genealogical Magazine*, [predecessor of *The American Genealogist*], Vol. 1, pp. 220, 212-213.

27. *This England*, Cheltenham, Gloucestershire, England, Spring 1976, p. 52.

CHAPTER 2

THE IDENTITY PROBLEM

True identity is collected from a multitude of signs.[1]
Sir Francis Bacon

In every question of pedigree as is well known to genealogists, one of the greatest difficulties is the proving of identity of persons of the same name belonging to a particular line. . . [2]
J. P. Earwaker, M.A., F.S.A.

What is the meaning of "identity," within the meaning of genealogical research? A leading court decision defines this word in clear and simple language, stating that it is "The proving that a person, subject, or article before the court is the very same that he or it is alleged."[3]

Actually ascertaining true identification is not that simple, as a true case history amply illustrates, as reported in a newspaper account in 1855:

"A melodrama has recently been enacted in St. Albans, Vermont, which may be denominated 'A Husband For A Day.' A short time ago, a lady whose husband has been in California about five years was agreeably surprised by the unexpected return of her better half as she supposed. He wore a heavy beard and moustache, and was familiar with many incidents of their early life, and so fully established himself in the capacity of her husband that he passed an agreeable day in her company, and obtained possession of some $300 previously remitted for her use. The happy pair were receiving the congratulations of their neighbors during the next day, when, lo! and behold, the joy of the lady was suddenly changed to bitterness by one who had recently returned from the gold region, and who proved to her satisfaction that the would-be husband was nothing more or less than a good imitation of the genuine article — bearing the same form and features, and having been an intimate friend of the true one. The marital impostor has been arrested and now awaits his examination for (so the indictment reads) 'assault and battery.' " (*Santa Barbara* [California] *Gazette*, June 28, 1855, page 1, column 5)

It is a difficult problem to establish the identity of living persons as current court proceedings disclose. Because genealogists are usually concerned with the identity of persons who lived in the past, and the only means of identity are names, places, dates, and relationships which are discovered in various publications, manuscripts, official records, and possibly information from living persons who possess personal knowledge of the family genealogy and history, a genealogist is burdened with great responsibility because of this identity problem.

A competent genealogist will not assume a person with the same or similar name is the same person mentioned in a book, manuscript, document, official records, or any other record source merely because of the similarity of names — even when the name or names are extremely unusual, as similarity of names in any case is a snare and a delusion if accepted without intensive research in every possible source.

A qualified genealogist will obtain all of the facts possible, analyze and judge them carefully, and then and only then, weigh all of the evidence before deciding the crucial problem and accept or reject the facts.

Consider the case of the following neophyte genealogist who wishes to trace his own ancestry. He has obtained almost complete information about his own parents and lesser information about his grandparents. He at least, however, has learned where his parents believe their ancestors lived before coming to California during the Gold Rush.

Assume that during an interview with his father, the latter tells what he knows concerning his ancestry:

"My grandfather was David Martin. He lived in Vermont. No, I don't know the date of his birth, or the name of the town or county. My father told me this years ago. That is *all* I know about the family, except in the 1800s my father, John Martin, who I suppose was born in Vermont came to California about 1850 to look for gold."

The genealogist now has traced his ancestry to his great-grandfather, David Martin, who lived in Vermont. With this information received from his family, which may or may not be correct, the genealogist feels he is now ready to begin his research.

The genealogist hurries to the local genealogical library to discover if there is anything in print about his family. He eagerly consults the card catalogue and discovers that the *Martin Genealogy* compiled by Thomas Arthur Hay was published in 1911. In consulting the index, to his dismay, he finds fifteen different persons with the name of David Martin. Which, if any of them, can he accept as his own ancestor David Martin? The answer, of course, is none of them. Unfortunately, the genealogist has an identification problem. Very simply, he does not possess sufficient identifying information to identify a particular David Martin as his ancestor. What the genealogist needs are place, dates of birth, marriage, death, and at least the names of the brothers and sisters (if any) of his ancestor David Martin to aid him in the identification process. He must continue his research in record sources in California, Vermont, federal records, and in the National Archives, not necessarily in that order. He will interview other members of the family. By process of elimination he may discover that one of the fifteen David Martins in the *Martin Genealogy* is his ancestor.

Assume the genealogist was told during the interview, above, that the grandfather David Martin was born in 1789 in Bennington, Vermont. In all probability, there was more than one David Martin born in that year and place. He cannot assume otherwise, so he still has an identification problem. Therefore, he must continue research in every possible source until he discovers substantial evidence to identify the right David Martin, or until he or his money supply is exhausted.

How often are the personal facts of people so identical that it is almost impossible to identify them? More often than is realized, as a few examples will disclose.

At a New York hospital a few years ago, Mrs. Richard Roe gave birth to a daughter on two successive days. The infants were not twins. The mothers were two different Mrs. Richard Roes. The two women were not related and did not know each other. To add to the confusion, the birth certificates of the children disclosed their fathers' names as Richard Roe. Both men were in military service, and to additionally confuse everybody, the names of the paternal grandfathers of these infants were the same, John Roe (true names withheld).

Similarity of name, even unusual names, such as "Xenocrates Y. Zzyzz," does not justify a genealogist to assume that another person by that name does not or did not exist.

Courts have expounded on this same principle in many appellate decisions. In a Pennsylvania case, a controversy arose over the right of various claimants to inherit the Link estate, which involved a considerable sum of money. In order for the claimants or any of them to inherit the estate, it was necessary for them to establish a genealogical relationship to John Link who emigrated from Bavaria to Pennsylvania. The crucial question was what part of Bavaria he came from.

The court's opinion of the evidence offered by the claimants' attempt to establish their right to inherit is revelatory of the problems which arise in many identity situations in genealogy. The court stated that:

> There is not a word of reliable testimony in this case to show from
> which one of the innumerable towns of the large political division of
> Germany known as Bavaria, John Link of Ross Township came.[4]

The court emphasized that similarity of names and isolated facts are not sufficient identification to establish ancestry as the court stated in its decision:

> The name "Link" is quite common. One can scarcely pick up a
> directory in a town of any size but that the name appears, therefore
> identity of names would not be helpful. Identity of names, religion,
> and nativity alone are insufficient to evidence family connection. The
> evidence to sustain relationship must bear on every material feature
> necessary to support a finding of kinship. It must be grounded on a
> reasonable certainty and come from witnesses [or reliable documents]
> whose truth and candor are not questioned.[5]

It is sheer folly to believe that because a surname is uncommon in your locality, that it is uncommon in a distant city. An example of this erroneous belief is illustrated by the fact that the central section of the Los Angeles telephone directory does not disclose anyone by the name of Tremblay. Some years ago on a visit to the Province of Quebec, Canada, in a village of 700 families, there were 300 persons by the name of Tremblay.

But these examples are not unique. The surname "Hunkin" is not included in Bardsley's *Dictionary of English and Welsh Surnames*, so it would seem unusual. It isn't listed in the central section of the Los Angeles telephone directory either, and this is surprising as this sprawling and populous city is noted as a place where people come to live from all over the world. Then one day there was a news item in a California newspaper:

Jim Hunkin of Mevagissey in Cornwall, England, threw a life preserver to Jim Hunkin (no relation) who had jumped into the water to save Jim Hunkin (no relation) who had fallen out of his rowboat.

However, the name is not missing in the Plymouth, Cornwall telephone directory which includes Mevagissey. There are thirty listings of persons by the name of Hunkin.

It isn't safe to assume that similarity of name, or the same name is sufficient to assume a relationship.

An interesting case involving identity and the evidence introduced to establish the identity of two men named John Hardy was heard by the United States Supreme Court in 1874. This question of identity was whether the John Hardy, a native of Canada, who left there in 1831 and came to California, was the same John Hardy who was the grantee of the Rancho Rio de Jesus Maria in Yolo County, California.

The evidence produced, which enabled the court to decide which one was which, was this: One John Hardy was "silent, reserved, and ungracious in his manners . . . frequently drunk and fond of the society of loose women." The other John Hardy was of "social disposition, genial, agreeable of good habits and good moral character."[6]

The problem of identification is critically complicated if similarities in addition to names are involved, as an actual case will illustrate.

Two men both named John A. Mason, unknown to each other, came to California in search of health and wealth during the Gold Rush of 1849. Both of them were wagon makers, their places of business were in the same block in Sacramento. Both of them left their respective wives at home in the East. Both had two children. Both of them failed to communicate with their families for twenty years.

After the death of both John A. Masons, the widow of one of them, who lived in Boston, learned that the estate of a John A. Mason (whom she assumed was her lost husband) was in the process of probate in Sacramento. A photograph of this John A. Mason was identified by twenty witnesses as her husband.

In the meantime, another widow from Illinois appeared on the scene and proved that this deceased John A. Mason was her husband and that she was entitled to all of the estate.

Later developments proved that the John A. Mason from Boston, died alone and friendless.[7]

IDENTIFICATION OF PRE-AMERICAN ANCESTORS

An interesting and yet difficult identification problem occurs when genealogists attempt to bridge the Atlantic and attempt to identify the family o the ancestors who emigrated from European countries to the New World. If the ancestors in the colonies did not disclose in some type of record where they came from, when and where they were born or baptized, or the names of their parents and their place of residence, nothing short of a miracle will cause it to be possible to trace their ancestry in their former homeland.

If the ancestors in the European or other country corresponded with the family in the colonies (or vice versa), and the correspondence was preserved disclosing genealogical data, identification may be effected.

Some families did preserve their ties with their families who remained in the homeland across the ocean, by correspondence or settlement of estates or legal matters; or they recorded the genealogical identification on the fly leaves of a book or family Bible, or at a later date on Bible record forms usually inserted between the Old and New Testaments.

Lawsuits for various causes of action sometimes commenced overseas disclosed genealogical data both here and in the foreign country. However, the most valuable source occurred when the estate of an overseas family was probated and the descendants in the colonies were legatees or devisees of a portion of the estate of the ancestor who did not emigrate, disclosing some genealogical data. In some instances the information is insufficient to identify the descendant in the colony and in other instances considerable genealogical details are disclosed.

A hypothetical case history will illustrate one type of the pre-American ancestry problem:

In one of the record offices in England, our hypothetical genealogist (the English counterpart) discovers the last will and testament of John Smith, of St. Giles in the Fields, London, England. The will is dated 11 August 1789. In the will is this recital: "I give to my son John Smith of Massachusetts in New England, the sum of ten pounds." There are no other clues in the records there. (All names, dates, and places are fictitious.)

The genealogist in the United States with some misgiving consults the U.S. 1790 Census for Massachusetts and is not surprised to find listed in that volume no less than sixty-one persons by the name of John Smith.

The identification is zero. But why not search the parish registers of St. Giles in the Fields? There are several problems involved. We don't know the exact year of birth or baptism of the John Smith in Massachusetts, and the number of John Smith baptisms in any one year is overwhelming.

THE CASE OF ROBERT WALKER OF BOSTON, MASSACHUSETTS

In the *New England Historical & Genealogical Register*, Volume 7, page 46, published in 1853, there is printed a document which purports to be a deposition dated 10 April 1679, of Robert Walker of Boston. He stated that he was a "Linnen Webster," aged 72 years. That about 56 years ago he was living with his father [not named] in the Town of Manchester, Lancashire, England. The purpose of the deposition was to aid Henry Sewall of Newberry to identify himself. Robert Walker and the Sewalls were "overthwart" neighbours 56 years prior to 1679. Robert Walker stated that Henry Sewall's father was Henry Sewall, but Robert Walker didn't bother to disclose the name of his father.

Anyone interested in the ancestry of Robert Walker will notice several important clues. No doubt the most important one is that he stated he was 72 years of age in 1679, therefore, his approximate date of birth was 1607.

The Manchester Cathedral Registers disclose that on 21 February 1607/08 a Robert Walker, son of Thomas Walker of Ardwick, was baptized.

Query: Is this Robert Walker the same Robert Walker who signed the deposition in 1679 in Boston? The answer to that question is "probably," but in my opinion his identity is not established by a preponderance or greater weight of the evidence. There are a number of reasons. The date of baptism is not always the same as the date of birth. Usually the baptism follows the birth within a few days, but there are exceptions. For example the lapse of time might be weeks or months or even years. This would be unusual in this case. Also, Robert Walker did not state any facts regarding his birth or baptism. A competent genealogist would not assume he was born or baptized in Manchester. Furthermore, we are only able to arrive at his approximate date of birth from his age unless he accurately states the number of years, months, and days.

Anyone interested in pre-American ancestry should read an article on this subject by an eminent authority, John I. Coddington, a competent genealogist and Fellow of the American Society of Genealogists. Mr. Coddington's discussion of Robert Walker's parentage was published in *The American Genealogist*, Volume 21, No. 1, July 1944, page 58 et seq., and anyone seriously interested in analyzing the identity of ancestors should read this classic.

Genealogists are the beneficiaries of the exhaustive research conducted by Henry F. Waters in the English archives commencing in 1883. Two large volumes representing much of his work have been published and are entitled *Genealogical Gleanings in England*. His principal research was searching probate records for a period of years when it was anticipated that ancestors in England would mention their descendants in the colonies. An examination of the results of his research as disclosed in the above mentioned volumes is extremely impressive.

Because the identification problem is so critical in tracing ancestors in the colonies and connecting them with their forebears in England, Waters' volumes are an important source to use for the identification process. Nobody represents that his volumes are perfect or complete or that they are a substitute for original research in England, but Waters must be searched in any serious quest for pre-American ancestry of colonists. If a document is relevant to the search, it is advisable to send for a copy of the original.

An example of the type of acceptable identifying information often disclosed in Waters' *Genealogical Gleanings in England* is disclosed in the will of Elizabeth Fawkner, County of Surrey, dated 4 June 1720: "I give and bequeath unto such the children or grandchildren of my uncles Edward Bulkley, Peter Bulkley, and Gersham Bulkley of New England as shall be living at the time of my decease the sum of five hundred pounds sterling."[8]

The information in this will is sufficient to identify the legatees in Massachusetts, or anywhere else in New England.[9]

A QUADRUPLE CASE OF ANCESTRAL MISIDENTIFICATION

The possibility of misidentification of ancestors is amply illustrated by researchers who were tracing the English ancestry of President John Adams. In 1925, J. Gardner Bartlett, one of the foremost specialists on English research wrote an article entitled "The English Home of Henry Adams of Braintree, Massachusetts," in which Mr. Bartlett stated that:

"During the past hundred years at least four erroneous claims have been made about the English home [and ancestry] of the well-known Adams family of Braintree, Massachusetts.

"In 1823 President John[5] Adams (John[4], Joseph[3], Joseph[2], Henry[1]) erected a monument in Quincy to Henry[1] Adams, his immigrant ancestor, the inscription stating that he 'took flight from the Dragon Persecution in Devonshire in England.'

"In 1853 a long pedigree purporting to exist in an original manuscript in England was printed in the *Register*, which set forth that Henry Adams was descended from a landed Adams family of Fenn and Waton in Stoke-Gabriel co. Devon, which it was claimed, was derived from the baronial family of Ap Adam of Tidenham and Beverstone co. Gloucester. The late Colonel Chester and others showed this pedigree to be a worthless forgery [References cited].

"Because Braintree, Massachusetts, was named for the parish of Braintree, co. Essex, England, the late Charles Francis Adams, about 1900, conjectured that Henry Adams might have come from Essex, and a Henry Adams was located near Chelmsford in that county who seemed to him to be, possibly, the emigrant to New England, but this supposition was certainly erroneous.

"In November 1923, the Sulgrave Institution publicly announced the purchase of an old farm cottage at Flore in Northamptonshire as the ancestral home of Henry Adams. The Institution was led into this unfortunate blunder by the misrepresentations of two English journalists, who had no knowledge of the Adams family. After a year of protest by the writer [Mr. Bartlett] and other persons who knew the true origin of Henry Adams, in Feb. 1925, the Sulgrave Institution, in syndicated newspaper articles, acknowledged its error, repudiated this Flore cottage as an Adams shrine, and directed it be sold.

"Henry[1] Adams, the founder of the Braintree family, was born about 1583 at Barton St. David co. Somerset. At least four generations of his ancestors resided there, and the Adams name is found on records in the immediate vicinity of that parish as far back as 1327. The Sulgrave Institution now intends to erect at Barton St. David a memorial to the Adams family and also to publish a correct account, compiled by [Mr. Bartlett] of the ancestry of Henry Adams." (*New England Historical and Genealogical Register*, Volume 79, page 217.)

PRE-AMERICAN ANCESTRY: PRECAUTIONARY RESEARCH

Beginning on page 30 of *Search and Research* (1977 edition) is a listing entitled "Reference Books: Pre-American Ancestry." It must be stressed that such a listing is for reference purposes only, and any clues included in these printed books are subject to verification.

Listed among these reference books is Banks, Charles Edward, *Topographical Dictionary of 2885 English Emigrants to New England, 1620-1650*. This book was compiled from Col. Banks' manuscripts in the Library of Congress and edited, indexed, and published by Elijah Ellsworth Brownell in 1937. It is risky to rely on the manuscript collections of a genealogist, as such an unpublished source would no doubt include many changes the compiler, such as Col. Banks would have effected if he had published the book instead of Brownell. Therefore, any genealogical data in this book is subject to verification, as the information published in it amounts to clues only, some of them erroneous. For detailed review of Col. Banks' manuscript collections, refer to "The Banks Manuscripts in the Library of Congress," by Milton Rubincam, F.A.S.G., *National Genealogical Society Quarterly*, Volume 33, pages 7-10, and specifically comments regarding Brownell's publication of Banks' *Topographical Dictionary* . . . on page 9.

Another source to beware of is included in Volume VII of the Virkus' *Compendium of American Genealogy* beginning on page 825 . . . *A list of 2500 Immigrants to America Before 1750.* This list was reprinted in a paperback edition in 1972, and in a book review of this opus, in *The American Genealogist*, Vol. 49, page 61, January 1973, it is stated "This is a reprint of the list in Vol. VII of Virkus' *Compendium of American Genealogy* and is chockfull of errors. The list should not have been reprinted any more than the work in which it was first published should have seen the light of day."

It isn't feasible to include all commercial genealogical publications of the character of the Virkus volumes, but there are two more of a similar nature which should be mentioned:

Mackenzie, George Norbury (ed), *Colonial Families of the United States of America*, New York (1907-1920), 7 volumes. In these volumes there is no indication of independent and critical research. There are many coats of arms and nothing except similarity of name to connect the arms with the families represented in the volumes.

Joel Munsell's Sons, *American Ancestry: Giving the Name and Descent in the Male Line of Americans Whose Ancestors Settled in the United States Previous to the Declaration of Independence, A.D. 1776*, Albany (1887-1899), 12 volumes. The publisher included information sent by individuals on forms provided for that purpose which did not provide for or request the sources of the genealogical data submitted to the publisher. Copies of these volumes were offered for sale to the public sending in their genealogical data and to others.

AGE AND IDENTITY

Advanced age of persons living or at time of death is often a difficult problem for genealogists.

"My grandfather was 114 years of age when he died. I have the proof," the relative tells you; or the same information is imparted to you in a genealogy or local history. It pays to be a skeptic. When the birth record in a family Bible, age in a census record, or baptismal certificate is involved, there is always the problem of deciding if the person mentioned in the records is the same person who died at age 114 years. Often these claims of advanced age are honest mistakes. Family Bible or other private records may intentionally misstate the age for a number of reasons. Dates may be changed to show that children were born after marriage. An old family Bible with blank record forms was sometimes used to falsify age to avoid military service — be suspect of family records written in pencil. People who engage in such practices are smart enough to find a Bible published in a year prior to the date of birth so the facts don't conflict.

With or without birth records, it isn't difficult for any person who so desires to falsify his or her age. A search of the old census or other records will always disclose a person with the same name, long since dead, and there is nothing to stop an individual desiring to appear older to adopt that record.

Beginning with somewhat complete registration of vital records has provided dishonest individuals with a means of not only changing their age, but also changing their identities. All that is required is to walk through a cemetery and find a gravestone of a person born on a date suitable to the seeker's need. If the place of birth is stated, or through other means the place of birth can be ascertained, such as on the subject's death certificate, persons in desperate need of a birth certificate simply go to the Bureau of Vital Statistics and obtain a certified copy of his "new" birth record. Nobody checks the death records or gravestone to ascertain that the child died at an early age. If there are living relatives of the deceased child, they are not notified, and it would be a miracle if they learned of the issuance of the birth certificate to a person who had no right to it. Therefore, there is nothing to stop conniving persons from obtaining the deceased child's birth certificate, assuming a new identity, using it to obtain a passport or for any number of illegal purposes. The only means to stop this ghoulish practice is to enter on all birth certificates the date the individual died. There is a legislative trend to require insertion of dates of death on birth certificates. For example, California has enacted a statute requiring registrars of vital statistics to do so. (California Statutes 1977, Chapter 1012, pages 3153-4). Unfortunately, legislation enacted at this late date will not prevent the past and some future fraudulent acts of dishonest persons.

LONGEVITY AND IDENTITY

Old age is often considered an honor. Soldiers, and the oldest residents of the city or town, receive special attention. This does encourage people to misstate their age, and when it is done often enough, it is even believed by the oldster. That this is not a fictional idea is evidenced by an article written by Zhores A. Medvedev, M.D. Dr. Medvedev's article is based on medical case histories and the essence of it is that elderly people who claim to be of exceptional old age of over 110 years are not to be believed. Physical examinations of living individuals claiming great age, and autopsies on the bodies of deceased persons disclosed that physical signs indicated they were much younger than claimed.[10]

Without denying the possibility of centenarians, the alleged cases of very advanced age are exceptional enough now to excuse an attitude of incredulity until proof [of age] is forthcoming.[11]

REPUTED CENTENARIANS

Many English parish registers contain an entry of the burial of a reputed centenarian, some registers contain several. All may be regarded as more than doubtful, as corroborative evidence is invariably wanting. In times when we know that the average duration of life was less than it is now, any old person who had outlived his contemporaries would be regarded by younger persons as older than he really was, and would be exceedingly apt to exaggerate his years in response to a demand for antiquity, and just as easily credited by those who wished to believe.[12]

In times, also, when parents not infrequently gave the same name to more than one child, the death of the elder would facilitate a claim by a younger to be considered his own elder brother. Mistaken identity may account for some reputed centenarians. Age was seldom recorded in a register unless it was advanced, and doubt was occasionally expressed.[13]

Some examples from parish registers support the evidence that the age of centenarians is often exaggerated:

> 1687. Nov. 8th Elizabeth Evans, widow, aged above 100 (ut computator) bur. [Harley Parish]
> 1718. Ellinor Ashpole, aged 120, bur. Jan. 11th [Little Brickhill]
> 1787. John Wood, of Farnham, Dec. 16th. 102-1/2 years, bur. [Farnham]

In the baptismal portion of the Farnham parish register, there are these entries:

> 1687. John, son of John Wood, bapt. Oct. 16th.
> 1697. John, son of William Wood, bapt. April 18th.

If the John Wood buried in 1787 was the person baptized in 1687, then he was 100, not 102-1/2 years of age, but he is just as likely to be the John Wood baptized ten years later in 1697, and his correct age at death would be 90 years.[14]

That there was doubt regarding advanced ages is evidenced by this entry in the Glasbury register:

> 1698. Charles —— of Pipton, aged 114, as common fame reports.[15]

If the examples quoted can be regarded as specimens of accuracy where verification of a sort seems possible, what sort of error may we expect where no supporting evidence can be found?[16]

IDENTIFICATION AND VARIATIONS IN SPELLING OF NAMES

Mere differences in spelling do not produce a different name. In the 16th century, and even much later, the number of letters a person included in his name was as much a matter of taste and choice as the number of flourishes added to the completed signature. The addition or subtraction of the final "e" about which so many moderns are punctilious, does not create a different name, e.g., Smyth(e), Green(e), Clark(e), Brown(e).[17]

Though referring to one and the same man or family, the following variants are found in the Stratford-on-Avon register: Shakespear(e), Shakspere, Shaxspere, Shaxpear, Shaxpere, Shakspeer, Shaksper, and in fifteen different variations in the Rowington parish register.[18]

People spelled names according to sound. Was Elkanah Bobbet (or Bobet) of the *Babbitt Genealogy*, by William B. Browne, a victim of misspelling? Bardsley's *Dictionary of English and Welsh Surnames* does not include the surname Babbitt, but it does include Bobbet and Bobbett. According to the doctrine of *idem sonans* or identical sounds, it is the same surname whichever way it is spelled.

Capable genealogists are aware of this problem and search the records for all possible spelling variations.

ADOPTION

An adoption of a person is a type of legal fiction whereby the relationship of parent and child is created. It is a fiction because adoption provides that the child is the literal issue of the adopting parents as modern birth certificates attest.

To prevent abuses, such as baby selling (which the law hasn't prevented in modern time), statutes were eventually enacted to regulate adoption.

The legal adoption by one person of the offspring of another giving him the status of a child and heir of the parent by adoption, was unknown to the law of England or of Scotland, but was recognized by the Roman law, and exists in many countries on the continent of Europe which derive their jurisprudence from that law. . . It was long ago introduced, from the law of France or of Spain, into Louisiana and Texas, and more recently, at various times and by different statutes throughout New England, and in New York, New Jersey, Pennsylvania, and a large proportion of the other states of the union. . . One of the first, if not the very first, of the States whose jurisprudence is based exclusively on the common law to introduce it, was Massachusetts [in] 1851.[19]

In jurisdictions, such as England where there was no statutory authority for adoptions until 1926, or in the colonies and later the States where there was no provision for adoption, there is no indication that informal adoptions were nonexistent. Fortunately, in probate and other court proceedings and records, children in this status were often referred to as "adopted" sons or daughters. But there is no guarantee that this precaution was always observed, and it is standard procedure to search every available source to compile a correct and complete record of a family, in order to confine the members of the family to biological children and identify those adopted.

Before more strict regulation, you cannot be sure that a person informally adopted did not change his surname to coincide with the "adopting parents" and there may be no indication of this fact of record. Birth and baptismal records (if baptism occurred during infancy and these records exist and are available) should produce a clue, providing the age or date of birth or baptism of the child is known. Be certain this date does not conflict with the order of birth of a child or children of a family. But if the date of birth is the same as one of the known children of a family, this would suggest twins.

During a lengthy legal career, it is a combination of pleasure and pain to represent numerous clients adopting children and in rare instances adults adopting adults. The pain arises due to the realization that there is a total loss of identity. Most people are aware that the records of the court are sealed and that a "new" birth certificate is issued stating that the adopting parents are the biological parents. Anyone who has tried to go behind those sealed records must obtain an order of the appropriate court. Too often, all an adoptee knows is that he or she was adopted and does not know the location of the court. It is sometimes possible to solve these cases, but the time, effort, expense, and strain is terrible. On the occasions people have consulted lawyers regarding this problem, counsel should quote the old legal maxim "No one should suffer by the act of another."[20] This doesn't help those suffering, but quote it to a judge or other official who hesitates to cooperate, if and when the occasion is appropriate.

SURNAME ORIGIN AND IDENTITY IN THE COLONIES

No doubt every genealogist has at some time during his or her career decided it was impossible to trace some ancestors in the seventeenth century or at a later time in the colonies. There is the possibility that those persons came to America without a surname.

In an address by Professor George M. Dutcher, LL.D. of Wesleyan University, he mentioned this problem, stating:

> A large proportion of immigrants between 1607 and 1840 belonged to the uneducated working classes and arrived without surname. Their first upward step in the land of opportunity was to acquire a family name, most often a patronymic or the name of their place of origin, such as Jackson, or Van Buren. . . Only a small proportion of Americans can trace their ancestry prior to 1600.[21]

Next time a genealogist encounters a genealogical cul-de-sac, it might be well to consider Dr. Dutcher's statement.

One solution is searching appropriate records for mention of bonded and indentured servants in local records.

CHANGE OF NAMES

Another identity problem occurs when immigrants (and others) before and after the colonial period changed their names. This practice was not confined to Schmidt from Germany changing his name to Smith, but also by someone by the name of Smith for some reason, he was not required to divulge, could change his name to Trowbridge, without the necessity of court proceedings or act of the legislature.

The common law past and present simply recognizes the right of persons to change their names.[22]

There is a restriction though, and that is that people are not permitted to change their names for dishonest or fraudulent reasons. Thus, in criminal proceedings, the defendant is required to state his true name, which would be his first, middle (if any), and surname.

This isn't necessarily the worst genealogical cul-de-sac as an examination of the early statutes of this country will disclose. The session laws and statutes at large of the fledgling jurisdictions which became the United States do include a large number of private acts which permitted individuals to change their names. The old names and the new names were disclosed.[23]

Ultimately the courts acquired jurisdiction in regard to change of names.

ILLEGITIMACY AND FOUNDLINGS

This aspect of identity is discussed in the chapter on Paternity and Maternity.

IDENTIFICATION UNCERTAIN DUE TO FIRST NAME

The head of a large family of only girls in Vermont told his wife that their next child soon due would be named Thomas Jefferson whether the infant was male or female. The child born was a girl and that is what was given for her first name. Fortunately, she was nicknamed "Jeffie."

It is obvious that proof of the existence of an individual will most commonly contain within itself proof of the sex of that individual. Although the name will be, in general, a strong indication of the sex, it cannot always be relied on; as instances are not infrequent of caprice, accident, or some other cause having led to the bestowal upon children of names not usually applied to their sex.[24]

Thus a son of the first Earl Powlett was called Anne Powlett, born 1711, died 1785. Other names usually appropriate to females have been borne by males. Some names, such as Evelyn, Sabine, and Christian, are borne indiscriminately by both sexes.[25]

In the register of Hanwell, in Middlesex, is the following entry: "Thomas, daughter of Thomas Messenger and Elizabeth his wife, was born and baptized Oct. 24, 1731, by the midwife at the font, called a boy, and named by the godfather Thomas, *but proved a girl.*[26]

When the given or baptismal name causes uncertainty, additional records must be searched to resolve any conflict, for example marriage records, land records if a deed is found describing the parties as husband and wife, probate records, death records, burial and cemetery monuments or gravestones, should solve the problem.

APPRENTICES AND SERVANTS

Identifying an apprentice may present a difficult problem unless it is possible to discover the contract or indenture creating the relationship of master and servant, or master and apprentice. Apprenticeship could be either voluntary or in some cases forced. Often these apprentices or servants were foundlings, illegitimates, orphans, and had no choice but to be bound out as apprentices, often the bottom of the social order and sometimes without a surname known to them. The terms "indentured servant," and "bond servant" may be confusing. The term "indenture" actually refers to the document or contract between the master and the apprentice or servant. The indenture actually means the wavy line caused when the two copies of the contract written on one piece of parchment, vellum, or paper was cut in two — one copy for each party.[27]

Apprentices were usually children or young minors, and the word apprentice is from the Latin to learn. The term of servitude lasted until a male was 21 years of age, a female eighteen.

Apprenticeship is of ancient origin. The English system provided for records and in the Guildhall Library in London is a fine collection of these records which disclose genealogical facts such as date of baptism, name of father, place names, dates incidental to the apprenticeship, and information regarding the trade or occupation.

In 1642 Massachusetts Bay (and other jurisdictions) enacted statutes regulating apprenticeship. Massachusetts required that town officers (selectmen) act to be sure that boys and girls were gainfully engaged in useful work, and the apprenticeship program was one method used to satisfy this requirement.[28]

Finding the written records regarding apprenticeship, if not recorded or in the absence of a court proceeding in the colonies is not easy searching, unless a collection of these records has been preserved in local or state archives.

A genealogist must be on guard to be aware of the possibility of change of names, or the acquisition of a surname when lacking one.

BOUND LABORERS, REDEMPTIONERS

During the colonial period, white immigrants, mostly from England, bound themselves to contracted or indentured servitude to pay for their passage from England to the colonies. This servitude might last for as much as seven years. After completing the term of their servitude, the redemptioners settled in the colonies. Their occupations were mostly farm laborers and servants, although some were skilled workmen.[29]

Although these indentures or contracts were supposed to be in writing, and no doubt were in most instances adequately written contracts, there is no guarantee that these documents were preserved by recording them in local offices. Also there is always the possibility of name changes to conceal identity, and if the name is genuine, locating their home parish across the Atlantic is difficult if not impossible for persons who belonged to the poorer class of people. Evidence disclosed in court and land records in the locality where the persons resided are among the most helpful sources. Passenger ship lists may help when the ship is known, if these still exist, and the date or approximate date of arrival in the colonies is known.

CONVICT IMMIGRANTS

The identity problem also involves the deportation of persons convicted of crimes in Britain and transported to the colonies. The total number up to 1775 was approximately 50,000 persons.[30]

When a genealogical researcher exclaims, "I am up against a stone wall," it is entirely possible that the reason is that the ancestor was a convict and solving his ancestry is a great challenge. Fortunately there are published records which may be consulted.[31]

Criminal court records should also be searched in appropriate areas.

IDENTITY BY REPUTATION – SURNAMES ILLEGITIMATE PERSON

It is customary for an illegitimate child to assume the surname of the mother, as without marriage the name of the biological father is not inherited. Thus, it is possible to gain a surname by reputation or usage, whether it is the mother's name, or by selection of a different surname.

Unfortunately, there is no provision for court proceedings for the purpose of establishing identity of ancestors for personal genealogical reasons only. The court decisions cited in this chapter and other chapters of this book which involve genealogical problems such as identity or identification were commenced for the purpose of protecting or securing personal and property rights; and in any instance where pedigree questions were the basis of the controversy, genealogy was incidental rather than the purpose of establishing ancestry for purely personal reasons.

A Comparative Identification Check List follows which should be of assistance in resolving identification problems.

COMPARATIVE IDENTIFICATION CHECK LIST

Name in Full:
(Include nicknames, aliases, changes of name — whether legal changes pursuant to private legislative act or court decree, assumed names, fictitious names. Also consider the testamentary demand for change. In a last will and testament the testator may require a legatee or devisee to change his/her name to that of the testator in order to qualify as a donee or beneficiary. In England this is known as the "Name and Arms Clause," if both name and the testator's coat of arms is involved.)

Variations in Spelling
Do not overlook the doctrine of identical sounds (*idem sonans*) or names which sound the same but are spelled differently. People who knew how to write did so phonetically, therefore, there is a great variation in the spelling of names and especially surnames. For example, *A Century of Population Growth. . .*, published by the Bureau of the Census in 1909 included nomenclature tables and at Page 254, the surname MORRILL is spelled eleven different ways in the 1790 Census.

Places of Residence and Dates

Date and Place of Birth

Date and Place of Baptism, Including Church

Church Affiliation: (Name of church(es) and locations)

Date and Place of Marriage(s): (Include maiden name of wife or wives)

Divorces: (date, place, court jurisdiction)

Date and Place of Death:
Date of Burial
Cemetery and Mortuary Records
Place of Burial: (town, city, name of cemetery).
If buried in a family plot, there should be circumstantial evidence of relationship.
Church affiliation at death: (name and location)
Obituary Information and Reference to Source

Occupation(s) or Profession(s):
Organization Affiliations: (Lodges, etc.)

Name of Father: (Include facts regarding his birth, marriage(s), death, burial, residence, occupation, and any other material facts you discover.)

Name of Mother: (Maiden name — include facts regarding her birth, marriage(s), death, burial, residence(s), occupation, and any other material facts you learn concerning her.

Names and details Regarding Subject's Brothers and Sisters:
(e.g., births, marriages, deaths, and any other facts of genealogical interest)

Names of Brothers and Sisters of Subject's Father:
(Include any genealogical facts concerning them)

Names of Brothers and Sisters of Subject's Mother:
(Include any genealogical facts you discover about them)

Subject's Grandparents or Earlier Ancestors:
(Include genealogical facts concerning them)

Official Records: (Partial list of sources)
Search official records for identifying facts regarding subject and do not limit the search to military records, such as service records and pension files. Search federal and state census records.

Consult land records, federal, state and local, and do not limit your search to tax rolls, deeds, mortgages, leases, liens, but also consult the miscellaneous record volumes every county recorder, registrar of deeds ought to have in his custody.

Court Records: Search federal, state, and local court records, and do not limit the search to probate, civil, and criminal records. Also search immigration and naturalization records. There are pension claims cases in the Court of Claims records.

Administrative Tribunals: To suggest a few — Department of the Interior, War Department, Inheritance Tax agencies in the various states.

Voter Registration Records

Poll Tax Records

Session Laws, Statutes at Large: In addition to record of change of name, divorce, legitimacy of marriage and children, all private laws.

Land Records: Title, possession and residence on specific land held by the family for generations and documents in the possession of the present owner occupant should be examined, when possible, as this is a very valuable method of establishing identity and a lengthy pedigree. (During a visit to Cornwall a few years ago, a local resident pointed to a farm and said the family in possession had held title down through the generations for seven hundred years.)

Reputation:
(1)   Reputation in the neighborhood for truth, honesty, integrity, sobriety, morality, and good behavior are identifying attributes a person of a similar name may not possess. Sometimes this information is disclosed in court and other official records.
(2)   Reputation of identity — that he or she is identified as the person he or she represents to be.

Note: If the person is not living, and existing persons do not know any facts, the only sources for identification will be official records, church records, family records (if available), printed sources, newspaper files, and perhaps the family burial plot.

Habits:
Similar to reputation and the same sources applicable to reputation should be considered and searched.

Physical Description and Physical Characteristics:
Examples: height, weight, color of eyes, color of hair, right or left handed, marks, scars, physical defects (such as loss of limbs, lisping, sight defects, deafness, or hard of hearing, etc.). Same sources to search as reputation.

Race and National Origin:
If no living witnesses, resort to records and other sources as in the case of reputation, supra.

Family Resemblance: (Also referred to as "Traces")
Comparison of family resemblance or lack of it. Refer also to medical evidence. Valuable only as a possible clue and not a substitute for intensive research.

Medical Evidence of Ancestry and Identity:
Inherited traits and defects are strong circumstantial evidence to establish identity and relationship. Harold Schwartz, M.D., a California physician, is an authority on this subject.

Handwriting Comparison:
Consult a document examiner if in doubt.

Vehicle Registration Records:
(Not of much assistance prior to recent times.)

Military Service Numbers:
Valuable, if available to you.

Social Security Numbers:
Of only recent value. There is some risk the same number has been issued to more than one person.[32]

Blood Types and Tissue Typing Tests:
If previous generations are involved, forget it. Not admissible in a court proceeding except under stringent conditions.

Polygraph (Lie Detector) Tests:
(Unfortunately of no use if the individual is deceased). Usually accurate, but still questioned. Not admissible in a court proceeding except under special circumstances. A congenital liar can "beat" the lie detector machine.

Fingerprints:
The only reliable system of identification, but unfortunately it is too late for genealogical problems of the past.

Notes and References

1. Sir Francis Bacon, *Maxims*, "Identitas vera colligitur ex multitudine signorum."

2. Earwaker, J.P., *A Lancashire Pedigree Case...*, Warrington, England 1887, p. 7.

3. *Hall v. Cotton*. 167 Kentucky Court Reports 464.

4. *In re Link's Estate*, 319 Pennsylvania Court Reports 513, 518, 522.

5. Ibid.

6. *Hardy v. Hardin*, 154 United States Supreme Court Reports 598.

7. Reed, Walter G. (ed), *History of Sacramento County*, California, 1923, p. 147.

8. Waters, Henry F., *Genealogical Gleanings in England*, 2 volumes, Vol. 1, 1901, p. 283.

9.   Jacobus, Donald Lines, *The Bulkeley Genealogy*, New Haven, 1933. This work is an excellent example of the analysis of identity problems and is worth studying for that reason.

10. Medvedev, Zhores A., M.D., "Caucasus and Atlay Longevity: A Biological or Social Problem?" *The Gerontologist*, London, October 1974, pp. 381-387.

11. Bradbrook, William, M.R.C.S., *The Parish Register*, London, 1910, pp. 58-60, 73-76.

12. Ibid.

13. Ibid.

14. Ibid.

15. Ibid.

16. Ibid.

17. Ibid.

18. Ibid.

19. *Ross v.* Ross (1878) 129 Massachusetts Reports 243, 262.

20. Ibid.

21. Dutcher, George M., LL.D., *New England Historical and Genealogical Register*, Volume 108, April 1954, pp. 105-108.

22. *In re Ross*, 8 California Supreme Court Reports, 2nd Series 608-09.

23. Stevenson, Noel C., "Genealogical Research in Session Laws and Statutes," *The New England Historical and Genealogical Register*, Vol. CX, 1956, p. 98 et seq.

24. Hubback, John, *A Treatise on the Evidence of Succession to Real and Personal Property and Peerages*, London 1844, pp. 425 et seq., and court decisions cited.

25. Ibid.

26. Ibid.

27. Blackstone, William, *Commentaries on the Laws of England*, Vol. 2, London 1809, pp. 295-296.

28. Massachusetts General Court: *The Lawes and Libertyes of Massachusetts* . . ., Cambridge 1648. Reprinted from the original in The Henry E. Huntington Library. Harvard University Press, 1929, p. 11.

29. Morris, Richard B., *Encyclopedia of American History*, Harper & Brothers, New York 1953, p. 518.

30. Ibid.

31. Coldham, Peter Wilson, F.A.S.G., *English Convicts in Colonial America*, Polyanthos, Inc., New Orleans 1977, 2 volumes.

32. Social security numbers are not the perfect identification device, as reported in the Los Angeles Times on January 22, 1979. A patient visited a dentist's office and submitted an insurance form with her social number in the usual box. The dentist looked at it and said that was his social security number. Patient and doctor compared the social security numbers on their respective cards and the numbers were identical!

CHAPTER 3

CLAIMS OF ROYAL LINEAGE
AND ANCIENT PEDIGREES

Occasional perusals of the Genealogical Department of the <u>Boston Evening Transcript</u> and other publications have convinced the writer of this article that, in spite of the fact that 'all men are created equal' and in spite of the good old American contempt for royalty and the 'effete nobility of Europe,' the American genealogical public have an exceedingly strong desire to deduce their descent by hook or by crook from the same 'effete' royal and noble houses of Europe. Furthermore, an investigation of these claims usually shows that not one in twenty of such pedigrees can stand up under the searching test of modern scientific investigation. These lines are usually based upon the standard [printed] works of Dugdale and their derivatives, upon printed county histories, and upon the notoriously inaccurate so-called Visitation pedigrees of the sixteenth and seventeenth centuries edited by the Harleian Society; and when these fail, the most wild and careless statements are relied upon.[1]

G. Andrews Moriarty

"Now it is quite certain that [the] Coplestone [family] or anybody else, must have had forefathers of some kind living in the year 1066. People who talk about old families sometimes forget the obvious fact that one family is really as old as another. Every family had some forefathers at any given moment since the beginning of the world. The only difference is that the 'old' family knows, or thinks that it knows, who its forefathers were at a particular time."[2]

Professor Edward A. Freeman

Mr. Moriarty and Professor Freeman wrote the foregoing statements before the universal use of microfilm, photocopiers, computers, electronic retrieval of genealogical data and the proliferation of family organizations to the extent that the Internal Revenue Service issued Revenue Ruling 71-580 providing that nonprofit family organizations established for the purpose of compiling genealogy for its members under certain conditions are exempt from income taxes.

It is doubtful if the foregoing examples of progress would unduly surprise them. Television was unknown, so it is doubtful if either of the gentlemen could have foreseen Alex Haley's *Roots*, either in book form or the televised version, and the subsequent pellmell rush of the general public to search for their ancestry. But what would not surprise them is the continued passion of Americans to search for genealogical connections linking them with royalty, especially William the Conqueror, Charlemagne, or at least the Magna Carta Barons.

A random examination of published family genealogies discloses this same desire to be connected with royalty and the selection and display of the family's claim to a coat of arms is standard procedure in most genealogies. A critical analysis discloses that the families of these genealogies have no legitimate claim to the royal lineage or the coat of arms, and historical investigation by experts dismiss these claims to royalty and coat armor.

J. Gardner Bartlett, an outstanding authority on English genealogical research, stated:

> Of the five thousand heads of families who came between 1620 and 1640, less than 50 or not 1% are known to have belonged to the upper gentry of England, and less than 250 more, or not 5%, can be considered as from the minor mercantile or landed gentry. No peers nor sons of peers, no baronets, nor their sons, but one knight and no sons of knights, were among the founders of New England.[3]

Ernest Flagg, a New Englander and more than familiar with this subject, commenting on the foregoing Bartlett quotation wrote:

> Yet if one were to credit the family genealogies he would conclude that the great majority were of gentle extraction. Sometimes it is only a crest or coat of arms that is claimed, but very often descent from the most prominent ancient English house whose surname is the same or similar to their own; and not a few in all seriousness, claim royal descent. At the public libraries, books purporting to show such connection for American families are fairly worn out by much handling.[4]

> Many people are inclined to think that because a statement is old it must be true. Even anonymous statements are accepted as gospel if old enough, . . . but one who examines critically, soon comes to the conclusion that in genealogy, at least, the art of lying has made little progress through the ages. . . Books on genealogy abound with statements furnished by interested parties which are not true. The writer [Mr. Flagg] has found many such in compiling this work.[5]

In his article on the "Wodhull, Odell, and Chetwode" families Mr. Jacobus emphasizes the folly of accepting as reliable genealogical data from early compilations. He states "There are obvious errors in the early generations, such as placing Nicholas de Wodhull (d. 1410) as son of Thomas (d. 1303), which would make Nicholas 107 years old at death if born even in the last year of his father's life."[6]

One of the favorite compilations utilized by researchers interested in tracing their ancestry to royalty is *Pedigrees of Some of the Emperor Charlemagne'. Descendants* (1941) by Marcellus D. R. von Redlich. The folly of relying on book of this character is discussed by Donald Lines Jacobus:

". . . von Redlich, pp. 237, 239, makes Richard Woodhull born at Thenford, 13 Sept. 1620 [no baptism is recorded there], the son of Lawrence Woodhull, younger son of Fulke Woodhull of Thenford Manor, and a royal line is traced through the Parr mother of Fulke. On page 239 Lawrence Woodhull is called 'of Thenford Manor,' which he never was, and in strict fact no evidence has yet been seen that he existed even as a younger son of Fulke of Thenford. Since this account follows the *Woodhull Genealogy* in assigning erroneous wives to the first three Richard Woodhulls in America, and bears no evidence of independent research, these statements and the alleged line of descent require verification from documentary sources before they can be accepted."[7]

"A few words about Burke may be apropos. Burke is excellent authority for recent generations of peerage and gentry families. For the earlier period, only genealogical novices rely on Burke. If the calendars which contain various classes of records, and which hence are the chief primary sources on which mediaeval pedigrees must be built, are not accessible to the trained genealogist, he relies on the works of Dugdale, of Round, of Cokayne, of Watson, of Farrer, and of other scholars who have used and who quote (as Burke does not) these documentary sources. Their writings are scattered through many books and in articles in a number of English journals such as *The Genealogist* and *The Ancestor*. So far as titled families are concerned, the *New Complete Peerage* begun in 1910 . . . is the outstanding compilation. Such works as those of Collins and Burke have their uses, but it is unsafe to place them in uncritical or inexperienced hands."[8]

Researchers who attempt to trace the ancestry of an immigrant to the American colonies more often than not must cope with a serious identification problem. If the ancestor's given and surname are common, the problem is compounded. But even in instances of uncommon or unique names, it is often impossible to locate his former home and parentage across the Atlantic. Even if the village or parish where the ancestor lived is located, successful genealogical research is dependent on records and if there are no records, it will not be possible to compile a pedigree.

This condition becomes more serious if there are no parish records. In some countries parish registers commenced earlier than others. In England parish registers supposedly started in 1538, but due to loss, destruction, war, theft, the elements, and negligence, parish records begin at various dates. Few can boast of the example of St. Giles in the Fields, a London parish whose magnificent registers of baptisms, marriages, and burials began in 1561. These registers are in beautiful condition, quite a record for a beginning over 400 years ago.

Assume it is possible to find parish registers and records, wills and administrations, documents relating to court proceedings, and other records of genealogical significance as early at 1538. Prior to this date there is a great paucity of records which disclose baptisms, marriages, and burials.

Another hazard which must be considered in regard to surviving parish registers and records is the possibility of changes due to erasures and the insertion of substituted names and dates, interlineations, and other changes inserted later — all forgery and fraudulent practices.

"It is not generally understood how little documentary evidence exists for the building of connected pedigrees between 1000 and 1200. This condition in some respects resembles that found in Virginia in the early decades, for often the first two to four generations of Virginia families have to be built on land evidences. In England, parish registers do not go back of the middle of the sixteenth century, and it is rarely possible to trace the general run of families further back than about 1490-1500. Land was owned by the aristocracy and descended from eldest son to eldest son. If the feofee died without issue, the next brother or nearest heir succeeded. If the feofee had no sons, but female issue, an only daughter was sole heiress, while several daughters shared the estates. When we read that an old family 'ended in an heiress,' only the landed eldest line is meant, and there may have been younger but often unpropertied male branches who mostly are untraceable because the records of the early period are concerned with the ownership and inheritance of landed estates.

The early generations of gentry families back of 1200, as given in county histories and other compilations, are often built on the mention of feofees of the same estates at intervals, and these names have been strung together in generation sequence. A study of dates will sometimes indicate that intervening generations have been omitted, as with the Chetwode pedigree which the present writer included in *The Bulkeley Genealogy* (New Haven, 1933), pp. 55-58, but with the expressed warning that the earlier generations could not be accepted as entirely correct.

Research in the primary sources may at times enable the student to rectify the early part of gentry pedigrees as heretofore published and accepted. But frequently the contemporary documents are too meagre to provide much additional information. However, because of land tenure, the student of mediaeval families may often be satisfied that a gentry family goes back earlier than can be proved by strict generation sequence. That is because we are dealing with land ownership, which descended through the eldest male line, and we know that each owner had to make proof of his right of inheritance, even though the records have not come down to us. This is a very different set of circumstances from a mere guess or assumption that one person named Wodhull or Odell descended from an earlier person named Wodhull or Odell, where identity of surname is the only evidence and where the inheritance of the same landed estate is not involved.

It is also a very different thing to attempt to prove a line of descent for an early American colonist from a king of England or a Magna Charta baron, because usually such lines go in some generations through younger sons, and invariably they go in some generations through females. Each successive step in such a pedigree has to be proved by competent evidence, because if a single link is false, the entire chain of descent breaks."[9]

"It is common knowledge among historical scholars that for many centuries during the Dark Ages no records were kept on which any authentic pedigree, bridging that period of time, can be based, and that no extant European family can be traced back of the sixth century of our era. To be sure, lofty pedigrees were later fabricated for the rulers descended from the able and ruthless men who founded dynasties during that chaotic period, but this was done as a matter of prestige, much as the rulers of Japan claim descent from the sun-goddess. There are no contemporary records or documents to substantiate any of them, and no serious historian or genealogist regards them as anything but mythology."[10]

"The most general mistake made by beginners in the field of genealogy is that of identifying surname with family. Admittedly, Wodhull and Odell are variants of the same name, but no contradiction is involved when we say that William Odell of Concord, Mass., and Fairfield, Conn., was not necessarily or even presumptively descended from the ancient Wodhull family. It is no contradiction at all, but a proper distinction between surname and lineal descent. Take the case of a name derived from a trade, such as Smith. Not even a tyro would assume that every Smith descends from one particular family of early Smiths, or that all Miners are of the same lineage. Although place-names did not give rise to such a multiplicity of families with identical surnames as the more common trade-names did, nevertheless families of diverse origin did often derive their surnames from the same place, and it is never entirely safe to make the assumption that a specific family of the name descends from the ancient family which once held the over-lordship of that place... [A]n assumption, made on surname identity alone, has no more weight than any other uninformed guess."[11]

The opinions of Messrs. Bartlett, Moriarty, and Jacobus on this subject have been presented. All of these gentlemen were prominent and exceptionally qualified American genealogists. Other outstanding genealogists, historians, and antiquarians have also written on this subject. Beginning with the previous century, Professor Edward A. Freeman (1823-1892) was pre-eminent because of his critical and competent discussion of royal lineages and other ancient pedigree claims. Freeman's qualifications are disclosed in the *Dictionary of National Biography* and qualified because of his education, experience, and reputation. Freeman expresses his viewpoint as an Englishman and this is important especially because of the period when he lived, and his passion for authenticity and research in original records.

Researchers and genealogists who depend on Burke's *Peerage and Baronetage of the British Empire* and similar tomes to link their ancestors with William the Conqueror and his companions, and otherwise compile what they believe are authoritative genealogies disclosing descent from other royal, noble, and ancient lineages, should be interested in what Professor Freeman said about Sir Bernard Burke and his contribution to genealogy, as several case histories from Freeman's eloquent writings will disclose.

Prefatory to the case histories Professor Freeman researched, it is important to know precisely Freeman's opinion of the volumes Burke compiled and published as disclosed in the following statements:

"What for instance can be the state of mind of Sir Bernard Burke? Does he know, or does he not know, the manifest falsehood of the tales which he reprints year after year? He may, one is tempted to say, be reasonably called on for a more critical examination than we can ask from people who simply send him the stories which they have been taught to believe about their own families. If he says that he is not responsible for them, that he simply puts into his book what is sent to him without examining into its truth, if he says that the responsibility for the truth or falsehood of the stories rests with those who send them to him, he shows a very imperfect notion of the duties of authorship and editorship, even in its lowest form. No man can have a right to publish, without contradiction or comment, as alleged fact and not as avowed fiction, a number of stories which are false on the face of them. The readers of the book accept the stories on the faith of the author or editor. If they think about the matter at all, they hold that it is his business to examine and verify the statements which are sent to him. Indeed Sir Bernard Burke himself tells us, in his 'Prefatory Notice' prefixed to the thirty-second edition of his *Peerage and Baronetage*, that he has 'again subjected its pages to searching revision and extensive amendment.' Here then Sir Bernard Burke distinctly takes on himself, what reason would have laid upon him even if he had not taken it on himself, namely responsibility for his own book."[12]

"We have no right to expect much historical criticism from the man who sends in the account of his own family which has for some generations, perhaps for some centuries, passed current as the history of that family. He very naturally accepts it as he finds it, without examination of any kind. It would indeed be kind of heroic sacrifice on behalf of truth, if he did critically examine what his father and grandfather and great-grandfather have handed down as something which tends to the honour of the family. He is in no way blameworthy simply for believing the fable in the first instance. He becomes blameworthy only if he sticks to the fable after it has been clearly shown to him that it is a fable. But a harsher measure must be dealt to the editor who year after year puts forth these monstrous fictions, without contradiction, commonly without qualification or hesitation of any kind. For it is practically no qualification to bring a story in with some such formula as 'it is said' or 'tradition affirms.' Readers, especially readers of books of this class, need to be told in very plain words that the stories are false, that they carry their own confutation with them. Nothing short of this clear warning will make the mass of people see the real state of the case; and this warning Sir Bernard Burke never gives them. The fault therefore lies wholly with those who invented the tales in past times, and with those who spread them abroad now without giving any help towards contradicting them. From Sir Bernard Burke we have a right to expect historical criticism, and we do not get it."[13]

Professor Freeman states that Burke claims he subjects his editions to searching revision and amendment. "But such is the abiding life of the fables that they live through all revision and amendment."[14]

The case histories which follow support Professor Freeman's criticism of Sir Bernard Burke's publications.

ALLEGED PEDIGREE OF THE STOURTON FAMILY

"In all these stories the pedigree-maker's power of invention did not go beyond mere invention of names, or the putting of real names in their wrong places. But there are pedigrees which take a much more daring flight, and which bring in large pieces of professed history which are nothing in the world but sheer invention. Take for instance the pedigree of the house of Stourton: —

'This noble family, which derives its surname from the town of Stourton, co. Wilts, was of considerable rank antecedently to the Conquest; for we find at that period one of its members, Botolph Stourton, the most active in disputing every inch of ground with the foreigner, and finally obtaining from the duke his own terms. Having broken down the seawalls of the Severn, and guarded the passes by land, Botolph entered Glastonbury when that victorious Norman had made his appearance in the West; and, thus protected, compelled William to grant whatsoever he demanded. From this patriotic and gallant soldier lineally descended' — such and such people without dates, till we come to a John de Stourton, who is placed in the time of Edward the Third, and who is likely enough to be a real man.

Now if we did not know that a pedigree-maker will do anything, it would really be past belief that anybody could have ventured on such monstrous fiction as this. . . Botolph Stourton and his exploits are invented of set purpose to swell the supposed credit of a family whose real beginnings seem to be in the fourteenth century. Here again we see the delusion of the surname. It was supposed that there could be before the Conquest a family of Stourton, one of whom was called Botolph, as another might be called John or Thomas. But the whole thing is a fiction. . . Botolph Stourton or any other Botolph is not to be found [in the Domesday Book]. . . . If William granted to Botolph whatever he demanded, it was clearly not land that he demanded, least of all the lands at Stourton. At page 72 of Domesday we find Stourton in Wilshire plainly enough; but its lord is not any Botolph. . . Of the two lordships in Wilshire held by Walsein of Douay, one of them has this fatal entry: 'Radulfus tenet de W. Stortone.' . . . . So Botolph Stourton vanishes from Stourton and he equally vanishes from every other spot; for not a man of the name appears in Domesday as holding or having held a rood of land anywhere. The tale is sheer invention; it is mere falsehood, which might at any time be [refuted] by the simple process of turning to Domesday."[15]

THE INVENTED PEDIGREE OF FITZWILLIAM

"When one is inventing falsehoods about a family, it is as easy to invent falsehoods to its credit as falsehoods to its dishonour. Whoever invented the pedigree of Earl Fitzwilliam was of another way of thinking. He had the strange fancy of wishing to be descended from a traitor. We there read: —

'Sir William Fitz-Godrick, cousin to King Edward the Confessor, left a son and heir,

'Sir William Fitzwilliam, who being ambassador at the court of William Duke of Normandy, attended that prince in his victorious expedition against England, as marshal of the army A.D. 1066 and for his valour at the battle of Hastings the Conqueror presented him with a scarf from his own arm. This Sir William was the father of

'Sir William Fitzwilliam, Knight, who married Eleanor, daughter and heir of Sir John Elmley, of Elmley and Sprotburgh, which lordships continued with the Fitzwilliams until the reign of Henry VIII, when they were carried, by co-heirs, to Suthill and Copley.'

It is perhaps needless to say that all this is a pure fable; but one really stands aghast at the utterly shameless nature of the fable. Sir William Fitzwilliam is supposed to be an English ambassador at the court of Normandy. The inventor of the fable had so little knowledge as not to see that the Sir, the first William, the Fitz, and the second William, was, each of them by itself, as much proof as could be needed that a man of whose name they formed any part could not have been an Englishman of the days of Eadward the Confessor. Furthermore it would seem that the inventor thought it honourable for an ambassador sent to a foreign prince to join that prince in an invasion of his own country, and to bear arms in battle against his own sovereign. As for the scarf from William's own arm, we need hardly look in the Bayeux Tapestry to prove that the Duke who knew so well how to wield his mace of iron did not cumber his arms with any frippery of scarves on the day of the great battle.

It is almost refining too much; but it is worth while to mark that this imaginary traitor is described as the grandson of Godric. The choice of the name is lucky; there was a traitor Godric in the fight at Maldon, and his doings are set forth in the song which records that fight. Those who like traitors for their forefathers may, if they think good, make choice of him."[16]

Professor Freeman queries "Can there be a wilder fable than this?" His answer is "Yes," and he continues to record the case histories.[17]

ALLEGED LINEAGE OF THE WAKE FAMILY

"In these stories [included by Burke] there seems to be a deliberate preference for traitors; in another we find a sublime indifference between an imaginary traitor and a real hero. This to be seen in the pedigree of the family of Wake. It stands thus [by] Sir Bernard Burke:

'The Wakes are mentioned by Brompton as in the immediate train of the Conqueror; but it is the opinion of antiquaries that the individual of the name of Wake recorded in the roll of Battle Abbey, was one of those who, being weary of Harold's rule, fled into Normandy, and invited Duke William, hence the family is supposed to have been of

importance prior to the Conquest. The celebrated Archbishop Wake
. . . wrote a history of the Wake family, in which he ascribes to
Hereward le Wake the feat of having successfully opposed and finally
made terms with William the Conqueror. As Augustine also mentions
Wakes in Normandy, it is probable that there were two parties in the
family at that time. An historical novel has been written on the feats
of Hereward in harassing the Normans and defending the abbey of
Brun after the Conquest. His tomb is still, or was to be seen, not many
years ago, in Lincolnshire. From "Baldwin Lord Wake, founder of the
abbey of Brun, who died 1156, descended, through a long line of
eminent ancestors, Richard Wake, Esq.' — who seemingly lived in the
sixteenth century."[18]

Professor Freeman states this is another example of genealogical fiction and
that the names of Brompton and Augustine are fictitious.[19]

ALLEGED ASHBURNHAM ANCESTRY

"Sir Bernard Burke gives two pedigrees of Ashburnham in the *Peerage and Baronetage*, and they both seem to go back to the sixteenth,
or perhaps the fifteenth century. This was not long enough ago; so
somebody invented an 'early progenitor' who is thus described:

'Bertram Ashburnham, a Baron of Kent, was Constable of Dover
Castle, A.D. 1066; which Bertram was beheaded by William the
Conqueror, because he did so valiantly defend the same against the
Duke of Normandy.'

Here again we have pure fiction, and impossible fiction. Bertram
Ashburnham, Baron and Constable, proves his imaginary character
by every word of his description. Dover Castle was not valiantly
defended by any one against the Duke of Normandy, and most
assuredly William the Great never beheaded any man for defending
any place valiantly against him."[20]

Professor Freeman concludes his discussion of this case as a "fable."[21]

ALLEGED BERKELEY FOREFATHERS

"Take another pedigree, that of Berkeley. This is a particular pedigree
concerning which I have given some attention to in my own work. I
trust I have shown (See History of the Norman Conquest, Vol. 4, pp.
755, 758, Second edition) that there is every probability that Robert
Fitz-Harding, the patriarch of the house of Berkeley, was son of a
Harding whose name often occurs in Domesday and elsewhere, and
grandson of Eadnoth the Staller, a man who, whether it be thought to
his credit or otherwise, having been a great officer under Edward and
Harold, passed after the Conquest into the service of William.
Eadnoth and Harding are perfectly well-ascertained men, and there is
no other Harding to whom we can so readily assign the otherwise
unknown parentage of Robert Fitz-Harding. But while other people
have been so anxious to devise for themselves imaginary English
forefathers, the Berkeleys seem anxious to get rid of their real English

forefathers. By Sir Bernard Burke all that we are told of the father of Robert Fitz-Harding, in other words of Harding, is that he was one of the companions of William the Conqueror. This is pure fiction; no such Harding can be found. Still it is something for Sir Bernard Burke to have foreborne to put in some of the grosser absurdities of the local antiquaries. Those who call Harding "Mayor of Bristol" say what is in one sense likely enough, though I do not know that there is any proof, and I cannot say off-hand whether Bristol had a Mayor so early. But the favourite thing is to call him a son of "the King of Denmark." Sometimes he is Mayor of Bristol, follower of the Conqueror, and son of the King of Denmark, all at once. It is amusing to ask a Gloucestershire antiquary what King of Denmark he means. You soon find that one King of Denmark is the same to him as another. The grotesque absurdity of William being accompanied by a son of the only possible King of Denmark, Sven Estrithsson, the cousin and ally of Harold, never comes into their heads."[22]

ALLEGED D'OYLY ANCESTRY

"The pedigree of D'Oyly is traced by Sir Bernard Burke though with a good many gaps, to the founder of Oxford Castle of Oily or Ouilly. . . .

But the pedigree does not bring in either the elder or younger Robert [of Oily or Ouilly] by name. . . Their particular doings all seem to go to the general credit of the family. The entry in [Burke] stands thus:

'This family, one of great eminence both in England and France, came to England at the period of the Conquest, and obtained the dignity of feudal baron of Hocknorton, in Oxfordshire, and hereditary constable of Oxford Castle (anno 1067), from William the Conqueror.'

Hence the pedigree runs about [suddenly] to people in the thirteenth, fifteenth and sixteenth centuries."[23]

These genealogical generation gaps of 300 to 500 years is a "record" which is not easily overlooked.

THE OBVIOUS IMPOSSIBLE CLAIM

If a pedigree states that an ancestor was granted land in Old Cumberland by William the Conqueror, this is easy to disprove because William the Conqueror never held Old Cumberland and therefore could not grant land or anything else there to anybody.[24]

"Thus when we are told, under the pedigree of the Earl of Bessborough that 'this family takes its surname from the lordship of Ponsonby, in Cumberland, which its patriarch acquired with other considerable estates at the time of the Conquest,' we may say with perfect safety that whenever this patriarch – of whom his tribe does not seem to know enough to give him a name – may have acquired its estates, [but] it was not at the time of the Conquest."[25]

"In most of these stories [or case histories] the great object was . . . to make out that the forefather of the family came in with William the Conqueror. That was the most striking and obvious proof of good birth. But alongside of this feeling there was another, a feeling for which Englishmen must have greater sympathy. On the principle that the longer the pedigree was the nobler it was, if it was something to trace the family back to a companion of the Conqueror, it was something more to trace it back to those who were here before the Conqueror came."[26] Hence, the mania to claim a Saxon or preconquest pedigree.

"Let no man believe a pedigree which goes further back than the last three or four centuries, unless he has the means of testing it by the touchstone of true history. It is something that the particular time which pedigree-makers have chosen for the display of their wildest pranks is the time when it is easier than at any other time to refute them by the easy process of turning to the great survey. Let no man believe him who says that his forefathers, bearing his name, were seated at such and such a place before the Conquest. Here there is no need to turn to the Survey; the impossible fiction refutes itself. And let no man believe him who says that his forefather received such and such land from the Conqueror, until he has looked in the Survey to see whether it be so. The assertion is not impossible, like the other; but in a vast number of cases it turns out to be no less false. Men are wiser if, in the absence of authentic records, they are satisfied with the certain fact that they must have had some forefathers in the eleventh century, and with the hope, which may be cherished till it is disproved, that those forefathers were neither Norman invaders nor English traitors. He may believe, in the absence of proof to the contrary, that he comes of the blood of some one who fought and died for England. But he must be satisfied with the reasonable hope; he cannot assert it as a fact which can be proved. If men read their history aright, the point of honour would be, not to make out that they are the descendants of the invaders, not that they are the descendants of those who kept their lands by submission to the invaders, but that they are the descendants of the men who gave their lives for their country, and whose sons lost their lands because they were sons of patriots."

"One word more, let no one deem that, because a false pedigree is a thing to be eschewed and scouted, therefore a true pedigree is a thing to be despised. A true pedigree, be it long or short, is a fact; and, like any other fact, it is to be respected. To those to whom it belongs it is a possession; and, like any other possession, it is to be respected. It is only the false imitation of the true which is to be despised. The inheritance of a really great name is a great inheritance, an inheritance which should be a matter, not of pride but of responsibility. . . . "[27]

THE BURDEN OF PROOF

Anyone who presents for consideration a pedigree, ancient or modern, is subject to the principle known as the "burden of proof." It is the duty of the proponent of the pedigree to prove every fact in the pedigree. He cannot say to someone "You can't disprove it." The compiler or person claiming the pedigree is bound with the duty to establish its authenticity.

"There is no country which offers such strong temptations to fiction in the way of pedigree as [England]. No other country in Europe has any event in its history which exactly answers to our Norman Conquest, an event which calls forth two veins of sentiment, the desire to trace up the pedigree to the conquerors and the desire to trace up the pedigree to something older than the conquerors. Between these two contending feelings our English genealogies have become a mass of fables."[28]

39

There are other peerage and baronetage publications currently published other than the Burke tomes. The format of these other publications are similar to Burke and there are no references to documentary sources.

The most comprehensive is *The Complete Peerage* commenced by G. E. Cokayne, the first editor, 13 volumes, 1910-1940. This monumental work is greatly respected. There are numerous footnotes referring to sources and annotations. But as in the case of all printed or published genealogies, all are subject to verification. This matter of verification applies to Sir William Dugdale (1605-1688) also. Although his *Baronage of England* published in 1675-76 is greatly respected, the *Dictionary of National Biography* (Page 141) states it has many errors. A practical example of this fact was demonstrated in 1685 when a trial court refused Dugdale's *Baronage* as evidence to prove a genealogical descent. (*Piercy's Case* 84 English Reports 1198.)

The mania or craze to compile pedigrees disclosing descent from ancestors living in 1066 (or earlier) presents a possible advantage researchers so interested may not have considered before: Anyone claiming to have established a pedigree which alleges descent from (for example) William the Conqueror, his companions, or others antedating 1066, can be certain to trace their alleged lineage through some kingly illegitimates, and are therefore eligible for membership in THE SOCIETY OF THE DESCENDANTS OF THE ROYAL BASTARDS.

These researchers are bound to eventually claim (for example) Charles II, who is credited with (at least) twelve illegitimate children. Henry I surpassed that record with nineteen illegitimate issue. Anyone of English descent who claims royal or noble lineage will eventually admit that any historical pedigree will disclose descent from these two virile royal ancestors.

There is dubious advantage in claiming an ancestor who lived 900 or 1000 years ago who was the son of the king's mistress, as it is doubtful the same individual would be enthusiastic if he learned today that his father or mother were illegitimate children of the mistress of an important personage.

Anyone interested in genealogical research soon learns that statistically he/she has 5,736 ancestors (half of which are ancestresses) if they traced their lineage for twelve generations. Actually, the number is much less than this if the families didn't move often, as cousins married cousins and that reduces the number of ancestors because of descent from a progenitor more than once. If genealogical researchers concentrated on their descent from ancestors born since 1600, they would soon discover that limiting the search for the ancestry of several hundred different progenitors would require research eight hours a day, seven days a week.

Also it would be beneficial in this respect: By restricting research to the last 377 years, the researcher would not need a large closet in which to hide the surplus skeletons and scandals which infest everybody's ancestry. The words of the great poet Anonymous express the benefits and advantages of restricted research with great eloquence:

> *There are cases when the simple truth is difficult to tell,*
> *When 'tis better that the truth should not be known,*
> *So we'd better leave her lying at the bottom of the well,*
> *And agree to let both truth and well alone.*[29]

Notes and References

1. Moriarty, G. Andrews, A.M., LL.B., "The Royal Descent of a New England Settler," *New England Historical and Genealogical Register*, Vol. 79, October 1925, p. 358.

2. Freeman, Professor Edward A., "Pedigrees and Pedigree Makers," *The Contemporary Review*, Vol. 30, London 1877, p. 21.

3. Flagg, Ernest, *Genealogical Notes on the Founding of New England. . .*, Hartford 1926, p. 107.

4. Ibid.

5. Ibid, p. 110.

6. Jacobus, Donald Lines, "Wodhull, Odell and Chetwode," *The American Genealogist*, Vol. 21, July 1944, p. 81.

7. Ibid, pp. 82-83.

8. Ibid, pp. 74-75.

9. Ibid, pp. 70-71.

10. Ibid, p. 70.

11. Ibid, p. 73.

12. Freeman, Edward A., "Pedigrees and Pedigree Makers," *The Contemporary Review*, Vol. 30, pp. 12-13.

13. Ibid, p. 13.

14. Ibid, p. 13.

15. Ibid, pp. 25-26.

16. Ibid, p. 29.

17. Ibid.

18. Ibid, pp. 31-32.

19. Ibid.

20. Ibid. p. 33.

21. Ibid.

22. Ibid. pp. 34-35.

23. Ibid. p. 35.

24. Ibid, p. 36.

25. Ibid, pp. 36-37.

26. Ibid, pp. 20-21.

27. Ibid, pp. 39-40.

28. Ibid, p. 41.

29. Norton-Kyshe, James William, *The Dictionary of Legal Quotations*, London 1904, p. 242, n. 2.

CHAPTER 4

THE SURNAME PROBLEM AND GENEALOGY

All countries of Western Europe seem to have adopted the same means of securing identification, or their neighbours did it for them. Wales [circa 1896] is the great exception. Here there is scarcely a trade name, only a few nicknames, no official surnames that I know of, just a sprinkling of local surnames, and the rest, quite 95 percent, are baptismal names. Hence the difficulty of identification in [Wales]. . . .

The English natural growth of distinct branches of hereditary surnames from, say, 1250 to 1450, fortunately escaped this obstacle to identification. The five classes mentioned above [local, baptismal, occupative, official, and nicknames] have proved amply sufficient for the purposes.[1]

Charles Wareing Bardsley, M.A.

In the times before the Conquest there were no hereditary surnames . . . as the hereditary surname of a family is utterly impossible before the Norman Conquest.[2]

Professor Edward A. Freeman

Obviously, prior to 1450, hopeful genealogists are handicapped as well as frustrated due to the lack of surnames. When there are surnames, there is the ever present problem of persons with the same given and surnames. Not the least of the problems is the lack of uniformity in spelling which creates what seems to be a different name altogether. Bardsley wrote an informative paragraph on this subject, stating that:

"One of the greatest difficulties in solving the origin of our surnames comes under the law of imitation. The parentage being forgotten, people naturally began to pronounce their names in such a way as seemed to convey a meaning. After the institution of Church Registers, the clerks wrote down accordingly. Hence the pitfall into which many stumble. Hence in co. Somerset, Greedy for Gredhay, Rainbird for Reynebaud, Trott for Troyt, Bacchus for Bakehouse, Toogood or Doogood for Thurgod, Goodyear for Goodier, Gospell for Gosbell, Physick for Fishwick, Potiphar for Pettifer, Pitchfork (co. Linc.) for Pitchforth (i.e., Pickford), Roylance for Rylands, Gudgeon for Goodson (cf. the pronunciation Hodgun for Hodgson in the North), Twentyman for Twinterman, Sister-son for Sissotson . . . Rayment for Raymond, Garment for Garmond, Forty for the old de la Fortheye of co. Oxford (which still exists as Forty in the City), and a host of others."[3]

"In many cases English surnames are a mere translation of Norman-French names: . . . Tallboys (i.e., Taillebois), Fairbrother for Beaufrere, Handsombody for Gentilcorps, or Whitebread (or Whitbread) for Blanchpain."[4]

The study of the history, origin, variations, and eccentricities in the spelling of names is of prime importance to anyone interested in genealogical research. One of the best sources and certainly the easiest to read is a judicial decision by Judge Daly of the New York Court of Common Pleas written in 1859.[5] Judge Daly wrote his decision pursuant to a petition for a change of name filed by a man who wanted his name changed from Snook to Pike. Judge Daly approved the change and deemed it necessary to relate the history and origin of surnames and the relevant portions of his decision are as follows:

A man's name is the mark or *indicia* by which he is distinguished from other men. By a practice now almost universal among civilized nations, it is composed of his christian or given name, and his surname. The one is the name given to him after birth, or at baptism; the other is the patronymic derived from the common name of his parents. In the case of illegitimates, they take the name or designation they have gained by reputation . . . . The christian or first name is, in the law, denominated the proper name; and a party can have but one, for middle or added names are not regarded . . . . Formerly, the christian name was the more important of the two. "Special heed," says Coke, "is to be taken of the name of baptism, as a man cannot have two, though he may have divers surnames." Coke Litt. 3, a(m).[6] Indeed, anciently in England, there was but one name, for surnames did not come into use until the middle of the fourteenth century, and even down to the time of Elizabeth, they were not considered of controlling importance. Thus Chief Justice Popham, in *Button v. Wrightman*, . . . speaking of grants, declares that "the law is not precise in the case of surnames, but for the christian name," he says, "this ought always to be perfect;" and throughout the early reports the christian name is uniformly referred to as the most certain mark of the identity of the individual in all deeds or instruments. Greater importance being attached to the christian name arose from the fact that it was the designation conferred by the religious rite of baptism, while the surname was frequently a chance appellation, assumed by the individual himself, or given to him by others, for some marked characteristic, such as his mental, moral or bodily qualities, some peculiarity or defect, or for some act he had done which attached to his descendants, while sometimes it did not. Camden[7] mentions an instance of a knight in Cheshire, each of whose sons took different surnames, whilst their sons, in turn, also took different names from their fathers. They altered their names, he says, in respect to habitation, to Egerton, Cotgrove, and Overton; in respect to color, to Gough, which is red; in respect to learning, to Ken-Clarke, (a knowing clerk or learned man); in respect to quality, to Goodman; in respect to stature, to Richard Little; and in respect to

43

the christian name of the father of one of them, to Richard son, though all were descended from William Belward; and the gentlemen of Cheshire, he adds, bearing those different names, would not easily believe that they were all the descendants of one man, were it not for an ancient roll, which Camden saw. Camden's Remains, (ed. of 1637), p. 141.[8] And Lord Coke refers to the Year Books to show that a man may have divers names, that is, surnames, at divers times.[9]

The insufficiency of the christian name to distinguish the particular individual, where there were many bearing the same name, led necessarily to the giving of surnames; and a man was distinguished, in addition to his christian name, in the great majority of cases, by the name of his estate, or the place where he was born, or where he dwelt, or from whence he had come. For example, the name Washington, originally Wessyngton, which, as its component parts indicate, means a person dwelling on the meadow land, where a creek runs in from the sea, or else from his calling, as John the smith, or William the tailor, in time abridged to John Smith and William Taylor. And as the son usually followed the pursuit of the father, the occupation became the family surname, or the son was distinguished from the father by calling him John's-son, or William's-son, which, among the Welsh, was abridged to 's,' as Edwards, Johns or Jones, or Peters, which, as familiar appellations, passed into surnames. The Normans added Fitz to the father's christian name, to distinguish the son, as Fitz-herbert or Fitz-gerald. Among the Celtic inhabitants of Ireland and Scotland, where each separate clan or tribe bore a surname to denote from what stock each family was descended, Mac was added to distinguish the son, and O to distinguish the grandson. Generally, where names were taken from a place, the relation of the individual to that place was indicated by a word put before the name, like the Dutch Van or French De, or a termination added at the end, which additions were in time merged into and formed but one word, until, from these various prefixes and suffixes, numerous names were formed and became permanent. So, as suggested, something in the appearance, character, or history of the individual gave rise to the surname, such as his color, as black John, brown John, white John, afterwards transposed to John Brown, &c.; or it arose from his bulk, heighth, or strength, as Little, Long, Hardy, or Strong; or his mental or moral attributes, as Good, Wiley, Gay, Moody, or Wise; or his qualities were poetically personified by applying to him the name of some animal, plant, or bird, as Fox or Wolf, Rose or Thorn, Martin or Swan; and it was in this way that the bulk of our surnames, that are not of foreign extraction, originated and became permanent. They grew into general use, without any law commanding their adoption, or prescribing any course or mode respecting them; for I know of but one instance of a positive statute commanding the taking of names or regulating the manner of selecting them, and that was limited to a particular locality. In the fourth year of the reign of Edward IV, an act was passed compelling every Irishman that dwelt within the English pale, to take an English surname, and enacting that it should be the name of some town, or of some color, as black or brown, or of some art or occupation, or of some office, which led to an extensive change of names in that part of Ireland, as a non-compliance was attended with a forfeiture of goods. But, though for several centuries the practice of giving or assuming surnames was general, it extended little farther than the particular individual of which it was the designation or mark. His descendants adopted it or not, at pleasure, or he assumed a new name himself, or others conferred upon him some characteristic appellation, which adhered to him and his descendants. This fluctuation and change, however, was materially arrested by a statute, passed 1 Henry V., c.5, called the Statute of Additions, which required not only the name of the individual to be inserted in every writ or indictment, but, in addition, his calling, his estate or degree, and the town, hamlet, or place to which he belonged. In the reign of Henry VIII, Cromwell, the secretary of the king, established a regulation, by which a record was required to be kept in every parish of births, marriages and deaths; a regulation which, in connection with the previous act, operated to check the caprice of individuals in the matter of their names, and to fix them as durable appellations, for every man's name thereafter became a matter of record at his birth, his marriage, and at his death; and this recording of such events in every family, led to the use of one name to designate the members of one family, which the record served to perpetuate; transmitting it from father to son, until the practice became general for all descendants to bear, and become known by, the name of a common ancestor. But this was the work of several centuries, and even [as late as 1859] in remote and sparsely settled districts of England and Wales, the practice is not entirely extinct of assuming and changing surnames. All this, it will be seen, was brought about without any positive provision of law, other than those that have been referred to. By a usage, sufficiently general to be called universal, the son now bears the name of the father, and in turn transmits it to his own male descendants. Surnames, from their infinite variety, have now become a more certain mark of identity than the first name, for the whole number of christian or first names now commonly in use do not exceed six hundred, while the directory of this city exhibits no less than twenty thousand varieties of surnames.[10] It is the combination of the christian and surname that now marks the individual's identity; and he is distinguished still more accurately by the use, now very general, of middle names or initial letters.

But though the custom is wide spread and universal, for all males to bear the name of their parents, there is nothing in the law prohibiting a man from taking another name if he chooses. There is no penalty or punishment for so doing, nor any consequence growing out of it, except so far as it may lead to or cause a confounding of his identity. In some countries it is otherwise. In France, a law was passed in the second year of the first revolution (L.6 Fructidor, Au.II.,) and another (19 Nivose, Au. VI.,) which is still in force (Codes Francais par Bourguignon et Royer — Collard, 34 and note; Dictionaire de Legislation Universal par Chabal — Chameane, vol. 2, p. 266,) forbidding any citizen to bear any first name (prenom) or surname, than that which is expressed in the registry of his birth, or to add any surname to his proper name; but no enactment of the kind has ever been passed in England or in this state, but, on the contrary, there have been many instances in which individuals have changed their names and held offices of public trust, and become distinguished by the name they adopted. The poet Mallet may be cited as an illustration. His father was of the clan of the Macgregors; and when that clan was suppressed, and its name abolished by law in consequence of the violent acts of Rob Roy, he took the name of Malloch, by which name the son was known until he came to London in his twenty-sixth year, when, disliking his Scotch patronymic, he adopted the French name of Mallet, and by this name held an office under government, became distinguished in literature, and transmitted the name to his descendants. That such instances rarely occur, may be readily accounted for in the fact of the absence, usually, of any object to induce a man to change his name. In the circumstance that there is generally a just and honorable pride in bearing the name of one's ancestors, and in the further fact that it is scarcely in the power of a man to change his name, unless he goes to a place where he is unknown; for as long as he continues to abide where he is known, people will continue to call him by the name to which they are accustomed.

It is this difficulty, I apprehend, mainly, that led to the practice of applying for the king's license, or the passage of a statute, in cases where the taking of a new name had become necessary in consequence of the devise of an estate upon that condition, as all persons will conform to what is decreed or enjoined by the sovereign authority of the state. Lord MANSFIELD seems to have thought, in *Gulliver v. Ashby*, (4 Bur. 1940), that the king's license, or an act of parliament, was essential to entitle a man to assume another name; but in later cases the right of an individual to take another name, without the king's license or an act of parliament, has been distinctly recognized; and the validity of acts done in the adopted name have been sustained even where they imposed a charge upon the public. In *The King v. The Inhabitants of Billinghurst*, (3 Maule & Sel. 250), the question was, whether a pauper, whose baptismal and surname was Abraham Langley, and who, by that name, had a legal settlement in Billinghurst, could, with his wife and family, be charged upon that parish. He was married in another parish by the name of George Smith, and had been known in that parish for three years before his marriage by that name. The wife and children had no settlement in Billinghurst, unless they had acquired one by the marriage, and the point involved was the validity of the pauper's marriage by the name of George Smith; the marriage act of 26 Geo. II. c. 33, rendering it essential to the validity of a marriage that there should be a publication beforehand of the "true christian and surnames" of the parties. It was insisted that this had not been done — that the marriage was, therefore, void, and that the wife and children were not

46

chargeable upon the parish of Billinghurst; but the court held that the publication of the banns by the name of George Smith — that being the name which the pauper had gained by reputation, and by which he was known at the time in the parish where he was married — was a publication of the true name within the meaning of the act. In a note at the end of this case, several decisions of Lord Stowell, in Consistory Court, are collected. In one of them (*Frankland v. Nicholson*) Ann Nicholson was married and the banns published by the name of Ann Ross. Sir WILLIAM SCOTT, in reply to the argument that the proper christian and surname of a party could not be altered except by the king's license or an act of the legislature said that there might be cases where names, acquired by general use and habit, would be taken as the true christian and surname of a party, but as there was not sufficient evidence in the case before him to show that the woman had ever been known by the name of Ross, he annulled the marriage. In another case before him, *Mayhew v. Mayhew*, which was a proceeding for a divorce upon the ground of adultery, the woman set up that she had never been legally married, having been described in the publication of the banns as Sarah Kelso, when her real name was Sarah White. It was shown, in reply, that she had gone by several different names, but was generally known by the name of Kelso before the marriage, and upon this evidence he held the marriage to be valid.

Doe v. Yates (5 Barn. & Ald. 544,) is a case still more distinctly in point. An estate was devised upon condition that the devisee should take the surname of the testator. The will provided that, within three years after the devisee arrived at the age of twenty-one, he should procure his name to be altered to the testator's name of Luscombe, by act of parliament or in some other effectual way. The devisee, before he was of age and before he entered upon or was let into the possession of the estate, took the name of Luscombe, which name he continued thereafter to bear. At twenty-one he took possession of the estate, but suffered the three years to go by, without applying for the king's license or an act of parliament, to entitle him to use the name of Luscombe, and he continued to hold and enjoy the estate for eight years thereafter, when he conveyed it to the defendants. It was insisted that he had forfeited the estate by having failed to comply with the testator's directions within the three years after he reached twenty-one, in not obtaining or applying for the king's license, or an act of parliament authorizing him to take the name of Luscombe. But the court gave judgment for the defendants, holding that the devisee had sufficiently taken the testator's name, and that it was not necessary for him to apply for an act of parliament or for the king's license. 'A name,' said Chief Justice ABBOTT, in delivering the judgment of the court, 'assumed by the voluntary act of a young man at his outset into life, adopted by all who knew him, and by which he is constantly called becomes, for all purposes that occur to my mind, as much and effectually his name as if he had obtained an act of parliament to confer it upon him;' and there are numerous cases, both in this country and in England, holding that where a man enters into a contract or does any act in a particular name, that he may be sued by the name that he used, whatever his true name may be, and generally that whenever a man has done an act in a particular name, or where he makes a grant, that it may always be shown in support of the validity of the act, that he was known by that name at and about the time when the act was done, though he may have been baptized or previously known by a different name. All that the law looks to is the identity of the individual, . . .[11]

Notes and References

1. Bardsley, Charles Wareing, M.A., *A Dictionary of English and Welsh Surnames* . . ., London 1901, p. 3.

2. Freeman, Edward A., D.C.L., LL.D., "Pedigrees and Pedigree Makers," *The Contemporary Review*, Volume 30, London 1877, p. 22.

3. Ibid, n. 1, pp. 2-3.

4. Ibid, n. 1, p. 8.

5. *In re Snook* (1859) 2 Hilton's Reports of Cases in the Common Pleas Reports for the City of New York 566 et seq. Justice Daly did not include the citations of two cases he cited in his decision, namely: *Button v. Wrightman*, 79 English Reports 1172 (cited on page 43) and *Mayhew v. Mayhew*, 105 English Reports 611 (cited on page 47).

6. Coke on Littleton, 3a — 3b, Eighth edition by John Rudall, Esq., London, 1822, pages 6, 7.

7. Camden, William (1551-1623), Clarenceux King of Arms.

8. Ibid.

9. Lord Coke's reference to the Year Books: These are reported court decisions which commenced in 1274.

10. The reference is to the New York City Directory.

11. *In re Snook*, n. 5, supra.

CHAPTER 5

EVIDENCE OF FALSE, FORGED AND
FABRICATED PEDIGREES

*Lying legends and false pedigrees may, under criticism, disappear
from our popular reference books for a time, but they are mostly
'scotched,' not killed; when the discussion has been forgotten for a few
years, hey presto! there they are, back again, as lively and mendacious
as ever.*[1]

W. Paley Baildon

John Martin Vincent, when a professor of European History at The Johns
Hopkins University, added his opinion to that of Mr. Baildon's, that:

"The list of written sources subject to falsification is by no means
exhausted in this brief review. Biography has offered a tempting field
for invention, and genealogy, which is in fact a condensed form of
biography and family history, has led many a writer into the realm of
fantasy and fraud. Primitive kings and potentates may be excused for
thinking that their race descended from the gods, but the desire to
maintain a long line of ancestry has not yet disappeared from the
world. A matter of pardonable pride has led to the perpetuation of
innumerable frauds. In the feudal period the possession of property
and honors depended largely on descent, hence the temptation to
fabricate was enormous. Under the old regime in France exemption
from taxation was a prerequisite of nobility, and any number of
patents were obtained by collusion and fraudulent representation of
long descent.

In modern days the genealogical tree is cultivated chiefly as an aid to
social prestige, and many a family line is assumed without due respect
to the facts. Indeed, throughout history there has been a tendency to
magnify the importance of the ancestor and to claim him with
confidence. There are great numbers of families with well established
descent through long periods of time, but in many cases of undoubted
validity there are at certain periods visible weaknesses in the
connecting rinks. The person who has followed his family back to a
point where the connection is in doubt is under great temptation to
bridge over a difficulty by assuming a relationship because of a
similarity of name or because the ascent appears to lead to
noteworthy people.

49

The weakness of many American genealogies lies at the point where they cross the Atlantic. The compiler with a certain degree of conscientiousness will say that "James Roe was *said to have been a son of Richard Roe*, at one time sheriff of Nottingham," and will then proceed to mount by another, perhaps authentic genealogical ladder to the thirteenth century, or to William the Conqueror. Families and even professional genealogists have been too easily satisfied with connections which lack *exact* proof. [Emphasis added] The adoption of a family tree or the assumption of a coat of arms is no longer a serious matter to the historian in America from the documentary point of view."[2]

A resume of laws to discourage fraud and forgery are a warning to researchers to be alert to the possibility that the records they search may not be authentic or genuine in whole or in part.

In 1413, Parliament enacted a statute providing for "The Penalty for Forging or Publishing a False Deed," providing that

". . . whereas many of the King's liege people which have manors, lands or tenements, by purchase or by descent of inheritance or in any other manner, intending to be in peace and rest in their said tenures as they were wont to be, divers evil disposed persons, some of their own head, and some by false conspiracy and covin, subtilly [sic] imagine and forge of new divers false deeds and muniments, and then do openly to be pronounced, published, and read, to trouble and change the lands of good people of the country, and to undo and trouble the possessions and titles of the said King's liege people, by the which imagination and falsity many of the aforesaid liege people be troubled and vexed, and at all times abiding in doubt of their possessions and estate: our sovereign lord the King willing to purvey a remedy in this case, by the advice and assent aforesaid, and at the request of the said commons hath ordained and established, that the party so grieved shall have his suit in that case, and recover his damages, and the party convict[ed] shall make fine and ransom at the King's pleasure."[3]

The provision that the penalty would be decided according to the "King's pleasure," was broad enough to fit the punishment to the crime.

During the reign of Queen Elizabeth I, the prevalence of this crime was so serious that in 1562 more drastic penalties were imposed to discourage forgery and another statute was enacted:

"Foreasmuch as the wicked, pernicious and dangerous practice of making, forging and publishing false and untrue charters, evidence, deeds and writings, hath of late time been very much more practised . . . than in times passed, not only to the high displeasure of God, but also to the great injury, wrong, hurt, damage, disherison and utter undoing of divers of the Queen's Majesty's subjects of this realm, and to the great subversion of justice and truth, which seems to have grown and happened chiefly by reason that the pains and punishments limited for such great and notable offences by the laws and statutes of this realm, before this time have been so small, mild and easy, that such evil people have not been nor yet are afraid to enterprise the practising and doing of such offences . . . "[4]

The statute provided that any person who forged any ". . .deed, charter or writing sealed, court roll or the will of any person. . . " with the specific intent of depriving anyone of their real property interests, was liable upon conviction, was responsible for double costs and damages, and was to be seated in the pillory to suffer both his ears cut off and his nostrils slit and seared with a heated iron as perpetual evidence of his crime and falsehood. He was also deprived of the profits of his land for life and subjected to perpetual imprisonment.

If the forgery involved personal property, the penalty was cutting off the ears and imprisonment for one year. A second conviction was the death penalty and forfeiture of all real and personal property.[5]

The "Great Act of Elizabeth I," as was frequently termed, ought to have been severe enough to stop forgery (which by the way may also involve fraud), but it was necessary to adopt more severe punishment. In the 1700's often referred to as the "Age of Reason," additional statutes were enacted which dispensed with the more picturesque forms of punishment by mutilation and forfeiture of property and placed reliance on the effectiveness of the death penalty to discourage forgers of deeds, wills, bonds, leases, and other documents.[6]

Following the "Age of Reason" the death penalty for the crime of forgery was eliminated in 1837 except for the forging of the Great Seal or public seals, and in 1861 the forgery of public seals did not provide for the death penalty.

The fabrication of false pedigrees may involve more than one crime, for example, obtaining money or property by false pretenses, forgery, fraud, as well as civil liability. When the death penalty was eliminated, the fabrication of pedigrees for profit by means of forgery was certain to attract dishonest persons. (However, not all fabricated or fraudulent pedigrees were the result of fraud and deceit or forgery because of the profit motive.)

Forgery is the false creation or alteration of a document which is represented to be legal or valid for the purpose it was made with the intention to defraud someone. It is doubtful if there is a place where this is not a felony, rather than a misdemeanor, which is a less serious crime.

Fraud is an intentional misrepresentation of a material fact, often referred to as "fraud and deceit," and it may be a crime, but it does imply or involve civil liability for money damages from a person who, for instance, represents that a pedigree is true and correct when in fact it is not.

A detailed study of fraud and forgery involving the compilation of genealogies is beyond the scope of this study, but it would be worthwhile for anyone seriously interested in genealogical research to learn of some actual instances of the occurrence of such unethical, dishonest, and criminal practices. Several English and United States case histories will suffice.

SPENCE PEDIGREE FORGERIES

William Sidney Spence was a famous, or more properly an infamous pedigree forger between 1844 and 1849. His modus operandi was to write letters to potential victims and represent that while engaged in inspecting and arranging the title deeds and other documents of Lady Cotgreave which belonged to the late

51

Sir John Cotgreave, he found an ancient pedigree of the Cotgreaves de Hargrave of Cheshire, which he represented was the work of the great William Camden in 1598 (or of Randle Holme 1672) and that this pedigree included names, dates, and places of genealogical events and armorial bearings. The letter ended with the assertion that he had permission to transcribe and compile pedigrees from the original, and believing that the potential client was a descendant of this or these ancient families, he would for a valuable consideration send the necessary extracts from the original pedigree upon receipt of the funds requested.

In due course experts denounced Spence's compilations as totally fraudulent, but in spite of this he managed to bilk at least sixteen different families.[7]

THE HARRISON ESTATE CASE

Mr. Richard Harrison of Warrington, Lancashire, England, a wealthy bachelor, owned extensive interests in real and personal property. To his knowledge he had no close relatives, and so determined that he would not bother to prepare a last will and testament, and let those who claimed any relationship to him prove their relationship. When he died in 1863 at the age of 79, the distribution of his estate was subject to the laws of succession. Therefore, the burden of ascertaining who were his nearest relatives was forced on them and the courts.

As to be expected, quite a number of persons claiming to be the rightful heirs rushed forward and filed documents in the court proceedings to establish their rights to the estate.

Although it is an indictable offense to tamper with entries in parish registers, it is only occasionally that such cases come before the courts. In this case, not only were there numerous entries by erasure and alteration, but entirely false entries were inserted, where there were vacant spaces on the pages of the registers. This was not done in one register only, but in at least three or four, and the official "transcripts" or certified copies, returned each year to the Bishop of Chester were changed. It was believed in some cases the records were destroyed. So extensive were these illegal entries, forgeries, or changes in the registers of Preston, Kirkham, Poulton, and Lytham, as well as the bishop's transcripts of Preston, Kirkham, and Penwortham, that the number totaled almost fifty.

The forgers (who by the time of the trial in 1886 were dead) also forged three marriage license bonds and forged with such skill that in spite of the fact that the writing had to conform with that of the 17th century, the detection of the forgeries was difficult.

If old Manorial Court Rolls had not been properly preserved and their custody guarded against forgery or destruction, the Harrison estate would have passed into the possession of those who were not entitled to the estate properties.

So clever were the activities of the forgers, that it was only by the fortunate discovery of one document, which had never been referred to at any of the trial sessions, that absolute proof was obtained of the manner in which the Penwortham transcripts had been tampered with.

Discovery of the rightful heirs entitled to the Harrison fortune was the result of the perserverance and genealogical skill of Mr. William Dampier Jeans who compiled a pedigree of the Harrison family extending over 200 years.[8]

REGINA V. DAVIES

In 1895, when Col. R. W. Shipway decided to inquire into the genealogy of his family, he was referred by a friend to a man who was introduced as Dr. H. Davies, Oxford, who represented that he was a qualified genealogist, and he was commissioned to undertake the research of the Shipway family history and genealogy. During the research process, Col. Shipway advanced Dr. Davies a sum equivalent to approximately $3,500 in U.S. dollars, which was a considerable amount of money in 1895.

Fortunately, W.P.W. Phillimore, a qualified genealogist, was consulted regarding the results of Dr. Davies' research and it was discovered that Col. Shipway was the victim of a monumental fabrication of his genealogy, and that the genealogy Davies had compiled was based on forgeries he had cleverly executed — in spite of the fact that he had fooled one of the experts of the British Museum and Col. Shipway's firm of solicitors who were furnished with certified copies of wills, entries from parish records, and other documents. Furthermore, Davies was not entitled to the degree of "doctor" and he was not a graduate of Oxford or any other institution of higher learning.

Davies was arrested and prosecuted for obtaining money by false pretenses. He was convicted and was sentenced to three years in prison.[9]

The Shipway case is an example of the danger of relying on certified copies. When the original documents and records are examined, they should be closely scrutinized for evidence of erasures and other irregularities, and if necessary, a document examiner should inspect them if there is any doubt regarding the genuineness of the records.

Fabrication, forgery and falsity, and related pedigree peccadillos are not limited to any particular country. Thanks to "great American know-how," the ability to locate missing heirs is probably unsurpassed. Or it is the reverse, the ability to locate the administration of a large estate cannot be equalled, and the number of persons claiming to be rightful heirs usually depends on how much money is available for distribution. This was particularly the situation in Pennsylvania and New York.

THE GARRETT ESTATE

When Henrietta E. Garrett, a resident of Philadelphia, died intestate on November 16, 1930, her estate was valued at $17,000,000. With that much money involved, plus the fact that the purchasing power in 1930 was so great, the news of the availability of this sum inspired people to file "nearly 26,000" claims in the Orphan's Court. The Court appointed a Master and Examiner who conducted some 2,000 hearings and heard the testimony of 1,100 witnesses. The record of the testimony and exhibits totalled 390 volumes containing 115,000 pages.

Because so many claims had to be considered, it wasn't until 1950, or 20 years after Henrietta Garrett died, that the Master decided that three first cousins were entitled to the estate which after the deduction of costs, expenses, and death taxes was considerably less than $17,000,000.

However, due to appeals to the Supreme Court of Pennsylvania, the estate was not closed and funds or property not distributed to the cousins until 1953.[10]

That there was perjury, forgery, fabrication of false genealogy as the court records disclose, there is no doubt. This is bound to happen when 26,000 claimants are clamoring for so much money. However, not all claims rejected were false, as for instance, the claims of second cousins who were not as closely related as the three first cousins.[11]

THE WENDEL ESTATES

More than one estate was involved in the Wendel family cases in New York. During the probate proceedings in progress in the early 1930's, "there was a total of two thousand three hundred and three in this group"[12] of claimants. This doesn't equal the number of claimants in the Garrett estate, but at first there was not as much money involved — a mere $5,000,000.

In 1936 Surrogate Foley said "This proceeding involves the latest and it is hoped the last attempt to impose a fraudulent claim of relationship upon the members of the family of ... Wendel ...." The surrogate also mentioned "... the unusual degree of fraud, perjury, and forged documents . . . presented in this proceeding and in other proceedings involving the Ella Wendel estate. . . . "[13]

One claimant the surrogate states "... that he had attempted to perpetrate a fraudulent marriage certificate of his alleged mother and father, a spurious will of his alleged father and other fabricated documents in order to [try and] substantiate his claim [to the estate]. The record in the case was directed by the surrogate to be transmitted to the district attorney ... for appropriate action ... [and this claimant] was indicted and convicted of conspiracy and sentenced to a term of three years [in prison]."[14]

If this claimant had succeeded he would have proven that crime does pay, as Surrogate Foley additionally stated: "The motive for the assertion [of this claimant to the estate] here is more sinister than appears upon its face. . . . If the [claimant] had succeeded in establishing his relationship [to the Wendel family, then out of three Wendel estates] he would have been able to obtain money and property valued at $40,000,000."[15]

It is paradoxical that a forged document may be of value to genealogists because the facts stated in the forgery may be true. This point must be credited to Professor Edward A. Freeman who wrote that

> "There is, we will say, a deed whatever may be its object — a sale of lands, a purchase of lands, a grant of lands, the enfranchisement of a villein, or anything else — which is done, say by John of Sutton, with the consent of his wife Agnes and his son Richard. There is another deed [executed] by Richard of Sutton with the consent of his mother Agnes and son William. Here is real evidence for three stages of the pedigree. Even if the deeds should chance to be forgeries, as many deeds are, they would still be [valid] evidence. For the object of the forger would not be to prove steps in the pedigree, but to make good some claim or other. He would have no motive for falsifying the pedigree, and, if he made any mistake in it, the mistake would be purely accidental.
>
> It must be remembered that there are deeds which seem to have been forged on purpose to make out false pedigrees. But I am speaking of deeds of the ordinary kinds, such as one finds in the cartularies of

54

monasteries, which, whether genuine or spurious, whether the claims which they meant to assert were good or bad, were not written to prove a pedigree. In either case the witness to genealogy is incidental, and has the value of incidental witness.

So, if a man is mentioned in a Pipe-roll, there is real evidence for the pedigree. So again, there may be the statements of credible chroniclers whose story may lead them to mention that such and such a man was the son or grandson of such or such another man. All these are different forms of real evidence; and the less the writer of the document was thinking of proving the pedigree, the further his statement goes toward proving it."[16]

Conclusion:

There is merit to what Professor Freeman wrote regarding forged documents which may state true facts; nevertheless, the problem of discerning what is "acceptable forgery" and what is unacceptable is a problem not easily overcome. It seems that a reasonable course of action is to judge every record with caution, scrutinizing and interpreting with more than average skill and judgment.

Notes and References

1. Baildon, W. Paley, *Law Quarterly Review*, Vol. 26, London, July 1910, p. 280.

2. Vincent, John Martin, *Historical Research — An Outline of Theory and Practice*, 1911, pp. 36-37.

3. *Statutes at Large*, I Henry V, Chapter 3, 1413.

4. *Statutes at Large*, 5 Elizabeth 1, Chapter 14, 1562.

5. Ibid.

6. *Statutes at Large*, 2 George II, Chapter 25, 1728-29, 7 George II, Chapter 22, 1733.

7. Stewart-Brown, R., M.A., F.S.A., "The Cotgreave Pedigree Forgeries," *The Genealogist's Magazine*, Volume 6, September 1933, No. 7, pp. 288-293.

8. Earwaker, J.P., M.A., F.S.A., *A Lancashire Pedigree Case: Or a History of the Various Trials for the Recovery of the Harrison Estates. . .*, Warrington 1887, pp. i, et seq.

9. Phillimore, W.P.W., M.A., B.C.L., The *"Principal Genealogical Specialist" Or Regina v. Davies and The Shipway Genealogy, Being the Story of a Remarkable Pedigree Fraud*, London 1899, p. 3 et seq.

10. *Garrett Estate* (1953) 372 Pennsylvania Reports 438, et seq.

11. Ibid.

12. *In the Matter of Wendel* (1933) 146 Miscellaneous Reports (N.Y.), 260, et seq; 159 Miscellaneous Reports (N.Y.), 443 et seq.

13. Ibid.

14. Ibid.

15. Ibid, n. 10, 146 Miscellaneous Reports (N.Y.), pp. 260, 273.

16. Freeman, Edward A., "Pedigrees and Pedigree Makers," *The Contemporary Review*, Volume 30, London 1877, p. 16.

CHAPTER 6

THE HERALDRY PROBLEM

The marshalling of coat-armour, which was formerly the pride and study of all the best families in the kingdom, is now greatly disregarded; and has fallen into the hands of certain officers and attendants ... called heralds, who consider it only as a matter of lucre and not of justice; whereby such falsity and confusion have crept into their records, (which ought to be the standing evidence of families, descents and coat-armour) that, though formerly some credit has been paid to their testimony, now even their common seal will not be received as evidence in any court of justice in the kingdom. But their original visitation books, compiled when progresses were solemnly and regularly made into every part of the kingdom, to inquire into the state of families, and to register such marriages and descents as were verified to them upon oath, are allowed to be good evidence of pedigrees.[1]

Sir William Blackstone

Blackstone wrote the foregoing quotation in 1765. It is fortunate for him that he isn't around today to learn of the craze of the American public to possess a "coat of arms," and their naive belief that sending a few dollars to one of the numerous commercial firms in the United States advertising for sale "the coat of arms of your family name," a product which is as phony as a three-dollar bill.

Unfortunately, the public does not know there is no such article as a "coat of arms of a family name." The public further would be surprised and perhaps shocked to learn that they do not possess the right to appropriate and display the coat of arms granted to some other person.

The general public does not know that similarity of surname is not sufficient to justify the adoption of a coat of arms. Persons with a common name believe they have the right to a wide range of choices, and therefore, select the arms which appears to their artistic sense. A person named Smith or someone with the surname of Winslow, for example, cannot simply consult a library book and appropriate the Winslow arms granted to some other person with the same surname. People who do this, or buy a coat of arms from one of the commercial firms would no doubt be surprised to learn that the right to bear or display heraldic devices is hereditary in England and other foreign countries, and to appropriate the arms to which they are not entitled subjects them to the possibility of a civil lawsuit or a restraining order and money damages, and under some circumstances criminal penalties.

Furthermore, in recent years a cause of civil action known as "invasion of the right of privacy" had developed which would involve an injunction restraining the use by a person not entitled to the coat of arms of someone who possessed the exclusive right to the use and display of the arms.

The fact is that the person who is legally entitled to the coat of arms in England and resides there, would not be prohibited from commencing a lawsuit against an infringer in the United States.

Although there is no provision for hereditary coat of arms in the United States and we have no official heralds, College of Heraldry, or Court of Chivalry, it should not be implied that courts in the United States will not protect the legal rights of persons who are entitled to arms and heraldic devices of people from foreign countries. It is possible for a person in the United States to use and display an original coat of arms designed for a person, if its appearance does not infringe the arms of another. If an original coat of arms was designed for a specific family, and it was reproduced in a family genealogy published in book form, it could be submitted for copyright protection. But why bother with a coat of arms which is of no hereditary or ancestry value or meaning? Milton Rubincam, one of the Fellows of The American Society of Genealogists, wrote this in regard to the unjustified *Assumption of Coats-of-Arms*:

> The right to bear arms is a source of mystification to many gen-
> ealogists, who adopt the armorial insignia of other families without
> proving their right thereto . . . . The fact that our ancestors bore the
> same surnames as armigerous families does not automatically permit
> us to assume the heraldic bearings of those families. We must prove
> that [we are] descended from families which had a legal right to use
> such insignia. . . . The United States is not governed by heraldic rules,
> hence anyone may adopt a coat-of-arms to his liking [subject to the
> possibility of legal action by the person or persons who resent the
> appropriation of their arms and decide to sue for the infringment].
> But the only honorable course is to prove descent from armigerous
> forefathers, and use their arms according to heraldic usage as
> described in the numerous manuals on the subject.[2]

The assumption of arms by persons not entitled to them, as described by Mr. Rubincam in his article, did not begin in the past few years. The practice of appropriating coat-of-arms and the genealogies by persons not legally, historically, or ethically entitled thereto has been plaguing competent genealogists and heraldic specialists before the beginning of this century and has continued until the present time. In an article by John D. Champlin, Jr., written in 1891 describing the tactics of the dishonest and unethical practitioners of heraldry and genealogy, he wrote this in regard to this problem:

> "When we consider that these genealogies spoken of by Mr. Freeman
> were manufactured in defiance of the law which condemned the

manufacturer of a pedigree to the loss of an ear [the penalty for forgery in England at one time], we shall be better able to appreciate the difficulties under which one labors in convention-ridden England, and the blessings of our own unlicensed liberty. Here [in the United States] the genealogist and herald hedged in by no ridiculous limitations, may make pedigrees and escutcheons to suit the taste and purse of the family consulting them. But while rejoicing in this, we shall do well to remember that the very freedom of institutions which has rendered possible the privileges we enjoy has developed a sharp wit which finds its target in the great, the good, and the rich. It behooves us, then, to avoid errors which have provoked criticism even among the duller transatlantic humorists, and to confine our pedigrees within the bounds of moderation and apparent truthfulness."[3]

Mr. Champlin continues with some examples to illustrate his point:

"A short time ago [circa 1879], a wealthy American family had their attention called to the fact that a trifling change in the orthography of their surname would enable them to make a connection with an ancient knightly [family], and to adopt its pedigree and arms. If they had contented themselves with publishing a genealogy in the ordinary way, and with carving the coat of arms on their own tombstones, all might have gone well; but vanity led them to put up in the church where reposed the ashes of the English family what had all the appearance of being an antique brazen tablet, in commemoration of their [the American] emigrant ancestor. The ordinary visitor would never have noticed any difference between this interloper and the brasses that had become mellowed by time instead of by acids; but the [English] family that had long enjoyed a monopoly of the funereal ornamentation of the church took umbrage at what they considered an invasion of their rights, and were mean enough to discover, and to proclaim the discovery, that the [American] tablet bore on its under edge the tell-tale legend,

'John Jones fecit 1879.'

Thus snuffed out in ridicule what might have been, but for culpable carelessness, a successful ingraftment."[4]

"Another American family, bearing a name famous in English history and exalted in one branch by a ducal title, concluded that similarity of surname gave them an equal right to the heraldic belongings of the family, and assumed the escutcheon, supporters and all. If their pride had been satisfied with the display of the insignia on their carriage panels, no one would have objected; but when it tempted them to assert publicly their right to the ducal title, which was then in abeyance, it aroused the curiosity of some prowling genealogists – those pests of society – who set about inquiries which, they asserted, proved that the American family was only of yeoman origin and of no possible connection with the ducal house. Thus did their vaulting ambition overleap itself, and to avoid ridicule they were obliged to suppress a magnificent table service of china and silver, on which they had displayed, at considerable expense, the ducal crest and coronet."[5]

Heraldry, it will thus be seen, is no trifling thing to be played with by everybody with impunity, but is subject to laws as strict as those of Medes and Persians."[6]

The law is in a constant state of change and development. The recognition and appreciation of the remedy of the right of privacy is an example and is now becoming quite popular in this litigious society. That right, and other available remedies (known to the legal profession) sooner or later will be the downfall of the hucksters who offer for sale horrendous heraldic devices to the public for a monetary consideration by misleading advertising by mail and magazine.[7]

Notes and References

1. Blackstone, Sir William, *Commentaries on the Laws of England*, Volume 3, London 1809, pp. 105-106.

2. Rubincam, Milton, "Pitfalls in Genealogical Research," *National Genealogical Society Quarterly*, Vol. 43, June 1955, No. 2, pp. 43-44.

3. Champlin, John D., "The Manufacture of Ancestors," *Forum*, Vol. X, January 1891, pp. 569-571.

4. Ibid.

5. Ibid.

6. Ibid.

7. Stevenson, Noel C., "Genealogy and the Right of Privacy," *The American Genealogist*, Volume 25, July 1949, No. 3, pp. 145-152.

PART II

RIGHT OF ACCESS TO OFFICIAL AND PUBLIC RECORDS

CHAPTER 7

OFFICIAL RECORDS — PUBLIC RECORDS

Official Records are those kept in the performance of duty by an [elected or appointed] officer even if not required by statute.

State v. Biscoe (1975)
112 Arizona 98, 99

A "public record," strictly speaking, is one made by a public officer in pursuance of a duty, the immediate purpose of which is to disseminate information to the public, or to serve as a memorial of official transactions for public reference.

People v. Olson
232 California Appellate 2nd 480, 486

The mere fact that a writing is in the possession of a public officer or public agency does not necessarily make it a public record.

People v. Olson, supra.

Public records housed in public buildings, in the custody of public officials, paid salaries from public funds; which public records are filed, recorded and maintained at the expense of the public for public use are available to the public to search and copy, if the public official decides the public is entitled to search and peruse the public records.

Anonymous

In other words, all official and public records are not available to you. No doubt the outstanding example is adoption records, because the records are sealed in accordance with existing law; and information from these records may not be disclosed without an order of a court of competent jurisdiction.

Another record source which in many offices access is denied is vital records, unless the official (or deputy) in charge is satisfied that the searcher is related to the family involved, or is authorized by the family member to represent them. In addition to these sources, U.S. Census records are subject to some restrictions in regard to use.

Fortunately, land records and court proceedings (other than adoptions) are supposed to be available to searchers. However, in some places genealogists or record searchers are not welcomed with enthusiasm, if they are strangers to the area.

If a public official refused to permit a search of the records or refused other lawful service, there is a remedy for a genealogist or record searcher and that is an action for a writ of mandamus to compel the official to do his duty.

ARE OFFICIAL AND PUBLIC RECORDS ORIGINAL RECORDS?

Not necessarily. For example, an original last will and testament filed in a probate court is an original record. This original filed will is also an official record. A copy of the original will recorded or written in a "Will Book," is not an original record. Deeds or other documents relating to real or personal property recorded in the Registry of Deeds, or the County Recorder's Office, are copies of the original. After recordation, the original is returned to the person entitled to it. Nevertheless, all of the records mentioned above are official or public records.

ARE FACTS IN OFFICIAL OR PUBLIC RECORDS ALWAYS CORRECT?

Unfortunately the answer is "No" because the human element is always involved. However, accuracy is encouraged because property and other legal rights are involved and often documents are signed under oath. This presumably encourages accuracy and honesty of all parties concerned — but there always will be exceptions. The law provides that certain official records shall be presumptive of the truth of their contents. (Robinson v. United Order of the Gold Cross, 77 App. Div. 215; 79 N.Y.S. 13, 16). This means that if there is doubt regarding the accuracy of a record, it is subject to rebuttal. However, this would require commencing a civil action to correct the record.

Conclusion:

Official records are the most reliable and dependable source for genealogy and family history, in spite of the fact that on numerous occasions there are reports of errors in birth, marriage, death certificates, and other records. Usually these are honest mistakes. The fact that individuals who are involved in the preparation of documents which become official records do so with some serious thought are frequently required to sign or otherwise represent the facts are true because they are under oath. For example, when an individual who is mentally alert prepares his will or instructs his lawyer to do so, it would be unusual for either of these persons to falsify any facts. The individual is supposed to read his will before signing. He (unless it is a holographic will which is written, dated, and signed in his own handwriting) signs the will before witnesses who attest to his signature and express an opinion in the attestation paragraph that this person is of "sound and disposing mind and memory."

There are other safeguards. In the event of litigation involving any type of official records, the principal safeguard is that witnesses are subject to cross examination as a test for the truth or falsity of their testimony. Likewise, documents are subject to be examined by expert witnesses for evidence of forgery and other indications that the document or any part of it is spurious.

Additionally, it is the practice of competent genealogists to consult as many sources as there are available to obtain substantial evidence before his/her research is valid.

In this book, only the most important official records will be considered due to space limitations. It will not be possible to discuss various tax records, such as real and personal property tax assessment rolls which are often used as a substitute for census records, or inheritance tax records which were first effective in Pennsylvania May 1, 1826 (Pennsylvania Laws (1825-26), Chapter 72). This set the precedent for other states to follow, to collect a new revenue. Poll taxes, when available, are another substitute for census records. Public school records according to court decisions are official records, but locating them is the problem. Military service records and pension applications are important and are official records. Pension applications are simply declarations or affidavits under oath and affidavits are often confused with depositions which are considered elsewhere in this book.

Naturalization records are within the category of court records which are considered in this chapter.

The status of passenger lists depends on who compiled them and their present custody.

Most or all official records will be discussed in the chapters devoted to the technical rules of evidence.

SUMMARY OF
FEDERAL AND LOCAL OFFICIAL RECORDS[1]

(1) Federal Records:[2]
   A. Land Records:
       1. Patents and other land records (National Archives)
       2. Bounty land warrants (National Archives)
           Bounty land affidavits (National Archives)
           Bounty land applications (National Archives)

   B. Military Records:
       1. Service records various wars (National Archives)
       2. Pension files and applications, various wars (National Archives)

   C. Census: (National Archives)
       1. 1790 census is printed and indexed and available in most libraries
       2. Microfilm copies of subsequent census records available in many libraries and Federal Record Centers throughout the U.S.

    D. Court Records: (Civil and Criminal)
1. U.S. District Court (Local federal clerks of courts and Federal Record Centers.)
2. Circuit Courts of Appeal (Federal Record Centers)
3. U.S. Supreme Court (National Archives)

    E. Legislative Records: (Journals, Laws, etc) (Published volumes)

    F. Miscellaneous Records: (Examples)
1. Shipping and passenger lists (National Archives)
2. Immigration records (National Archives)
3. Passport records and applications (1791-1879 — National Archives)
4. Naturalization records (Federal Archives and local court records)

(2) State Records: (Also Territorial Records)
1. Vital statistics, births, deaths, and marriage certificates
2. Files and reports of appellate courts
3. State libraries and archives
4. Census and records taken by state authority
5. State land office records
6. Records of Secretary of State (often this officer is also the custodian of miscellaneous collections of early official records from different parts of a state)
7. Legislative Journals (Published volumes)
8. Session laws (Published volumes)
9. Court reports (Published volumes)
10. Administrative records (e.g., inheritance tax files: try state archives)
11. Executive records (Secretaries of various states and archives)

(3) County, Town, and Other Local Records:
    A. Court records: (Civil and Criminal)
        (Custodian: generally the county clerk)
1. Probate files and record volumes
   a. Wills
   b. Petitions for letters testamentary
   c. Petitions for letters of administration
   d. Decrees of distribution and orders
   e. Inventories
   f. Miscellaneous affidavits
   g. Petitions to determine heirship
   h. Guardianship matters
   i. Adoption proceedings
   j. Affidavits and depositions
2. Civil Actions: (other than probate) law and equity (Consult files and record volumes)
   a. Partition
   b. Quiet title
   c. Divorce

      d. Foreclosures

      e. Actions for possession of real and personal property

      f. Other actions too numerous to mention

3. Vital Records:

      a. Birth certificates

      b. Marriage licenses and intentions to marry

      c. Marriage records

      d. Death certificates

4. Land Records: (Custodian generally county recorder)

      a. Deeds

      b. Mortgages

      c. Leases

      d. Recorded wills

      e. Powers of attorney

      f. Miscellaneous affidavits

      g. Judgments and decrees affecting realty

      h. Contracts pertaining to real property

5. Miscellaneous Records:

      a. Assessment and tax rolls

      b. Register of voters

      c. In every record office, particularly in the land records there is to be found a mass of miscellaneous records that do not fit in any of the above sources. They are recorded in separate volumes. A good example is an agreement for support of children.

      d. Coroner's files

      e. Maps and plats

6. Town and Municipal Records:

      a. Vital records — birth, marriage, and death records (Local and state offices)

      b. Court records of various types (Clerk of specific court)

      c. Land records are kept in some towns and cities (Town or City Clerk)

      d. Miscellaneous records (often the same type of records are in custody of the town clerk as the county recorder or the county clerk has — depending on the state) (Town or City Clerk)

Notes and References

1. Adapted from *Search and Research,* by Noel C. Stevenson, F.A.S.G., Deseret Book Company, Salt Lake City, 1977.

2. Colket, Meredith B., Jr., and Bridgers, Frank E., *Guide to Genealogical Records in the National Archives,* Washington 1964, an excellent research guide to federal records.

CHAPTER 8

VITAL RECORDS

*Almost two centuries before the passage of the Statute of William IV
[registration of births, marriages, and deaths, effective in 1837], the
founders of the Massachusetts Colony, though not less attached than
other Englishmen to their own forms of religious worship, had the
wisdom to perceive that it was more important for the civil government
to preserve exact records of the dates of births and deaths, than of
religious ceremonies from which they might be imperfectly inferred;
and that the importance of recording those facts did not depend on the
particular creed or church government of the individual, but applied
equally to the whole people. They accordingly left the baptism of the
living and the burial of the dead to the churches; but by an ordinance
of 1639 enacted 'that there be records kept of the days of every
marriage, birth and death of every person within this jurisdiction;'
and similar statutes have been ever since in force in Massachusetts.*
                               Justice Gray, <u>Kennedy v. Doyle</u>
                               (1865) 92 Massachusetts Reports, 161, 164

The term vital records indicates evidence of births, marriages, and deaths.
Some custodians of vital records are the source for divorce and dissolution of
marriage records.

Christening and baptism records are not evidence of birth,[1] although they
are evidence that the person has been born. This is obvious, as the date of
baptism may occur many years after the date of birth. A church marriage record
is not an official record unless the church is the established church and the
church records recognized as official records of the realm. The date of a burial
record is not evidence of the date of death, although it is certainly evidence that
the person is dead. It should not be implied that baptismal and other church
records are to be ignored. Discussion of christenings, baptisms, church
marriages, banns and burials will be included in a chapter on church records.
Burial records also will be discussed in cemetery records. Marriage and marriage
records, divorce and annulment are included in more detail in a separate chapter
of this book. Here we are concerned only with births, marriages, and deaths.

According to Kane's *Famous First Facts*,[2] the first state "Birth Registration Law" was passed by the State of Georgia December 19, 1823.[3] This was much earlier than most state action on this subject (some of the states during colonial times began registration much earlier than the 1823 date). Note that this statute applies to birth record registration only. There are some marriage and death records in the Georgia counties prior to 1823, but the dates of commencement vary in the various counties.

This 1823 date for any registration of vital records is early, but Georgia's record is not all that impressive, as a survey of all of the 159 counties in that state disclosed. Of the 159, sixty-nine counties returned a questionnaire sent to them.

The purpose of the survey was to ascertain how responsive the various counties were in registering births following the enactment of the statute on December 19, 1823. Presumably the effective date would be January 1, 1824. None of the counties in existence on that date commenced registration in 1824. The first one to comply was Harris County, and it did not do so until 1828 – one year after it was organized. Sixty-five out of the sixty-nine counties reporting did not begin registration of birth records until after 1900, and sixty-three counties did not begin until after 1915. Unfortunately this record is common; a majority of the states failed to register evidence of early births, marriages, and deaths.

The legislative purpose in enacting the Georgia Statute was very laudable:

> Whereas, much inconvenience has been experienced in this State from the difficulty of obtaining testimony of the ages of persons interested in questions of rights before our courts; and whereas, embarrassing difficulties frequently impede the correct administration of justice on this subject: for remedy whereof, Be it enacted. . . [provision for registration of births followed].

The registration of birth, marriage, and death records in the United States in the past has been a dismal failure. This important function at an early date was ignored, delegated to local officials, and registration at a central location in each of the states was not undertaken, in some instances, until after 1900.

Compared to Great Britain and other European counties which started registration of baptisms, marriages, and burials as early as the sixteenth century, and vital records at later dates, local jurisdictions of the United States have been derelict in their duty to perform this important function.

Fortunately, there are a few jurisdictions that registered births, marriages, and deaths at an early date. The General Court of Massachusetts as a Colony ordered registration of vital records in 1639.[4] However, registration of vital records in what is now Massachusetts commenced earlier than the legislation of the General Court. For example, Boston and Plymouth Colony records antedate 1639.

Also, the vital records of Connecticut, New Hampshire, Rhode Island, and Vermont were recorded at varying dates. In the South and other parts of the country, the citizenry and officials failed us.

In the South, Virginia is an exception. The General Assembly at its February, 1631-32 session ordered registration of "all burials, christenings, & marriages. . . ."[5] Although baptisms and christenings are not proof of birth, and burials are not evidence of the date of death, they are at least evidence that someone has been born or died. It wasn't until the session of March, 1659-60, of the "Grand Assemblie," that a statute was enacted "That every parish shall well, truly, and plainly record and sett downe in a booke provided for that purpose, all marriages, deaths and births that shall happen within the precincts of the parish, and in the month of March in every yeare, the person appointed by the parish so to do, shall make true certificate into the clerke of every county to the intent the same may there remaine on record for ever." The statute also provided that if the master of any family failed to report within one month any birth, marriage, or death, he shall forfeit one hundred pounds of tobacco.[6] Fortunately, the legislators were not concerned with the law requiring separation of church and state.

The enactment of statutes by the Virginia Assembly at such an early date is encouraging; but if the law was enforced, Virginia's government warehouses should have been bulging with tobacco forfeited because the births, marriages, and deaths were not reported at an early date except for one county. A survey of all of Virginia's counties disclosed (68 out of 127 counties responded to a questionnaire) only Middlesex County's efforts to comply with the law are impressive. The clerk of Middlesex County wrote "We have Parish Registers which give Birth, Death, and Marriage records from 1653-1812." Richmond County is second; the clerk reported that birth, marriage, and death records commenced in 1672. Marriage records in some counties commence at early dates in the counties reporting. For example, in Richmond County they begin as early as 1672. But the records of births and deaths for most counties are woefully inadequate. It is possible that counties not reporting may have early records.

Some Southern States are not noted for early registration of vital records. North Carolina is just one of the states in this category. Seventy-two counties out of one hundred responded to a survey questionnaire. Only one county, Caswell (formed in 1777) reported any birth and death records and these did not commence until 1913. The marriage records are an exception, as these commenced in 1777. Some interesting news was received (January 12, 1977) from Mr. J. B. Blaylock, P.O. Box 147, Yanceyville, North Carolina, 27379, who held the position of Register of Deeds of Caswell County for forty-two years until he retired recently. During his tenure in office, he collected over 675 Bible and other family records. Mr. Blaylock will respond to inquiries regarding his collection, but correspondents must enclose a stamped and addressed envelope and expect to pay for information if he has it. His records are not confined to people of Caswell County.

> Eventually, the various states adopted central registration of birth, marriage, and death records. The dates of adoption of a uniform system of central registration vary from state to state. It is necessary therefore to consult reference books to ascertain the date of earliest registration in any specific state.[7]

Notes and References

1. *Kennedy v. Doyle* (Mass, 1865) 10 Allen 161, 162.
2. Kane, Joseph Nathan, *Famous First Facts*, New York 1950, p. 83.
3. Dawson, William C. (compiler), *A Compilation of the Laws of the State of Georgia Passed by the General Assembly. . . 1819-1829*, 1831, p. 113.
4. Massachusetts General Court, The Book of the Laws and Libertyes of Massachusets Concerning the Inhabitants of the Massachusets [sic] . . . , Cambridge 1648, pp. 46-47. Facsimile edition reprinted from the original in the Henry E. Huntington Library, Cambridge 1929.
5. Virginia Grand Assembly, The Statutes at Large; Being a Collection of All the Laws of Virginia, From the First Session of the Legislature in the Year 1619, compiled by William Waller Hening, Volume 1, February 1631-2, 7th Charles 1st, Act III.
6. Ibid, note 5, March 1659-60 — 11th [year] of Commonwealth, p. 542.
7. Stevenson, Noel C., *Search and Research*, 1977, is one of the reference books which disclose the dates of central registration in the various states.

CHAPTER 9

HOW ACCURATE ARE VITAL RECORDS?

Records kept by the registrar of vital records are vital to the general welfare, and the registration of a birth right must be given as much sanctity in the law as the registration of a property right.
State ex rel Schlumbrecht v. Louisiana State Board of Health
(1970) 231 Southern 2nd Reporter 730, 732

The foregoing quotation from a decision of the Louisiana Supreme Court presents a beautiful ideal. An ideal, however, is not real life, so be prepared for disillusionment.

One of the first shocks experienced by anyone interested in genealogical research is the sad realization that records of births, marriages, and deaths are not universally accurate. (This unfortunate situation is not limited to vital records.) Why? Tragic, but true, records are not compiled for the principal purpose of preserving genealogy and family history. A writer on this subject discusses "The Uses of Vital Statistics" and states that

> The information collected at vital registration is used principally in the study of population movements. Since censuses can only be taken periodically (often at decennial intervals), vital statistics serve as the principal instrument for making intercensal estimates of population. The decomposition of population growth into births, deaths and migration is essential if its nature and causes are to be fully understood, and a knowledge of mortality and fertility rates is also necessary if reasonable assumptions are to be made for projection of population trends. (Grebenik, Eugene, "The Uses of Vital Statistics," in the *International Encyclopedia of Social Sciences*, Volume 16, Macmillan Publishing Corporation, New York 1968, p. 342.)

Obviously the author of that paragraph did not consider the genealogical or historical importance of vital records. Registration of birth, marriage, and death records throughout the United States was principally motivated for statistical and public health purposes. If as much attention was devoted to genealogical purposes as social, statistical, and public health purposes, the possibility of accuracy of genealogical facts would be enhanced greatly. If genealogical facts, such as parentage, and dates and places of birth, marriage, and death were recorded as accurately as medical and other health facts, genealogists would be able to utilize vital records with much more confidence.

Who prepares the certificate forms for these important events? Usually clerks. The physician is interested in the medical aspects of birth or death. The clerk issuing a marriage license is not interested in genealogical detail. As a result almost one hundred percent of the time, birth, marriage, and death certificates are incomplete. Usually the names are complete and correct and for additional identification in recent years, a social security number is required. Age at birth is no problem, but at marriage and death there may be some doubt. The date of birth on birth, marriage or death certificates may be wrong. The maiden names of females are often ignored because the informant's knowledge of the family relationships is inadequate, and in the rush and hurry of modern life, nobody will wait for someone to ascertain the facts. The place of birth is a common instance where little care or attention prevails. There isn't space enough on the forms for including the city, town, or county, so the state or country of birth is entered if the informant knows that much. Assume the informant told the clerk or official recording the information, detailed information of this character, it would rarely be recorded on the form. Assume an informant told the clerk the subject's parents were born in Scituate, Massachusetts. In most places the clerk could not spell "Scituate," so he/she would enter "Mass." However, now that we have the zip system, the entry would no doubt be "MA" as the place of birth. If the clerk could spell the town or city, this information probably would be ignored. The attitude is that information is not necessary for statistical purposes.

The foregoing applies especially to our modern compilation of birth, marriage, and death records. Records of previous centuries are discussed elsewhere in this book.

Discrepancies, omissions, and mistakes in the early vital records occurred frequently. Until strict laws were enacted forcing duty on physicians, midwives, and others to exercise some care and diligence in regard to vital records, few officials or citizens were concerned whether accurate records were maintained, or information regarding these events were reported for registration. When the information was reported, glaring examples of carelessness were often the result.

For example, an 1872 Ohio birth record stated that the child was a "female;" the family Bible record stated the child was a "male." This discrepancy was, of course, frustrating but the problem worsened because the inscription on the gravestone of the child read "Infant Lippincott."

The late H. Minot Pitman, a qualified genealogist, was cautious in accepting the facts stated in vital records as universally true, stating that

> "The vital records of a town or health department of a city or state are usually accepted as satisfactory proof, but they are not always correct. This may be due to errors of recording on the part of the clerk, or to false statements, intentional or not, of the relative furnishing the information. Recently in searching for the parents of a man listed in *Who's Who in America*, I found his mother given as Jane Doe [true name withheld]. "Jane Doe" was repeated [as his mother] in the man's death certificate. But on looking up the "mother's" will, she

referred to the man as her stepson, a relationship which was repeated
in the petition for probate of her estate, and confirmed by her ninety-
year old son when I finally located him, the mother really being
"Charity Roe [not the true name], his father's first wife."
(*Genealogical Proof* . . . , by H. Minot Pitman, LL.B., F.A.S.G., *The
American Genealogist*, Vol. 37, October 1961, p. 193.)

JUDGING THE ACCURACY OF FACTS IN VITAL RECORDS

The personal knowledge of the individual who furnishes the information for
birth, marriage, and death certificates is the basis for judging the accuracy of
these records. Therefore, the first consideration in exercising judgment is the
relationship of the informant to the person born, married, or dead. If the
informant is closely related, such as a father, mother, brother, or sister, the facts
on the certificate are probably accurate or as accurate as can be expected from
relatives. There are exceptions, such as the rare instance of a neighbor, or distant
relative, who knows more about the family history than close relatives.
Unfortunately, this unusual feature cannot be ascertained without a personal
interview and often it is too late because of the passage of time. Certainly parents
who are informants for birth records ought to know the facts, and relate them
freely unless they are concealing some unfortunate incident.

It is usually safe to assume that a bride and groom know that the facts
included in their marriage record are correct, as they presumably supplied those
facts. The only exception might be with respect to "age information" — for
obvious reasons. The question of paternity and maternity is discussed in another
chapter.

Death records in regard to the date of death are usually correct because there
is an official interest in how, when, and where the decedent died. But the
accuracy of the rest of the information is dependent on the knowledge of the
informant.

Informants supplying genealogical facts, if a relative, usually know the facts
and if they do not, they probably have no reason to misrepresent them. If the
informant does not know a specific fact, the space for that will state "unknown."
If the informant is a close relative and there aren't many "unknown" facts, the
information may be rated as probably accurate. If the informant is a distant
relative or a stranger, there is much more possibility of error.

If the informant's answers as disclosed on the certificate are stated as
"unknown" in several places, the value of the entire record should be questioned,
and if possible, close relatives should be located or other records searched in
order to discover the facts. The funeral directors often maintain complete records
including names and addresses of close members of the family. An examination
of the probate and land records should be undertaken. Also, civil court records
and any other records available should not be overlooked. Additional
investigation is always justified.

If the informant is a stranger, this presents a problem unless you are able
through independent investigation to ascertain how many years the informant
knew the subject of the death. It must be recognized that often a neighbor or
friend of the person knew more about the family than some relatives.

FALSE AND FRAUDULENT RECORDS

Recognizing that records are false is difficult and this fact is disclosed only due to some information on the certificate or from other sources, but it does happen.

Richard Roe and Jane Roe consulted me for legal advice. They informed me they were husband and wife and had decided to separate. During the interview they said there were no children, but that one was expected. Further questioning disclosed the fact that the expected child was sired before they were married by John Doe, the wife's former husband from whom she was divorced. They planned on representing this child as theirs and intended that the birth certificate would state that the child (whom I shall call Woe Doe), was the issue of Richard Roe. When I refused to prepare documents misrepresenting the paternity of the expected child, they decided they did not want me to represent them as an attorney. I have often wondered what happened to Woe Doe, who was misnamed Woe Roe, and also wondered how many birth records are false in whole or in part. There is not a satisfactory answer, but without a doubt there are many such cases. (Refer to the chapter on Paternity)

ADOPTIONS

Adoptions are so numerous that it would require a very large computer to ascertain the number of instances where reissued birth certificates misstate the names of the parents of children. The system of issuing new birth certificates naming the adopting "parents" as the biological parents has created problems for which there is no adequate solution for genealogists.

IDENTITY

This is one of the serious problems due to similarity of names. Refer to the chapter on this subject.

SPELLING OF NAMES

Due to the fact that in the past and in the present people are inclined to spell phonetically, a serious problem arises. For a valuable guide to ascertain the various spelling of surnames, consult *A Century of Population Growth . . 1790-1900*, Washington 1909, published by the Department of Commerce and Labor, Bureau of the Census. Beginning on page 227 is a nomenclature table listing surnames included in the 1790 census. The number of different spellings for common names is astounding and is an example of phonetic spelling of that period. For instance, the surname Reynolds was spelled thirty-four different ways by the census enumerators.

PUBLISHED VITAL RECORDS

Presumably, the only defects in these records result from incorrect deciphering of handwriting of the official or original records, scrivener's errors, and printing errors. But that is not all. Researchers are usually aware of the hazard of what happens when information in official record volumes (e.g., land records) is copied and converted from that form into copied manuscripts and printed books. Not all researchers consider that when birth, marriage, and death records such as those of Massachusetts towns are copied and printed, frequently family groups are separated into alphabetical listings. Many vital records are published alphabetically by surname and in that form if the original record is in a family group, a valuable means of ascertaining relationship of the children to the parents is destroyed. To compensate for this defect, it is often necessary to search the original records. Published vital records should be used only as a guide, for the reasons mentioned above.

An example of this practice of family grouping is one I found in Castine, Maine. In the 1700's, the town clerk not only entered the children born in Castine in family group form, but also included children born elsewhere. Technically, the children born other than in Castine could not be classified as part of an official record, but from a practical aspect there was no reason for not accepting the record of the entire family as correct as one could possibly expect.

INDICES TO VITAL RECORDS

An index is not an official record of births, marriages, or deaths. At the Connecticut State Library, for instance, the Barbour Index is a great aid to research as it includes the entire state in one search of the index. However, this is not an official record; it includes church and other private records in addition to the index of vital records in the various towns.

Also, do not overlook the fact that there are bound to be errors of various kinds in the indices, and on occasion, names have been omitted.

CHURCH RECORDS

Church records which include births, baptisms, banns, marriages, deaths, and burials are not official vital records (at least not in the United States) and are not valid substitutes for official vital records. There are a few exceptions; during the colonial period the legislative body ordered registration of christenings or baptisms, marriages, and burials. This occurred in Virginia, and it may be argued that these records would be official records. If official records are not available, church records may be substituted.

AGE

This is a problem frequently encountered and especially in death certificates. When a record states that an old pioneer died at age 114 years, be skeptical. Such an ancient age is possible, but not probable. Additional research in other sources should disclose the error.

BIRTH AND MARRIAGE CERTIFICATES

A birth certificate is evidence that the person mentioned in it was born on the date stated. Assuming the name and date is correct, additional evidence is still required to establish that the person named in the birth certificate is the same person mentioned in your record. The same precaution also applies to marriage and death records, as there is always an identity problem due to similarity of names. The subject of identity is discussed in a separate chapter.

Conclusion:

In most instances registering officials are conscientious in their efforts to compile accurate records, but they are dependent upon informants for the accuracy of the facts. Under no circumstances should a pedigree be based solely on vital records or parish registers.

Searching printed, typewritten, or manuscript copies of the official vital records (e.g., published vital records of Massachusetts towns) is not a search of the official vital records.

Since the turn of the century, there has been considerable progress in providing for accuracy in the registration of birth, marriage, and death records. However, accuracy in regard to genealogical facts is dependent on the knowledge of the informant providing the information regarding relationships and other data. Therefore, the relationship (if any) of the informant to the persons mentioned in the certificate of birth or death should be considered. In the case of marriage records, the informants are supposed to be the bride and groom, and at least the information stated by them should be correct. You may anticipate there are instances when the bride or the groom will misrepresent his or her age for personal reasons.

Of course early vital records do not state from what person the information was obtained. In small towns and parishes, the registrar often knew from family or general reputation facts regarding parentage, marriage, and deaths or burials.

An assumption cannot be made that facts stated in vital records are always correct. Some of the defects have been disclosed by personal research and court decisions:

Adoption problems: Uncertainty of paternity: *Adoption of Bonner* (1968) (California Court of Appeal) 260 A.C.A. 17.

Paternity Questioned: S.D.W. etc. v. Holden (1969) (California Court of Appeal) 80 California Reporter 269.

Birth Certificates do not necessarily disclose the true father: Schumm v. Berg (1951) (California Supreme Court) 37 C.2d 174.

CHAPTER 10

VITAL RECORDS — EVIDENCE OF MARRIAGE

If there is one thing that the people are entitled to expect from their lawmakers, it is rules of law that will enable individuals to tell whether they are married and, if so, to whom.
Robert H. Jackson, Associate Justice U.S. Supreme Court
Estin v. Estin (1947) 334 U.S. 541, 553

Establishing the fact of marriages is one of the most important features of genealogical research. Illustrative of this principle is an incident related by Lord Eldon, one of England's great jurists during the 18th and 19th centuries, and Lord Chancellor for three decades. Lord Eldon was conversing with an Irish Peer who wanted to sit in the House of Lords. He explained to the peer that by act of Parliament, a peer has that right, but first must establish his pedigree disclosing ancestry which would entitle him to the seat.

The peer asked him how the marriage of his grandfather was to be proved. Lord Eldon said, "I told him that it must be proved in the usual manner by production of the Register of the Parish, where the marriage was celebrated." 'But my dear, says he, in Ireland there are very few parish registers – I don't know in what parish my grandfather was married, but it has no register.' How do you know that, said I, if you do not know the parish? 'Oh, aye, said he, that's true – it did not occur to me. But it is, he added, very hard, my Lord – won't my testimony, my dear, be sufficient to prove my grandfather's marriage?' Certainly, my Lord, said I, if you were present at your grandfather's marriage – otherwise not. 'Well then, says he, what can be done?' "[1]

The solving of the proof of marriage has not improved since Lord Eldon's lifetime, but this chapter should aid in deciding "what can be done."

The first thing to be done here then is to define marriage and some other terms relating to marriage.

Marriage is the civil status of one man and one woman capable of contracting, united by contract and mutual consent for life, for the discharge to each other and to the community, of the duties legally incumbent on those whose association is founded on the distinction of sex.[2]

Genealogists constantly encounter marriage problems such as the following:

1. Location of the marriage record, if this is possible. The first logical source to search is the office where marriages are recorded.

2. Many marriage records are not recorded in the official vital records, or in church records and family records. Therefore, the search must be conducted elsewhere. Other sources will be considered in this chapter.

3. If there is an identity problem due to common names, this must be resolved, if possible. Common names such as John Smith marrying Mary Jones is the usual identity problem. However, an assumption cannot be made that because names are unusual, there is only one person by that name. Uriah Tipple is an unusual name, but there may be more than one person by that name.

4. The validity of a marriage may be a problem, even when it is registered in the official records. For instance, were the parties of legal age? Or was there some other defect present which would affect their capacity to marry? Usually the only source where lack of capacity will be discovered is in court records where the validity of the marriage is challenged. Validity of the marriage is extremely important when compilation of the genealogy is for evidence in a court proceeding, or the preparation of an application for membership in a hereditary society.

One of the purposes of this chapter is to aid you in recognizing and solving the marriage problems which confront you in genealogical research.

CAPACITY TO MARRY

Historically, there are certain conditions or incapacity which prohibit parties from marrying, for example, certain degrees of relationship or consanguinity and affinity, age, insanity, physical incapacity, certain diseases, miscegenation, marriage out of the residential jurisdiction to evade local laws, bigamy, polygamy, use of force, duress or fraud, false impersonation, persons under the influence of intoxicating liquor or drugs, drug addicts, drunkards, paupers, indigents, and habitual criminals.

MARRIAGEABLE AGE

It is not safe to assume that the modern legal age for marriage may be applied in the past. Some historical examples will demonstrate this fact. In 1160, Henry II arranged the marriage of his eldest son, then five years of age, to Princess Marguerite of France, age three. Henry Fitzroy, the first Duke of Grafton (1663-1690), second son of Charles II, was nine years old when he was married to Isabella, daughter and heiress of Henry Bennett, Earl of Arlington, when she was but five years of age. It is not believable that these parties lived together as husband and wife.

A court decision of Federal District Court in 1942 entitled *Hitchens v. Hitchens*, reported in 47 Federal Supplement 73, at page 76, confirms the fact that early marriages were not entirely fictional, as it is stated that the common law provided that "... if either spouse was under the age of seven the marriage was void, and if the female was between the ages of seven and twelve and the male seven and fourteen, the marriage was voidable."

As stated by Blackstone in his *Commentaries*, Volume 1, page 436, the legal age for marriage at common law was fourteen years for males and twelve years for females. Any marriage under this age was voidable, and as mentioned above, if under the age of seven, it was a void marriage.

MARRIAGES PROHIBITED
DUE TO CONSANGUINITY AND AFFINITY

In 1563, Archbishop Parker published a table of prohibited degrees which discloses the relations man or woman could not marry due to consanguinity or affinity:

A man may not marry his	A woman may not marry her
1. *Grandmother*	1. *Grandfather*
2. *Grandfather's wife*	2. *Grandmother's husband*
3. *Wife's grandmother*	3. *Husband's grandfather*
4. *Father's sister*	4. *Mother's brother*
5. *Mother's sister*	5. *Father's brother*
6. *Father's brother's wife*	6. *Father's sister's husband*
7. *Mother's brother's wife*	7. *Mother's sister's husband*
8. *Wife's father's sister*	8. *Husband's father's brother*
9. *Wife's mother's sister*	9. *Husband's mother's brother*
10. *Mother*	10. *Father*
11. *Step-mother*	11. *Step-father*
12. *Wife's mother*	12. *Husband's father*
13. *Daughter*	13. *Son*
14. *Wife's daughter*	14. *Husband's son*
15. *Son's wife*	15. *Daughter's husband*
16. *Sister*	16. *Brother*
17. *Wife's sister*	17. *Husband's brother*
18. *Brother's wife*	18. *Sister's husband*
19. *Son's daughter*	19. *Son's son*
20. *Daughter's daughter*	20. *Daughter's son*
21. *Son's son's wife*	21. *Son's daughter's husband*
22. *Daughter's son's wife*	22. *Daughter's daughter's husband*
23. *Wife's son's daughter*	23. *Husband's son's son*
24. *Wife's daughter's daughter*	24. *Husband's daughter's son*
25. *Brother's daughter*	25. *Brother's son*
26. *Sister's daughter*	26. *Sister's son*
27. *Sister's son's wife*	27. *Brother's daughter's husband*
28. *Brother's son's wife*	28. *Sister's daughter's husband*
29. *Wife's brother's daughter*	29. *Husband's brother's son*
30. *Wife's sister's daughter*	30. *Husband's sister's son*

Although this table is of only partial legal significance modernly, it is historically important. It will aid you in eliminating relationships of parties which the records disclose are married. However, these prohibitions did not always prevent persons within the prohibited degree from marrying. Frequently court records disclose such prohibited alliances.

There are several types of marriage, or more properly stated, there are different means of entering into the marriage relationship, some of which are at this late date relics of history, but of interest and importance to genealogists.

STATUTORY MARRIAGE

The states of the union provide for statutory requirements for marriage which regulate licensing and solemnization of marriages. The purpose of these statutes is to prevent persons from marrying without the consent of the church or state. Therefore, parties wishing to marry are supposed to obtain a license, or in other respects, comply with the law regulating marriage.

Some of the statutes are directory only and, in that event, marriages such as common law marriages may be contracted without a license, and because the law is directory and not mandatory, these "self marriages," informal, or common law marriages are valid. In some jurisdictions there is a penalty for not obtaining a marriage license and complying with the statute, but this does not invalidate the marriage. However, there are some states in which the law must be strictly complied with or the marriage is void.[3]

COMMON LAW MARRIAGE

Common law marriage may be defined as a civil contract between a man and woman competent to contract, who mutually consent and agree to be husband and wife, to live with each other during their joint lives, and to discharge the duties of husband and wife.[4]

If the man and woman agree in words of the present tense (*per verba praesenti*) by saying to each other that from that moment they are and will be husband and wife, that is sufficient in some jurisdictions. In other jurisdictions open cohabitation is also necessary.[5]

If the man and woman state in words of the future tense (*per verba futuro*), there is no marriage until the marriage is consummated.[6]

The parties may agree orally or the agreement may be in writing signed by them, with or without witnesses, and without the necessity of recordation of a written document in a public record office.

The man and woman could agree to the marriage in private, or in the presence of a witness or witnesses. The common law did not require banns, license, a cleric, judge, or justice. The marriage was valid without any intervention or assistance of any third person. A ceremony of any description is not required for the validity of a common law marriage.

Because a common law marriage thus did not require a ceremony, witnesses were not necessary. However, there was no legal objection to the presence of witnesses if desired. Proof has always been a critical problem when parties resort to common law marriage, and often the only means of establishing the fact of marriage has been through litigation in the courts before a judge or jury; and court records abound with lawsuits because one or both of the parties were forced to prove the common law marriage. This was (and is) accomplished by the testimony of witnesses (if living), documentary evidence, proof of cohabitation by witnesses, and to a lesser extent by circumstantial evidence.

A more serious problem results when either one or both the man and woman are dead. If there is any doubt regarding the existence or validity of the marriage, litigation is almost certain to ensue. The executors or administrators, surviving children, and sometimes creditors of the deceased commence the lawsuit and present whatever evidence is available to prove marriage or the lack of it. Frequently the testimonial and documentary evidence is voluminous.

Court records are often the only source for establishing the fact of the existence or nonexistence of marriages.

The law is not uniform in all jurisdictions regarding common law marriage, but generally the following minimum requirements are necessary to constitute a valid common law marriage:

1. There must be mutual consent and agreement, expressed in words of the present tense, either orally or in writing, between the man and woman to be husband and wife.

2. The parties must consummate the marriage and cohabit as husband and wife.

3. The man and woman must acquire the reputation in the community in which they live that they are husband and wife.

4. Common law marriage must be valid where contracted.

The fact that a minister of the gospel need not be present prompts a brief discussion of private records, such as an entry of a marriage record in a family Bible. Such a union could well be a common law marriage and this would be so if the parties joined in marriage in a jurisdiction where there was no provision for a statutory marriage which the law requires the marriage to be performed pursuant to license or a ceremony before a clergyman, judge or justice of the peace. If a minister were present, he could be termed a witness even if he conducted a ceremony, as the important element necessary for the validity of a common law marriage is not the clergyman; it is the mutual agreement expressed in words of the present tense of the man and woman, with or without witnesses.

That there has been a general belief that a common law marriage is an illicit relationship in which a man and woman are living out of wedlock is evidenced by the fact that a prominent hereditary society refused to admit to membership persons who were the descendants or issue of a man and woman who had entered into a common law marriage. Unfortunately, officers in charge of admissions did not know that a common law marriage in many states is just as legal as a statutory marriage which requires a license, ceremony, etc.

A marriage if entered into according to the principles of law regarding common law marriage is as valid as one arising by complying with all of the formalities required for a statutory marriage, which require a license, judge, clergyman, or other officer designated by law of the jurisdiction where the marriage is solemnized.

"A marriage at common law [requires] no particular form or ceremony to make it valid, but enough [must] be said to make it a contract. It [is] even more than a contract. It [is] a status created by contract."[7]

Whatever the form of ceremony, or even if all ceremony is dispensed with, if the parties agree presently to take each other for husband and wife and from that time live together in that relation, proof of these facts is sufficient to constitute proof of a marriage binding on all parties.[8]

Obviously, the hereditary society was in dire need of legal advice. An actual case history will demonstrate the folly and inconsistency of their rule.

The facts of this case history commenced in 1900, and the man and woman, no doubt, have been transferred to a different sphere. However, a child was born and may be living somewhere on this planet where lawsuits are becoming more and more a popular pursuit. Therefore, it will be prudent to resort to fictitious names. However, other than changing the names, the decision of the court which considered the facts on appeal are quoted verbatim.

Joshua was divorced by his wife, and at least one of the reasons for the divorce was his attention to Mabel. Mabel at a later date testified that after Joshua's divorce he said to her:

" 'Mabel, you got the blame and we might as well have the game. We'll be married.' It went on then till in May .... Josh then said to me: 'The Court won't give us no license,' and he took my hand and said, 'I pledge myself as true and lawful husband to you the longest day I live,' and I said to Josh, 'I pledge myself as true and lawful wife to you the longest day I live,' and he slipped his mother's wedding ring on my finger, and he kissed me, and he said, 'If we ever have any children, they will hold us together.' "

The highest court in the state where this decision was rendered held that the marriage between Joshua and Mabel was valid. But the hereditary society would rule that Joshua and Mabel were not married and lived out of wedlock.

But assume that Joshua and Mabel asked a local clergyman to be present and perform a ceremony without the issuance of a license (which is not required), and further assume that a record of this marriage was entered in a family Bible, the hereditary society would accept this as a valid proof of the marriage of Joshua and Mabel. It is still a common law marriage. The presence of the clergyman was not necessary. He would be considered as a witness as his function was not at all essential. In every marriage it is the agreement or contract of the parties that binds them in marriage. Marriage is a contract which changes into a relationship.

There is a general belief that self-marriage, marriage by mutual consent, or what is known as common law marriage originated in what is now continental United States. That is not true. Marriage based on the consent of the parties, without witnesses or a ceremony conducted by the clergy or civil officer, and usually by oral agreement, was practiced before and after the Norman Conquest.[9]

There was no solemnization of marriage in the Church before an ordinance of Pope Innocent III (c. 1060-1216) before which the man came to the house where the woman lived and carried her to his house, and this was the ceremony.[10]

Marriage ceremonies were not required to be solemnized by the clergy in or out of the parish church. The Roman Church continued to recognize these informal or what are generally termed common law marriages until the Council of Trent in 1563, and this condition prevailed in all of Europe insofar as ecclesiastical law was concerned. However, the provisions of the Council of Trent did not bind the Church of England. These informal marriages were not approved by the Church of England and parties who did not have the marriage blessed by it were subject to punishment; but in spite of the disobedience of the men and women who resorted to informal marriages, the Church recognized the marriage as valid.

A famous example of a disobedient member was Sir Edward Coke who was married in 1598 without publication of banns or bishop's license. He was subjected to penance, but the marriage was valid.

In 1753 Lord Hardwicke's Act became law and provided that marriages not solemnized in the parish church of one of the parishioners by an ordained priest, pursuant to publication of banns or by bishop's license, was null and void.[11]

At the Fleet Prison and nearby were numerous "marriage houses," where clandestine marriages were performed by persons pretending to be priests, although some probably were ordained priests, who married couples in defiance of the Church. The first marriages date as early as 1613. Logically there can be no doubt that there are people living today who descend from ancestors who married by a Fleet "parson." There were thousands of these marriages performed between 1613 and 1754 when these clandestine marriages were prohibited by Lord Hardwicke's Act.[12] The Public Record Office in London has collected a large number of these marriage registers.

Courts have usually refused to admit these marriage registers in evidence, not only because they are hearsay evidence, but also their credibility is questioned. However, there have been instances when courts did admit them in evidence, but the question of credibility is still a question for a judge or jury to decide.[13]

The passage of Lord Hardwicke's Act did not prevent couples in a hurry, dissenters, or anyone else from crossing the border into Scotland and entering into an informal marriage by consent and agreement, which is simply a common law marriage, as the law of Scotland did not require formal or ecclesiastical marriage ceremonies. Hence the Gretna Green marriages flourished.

But Lord Hardwicke's Act did stop the Fleet and other marriage shops from conducting clandestine marriages; the registers of which are for the most part notoriously undependable, although the English courts were divided in regard to the admissibility in evidence of these registers. Some of the registers were accurate and some were not, and the decision as to whether to accept or reject a marriage record in one of these registers must be decided on the facts of a specific case.[14]

It has been held sufficient for the man to say to the woman "This is your wedding ring, we are married," and they thereafter live together as husband and wife.[15] But there had better be more evidence of marriage than that. It is true this is sufficient to prove their secret marriage, if at some future date they are around to testify to their mutual consent and agreement and that they intended to live together from the moment he put the ring on her finger as husband and wife. Unfortunately, many couples do not add to the meagre evidence of the marriage. Here is what they should have done to eliminate any doubt. The most valuable feature would be to sign a simple agreement such as this actual example.[16]

"Providence, R.I., August 18, 1859

This is to certify that we, H. C. Mathewson and Sarah D. Mathewson, both of Providence, R.I., do hereby acknowledge ourselves to be man and wife.

Signed in the presence of

H. C. Mathewson	C. A. Carpenter
Sarah D. Mathewson	S. J. Horton"

If they recorded this with the town clerk, and especially if they signed under oath, this evidence would be the most anyone could hope for.

But assume the parties do not do this, then hope that they represented to the people of the community that they were in fact married. This would gain them the reputation in the neighborhood that they were living openly as husband and wife. To add to the evidence, they introduce each other as married. Their respective families and neighbors recognize them as married. Children are born to them and are recognized by them and the neighbors as legitimate issue of the marriage. Documentary evidence, such as deeds to land describe them as husband and wife, and this is at least circumstantial evidence of the marriage. Hopefully, there are other records which offer evidence of the marriage. This is the ideal evidence to prove a common law marriage. You will not find this evidence in the usual marriage records in the courthouse. Court records are the best source, and if you do not discover a record there, your only choice is to search every other type of record available, official, public, or private.

Considering the many centuries that marriage relationships have been in existence, it is paradoxical that there has been such a paucity of guidance from religious and civil sources. Sir William Scott in the leading English decision in 1811 stated that "It is not unworthy of remark that, amidst the manifold ritual provisions, made by the Divine Lawgiver of the Jews for various offenses and transactions of life, there is no ceremony prescribed for the celebration of marriage." "... And it is equally true that none is prescribed by the common law, or our statutes in relation to marriage."[17]

Living together out of wedlock, or concubinage will not result in the formation of a common law marriage regardless of how long the arrangement continues. In the jurisdictions where common law marriage is recognized, there must be the intention, the mutual agreement to be husband and wife, cohabitation, the representation that they are husband and wife, therefore, the couple had better tell the neighbors that they are married. There are some states of the United States where it is still possible to enter into common law marriage, and they are valid. In some states common law marriages will be recognized, but there is a penalty if the parties ignore the formalities required by state statutes. In other states, common law marriage is not recognized, is prohibited, and will never be recognized no matter how long the parties live together or how many children they produce.

The Lord Hardwicke Marriage Act of 1753 did not affect the colonies. Therefore, the common law and hence common law marriage was valid in the colonies and continued to be legal in all of the colonies, and subsequently the States after formation of the Union, unless abrogated by the colonies or by the States.[18] When territory, which was not a part of the colonies before and after they became States, adopted the common law as the basis of their legal system, they automatically recognized common law marriage, unless and until it was declared invalid. Louisiana is an exception as it did not adopt the common law; its legal system is based on the civil law of Rome.

Therefore, common law marriages were valid if entered into before laws were enacted in any of the colonies, territories, or states attempting to prohibit or discourage these informal marriages. Laws have never wholly prevented men and women from entering into common law marriages; they have frequently knowingly and more often unknowingly ignored or circumvented the marriage statutes which fact is abundantly disclosed by the massive amount of litigation to establish the validity or invalidity of marriage relationships.

Legislators are responsible for this paradoxical condition. This is because the laws often provide a choice for the anxious bride and groom, even though they are not aware of it. Laws regulating marriage are either "mandatory" or "directory."

If the law is "mandatory", any attempted marriage which does not strictly comply with the statute is absolutely void. For example, the state law reads "Buy a license first or the marriage is void." Then if the parties do not comply, the marriage is void. If they do not want to comply, they have a choice of going elsewhere. They might leave North Carolina where common law marriage is not recognized and resort to a "Gretna Green" marriage by crossing the border to South Carolina where common law marriages have always been legal.

If the law is "directory" only which amounts to the statute stating "go buy a marriage license," this wording is "directory" if that is the only wording. The statute must specifically state that the marriage is void in order for the provision to be mandatory. In some jurisdictions the statute provides that if the license is not bought and in other respects the laws regulating marriage are not complied with, the man and woman may be punished by fine or imprisonment (or both), but the marriage is still valid.

In many jurisdictions in the past and at present, there is still a clear choice: Buy a license, or save the money and enter into an agreement in words of the present tense to be husband and wife, cohabit, openly live together in the community, and gain the reputation that the relationship of the parties is that of husband and wife. The law in this type of jurisdiction does not impose a penalty for ignoring the statute.

States which do not recognize common law marriage will generally recognize its validity if the marriage occurred in a State which does. For instance, assume a man and woman entered into a common law marriage in Kansas where common law marriages are recognized and they later move to Illinois where statutory marriages are required. Illinois will recognize the common law marriage of the parties from Kansas.[19]

One of the disadvantages of common law marriage (or any other marriage of which there is no record) is that there is no requirement to record in writing the names, dates, place, and other facts of marriage. It is therefore often difficult to establish the existence of the marriage even when the parties and witnesses are living and available to testify. Marshal Van Winkle of the New Jersey Court of Chancery wrote that "A claim that a common law marriage exists, usually follows a funeral; and in nearly every case the claim comes as a great surprise."[20]

At this late date, the only means of establishing the fact of a marriage is searching all records, official, public or private, and hope for success. The research methods and sources available for this purpose will be discussed in another part of this chapter.

GRETNA GREEN MARRIAGES

After Lord Hardwicke's Marriage Act of 1753, it was impossible to validly marry in England without either publication of banns or by issuance of a special license. This Act did not affect Scotland where it was possible to enter into a marriage by consent and mutual agreement of the man and woman before witnesses without any other formality. For the couple in a hurry, for dissenters and those with any other reason, it was easy for them to cross the border to Gretna Green which bordered on Cumberland and contract a valid marriage sans red tape.

The 1856 Marriage Act of Scotland ended this convenience unless at least one of the parties resided or had been in Scotland at least twenty-one days preceding the marriage ceremony.[21]

MARRIAGE BY PROXY

Marriage by proxy was allowed by Roman Law and by Canon Law. It was possible for a man who was away from home to marry a woman by letter or messenger. For example, the proxy in the presence of the woman and witnesses said, "I being the proxy of John Doe, take thee to be his wife." The woman would then say, "I do take John Doe to be my husband, by thee being his proxy."[22]

BOGUS AND MOCK MARRIAGES

"It has been [determined] that in Wisconsin a marriage ceremony performed in a play is just as binding as if it were performed by a minister in a church. If a man and woman acknowledge themselves to be man and wife before competent witnesses that settles it according to the law, and therefore two players, during a performance, refer to each other as husband and wife, they are legally married unless there is no one in the audience," as reported in the *Weekly Red Bluff* [California] *News*, November 19, 1892. It is true that prior to 1917 in Wisconsin, common law marriages were valid. However, it seems that this is too much to believe as the intentions of the man and woman must be considered and the audience certainly knew they were attending a play.

John F. Morland, the editor of the third edition of *Keezer On the Law of Marriage and Divorce*, on page 153 states:

> A pretended marriage, though legal in form but entered into in jest, with no intention of entering into the actual marriage status and with a clear understanding that the parties are not bound and the ceremony is not followed by any conduct indicating a purpose to enter into such a relation is held subject to annulment at the suit of the parties to such a pretended marriage.

However, there are court decisions which hold that mock or bogus marriages are valid if an innocent party to the marriage was deceived.

SECRET MARRIAGES

There is a presumption against the validity of secret marriages, if and when discovered. This presumption is not conclusive, it is rebuttable if sufficient evidence is presented.[23] A secret marriage may never be disclosed, and usually the disclosure results when the validity or claim of invalidity is questioned in a court proceeding. Disclosure may also result from private or public record sources.

IRREGULAR MARRIAGES

These marriages do not comply with the law, but are usually recognized as valid.

HANDFAST MARRIAGE

An early definition of "handfast" is the custom of handfasting, or contracting marriage.[24] A more recent definition is to bind by joining hands. Handfasting is a form of irregular or probationary marriage, contracted by the parties joining hands and agreeing to live together as man and wife according to agreement, resulting in a common law marriage.[25]

Handfast marriage is mentioned as early as the 13th century according to the O.E.D. Handfast also means to betroth, and to enter into a contract of marriage.

This type of marriage originated in Europe and was known in Scotland and England. In jurisdictions requiring banns, license, religious ceremony, or some form of statutory compliance, it would be irregular, but not void unless specifically stated invalid by statute.

There are instances of handfast marriages in New England which are of record because of court proceedings commenced to punish the parties who did not comply with the regular form of marriage ceremony prescribed by statute. A French refugee who visited Boston c. 1687 wrote that "there are those who practice no formality of marriage except joining hands, and so live in common."[26]

Handfast marriages could qualify as a common law marriage, if the man and woman agreed to be married in the present, cohabited, and were recognized in the community as husband and wife these elements would qualify it as such. Clasping hands would not be necessary, but it would add to the agreement.

This is another example of why court records should be searched to find evidence of marriage.

FICTITIOUS MARRIAGE

A fictitious marriage occurred when an English subject decided to marry a person within a prohibited relationship, for example, a man marrying the sister of his deceased wife. The parties married in Denmark, or some other country where such a marriage was not prohibited and therefore valid. After the ceremony, the parties returned to England. In England if the validity of the marriage was tested, it was adjudged void. Unless the marriage of the parties was questioned in a court proceeding, it is unlikely that this fact would ever be discovered, especially in a community where the man and woman were not known prior to the marriage.[27]

MARRIAGES AT SEA

The ship on which the marriage is performed is subject to the law of its place of registration represented by the flag it is flying. The major problem is locating the records of the ship involved.

The Merchant Shipping Act, 17 & 18 Victoria, c. 104, enacted in 1854, provides for marriages on board British merchant ships. The law provides for entries of the marriages in the official log book of the ship.

SLAVE MARRIAGES

Slaves were permitted to marry with the consent of their masters, according to early case law. However, there is legal authority that such marriages were not valid as slaves could not enter into a contract and without a mutual agreement recognized by the law, there could not be a legal marriage.[28] In my opinion, genealogists should recognize these unions as valid marriages. Authority for this opinion is supported by case law, to the effect that documentary evidence such as a marriage certificate was not necessary, that a marriage between slaves was valid if based on agreement of the parties, and the marriage was recognized by residents of their neighborhood. In other words it was a marriage based on consent of the man and woman, custom, and reputation in the community that they were married, therefore, these elements or features constituted a common law marriage.[29]

After slavery was abolished, any doubt regarding the legality of slave marriages was removed upon their attaining the legal status of free persons.[30]

INDIAN TRIBAL MARRIAGES

If the formalities, customs, and usage of the tribe are complied with the tribal marriages are valid.

In my opinion, genealogists should ignore the strict rules of evidence and "bend over backwards" to accept any reasonable evidence to establish the validity of marriages. There is an exception, if you are preparing a pedigree for evidence in a court proceeding, you must be bound by the applicable rules of evidence which will be discussed in another part of this book.

CHECK LIST OF RECORD SOURCES
FOR ESTABLISHING EVIDENCE OF MARRIAGES

(A partial listing)

1. A certified copy of the marriage record issued by the official custodian of the vital records. This is an official record and admissible in court proceedings. The fact that the certified copy is admitted in evidence does not prove the fact of the marriage. The evidence may be rebutted by an adverse party. For example, the identity of the persons described in the marriage record is subject to question.

2. Church marriage registers are private records, except the records of an established church. For example, the registers of the Church of England would be considered an official record.

3. Witnesses present at the time of the ceremony. Courts consider the testimony of "eye witnesses" as the most reliable evidence. The reasoning of this principle is that documentary evidence is not the best proof of marriage. A witness who swears to have been present and observed the

marriage ceremony, assuming of course he or she is telling the truth and testifies to facts that indicate a valid marriage took place, is considered more reliable than documentary evidence. But "eye witnesses" are not the perfect answer to the problem. There is still the question of identity of the marriage partners if considerable time has elapsed, the honesty and capability of the witness, and the final blow — that witnesses eventually pass on to another realm.

4. Family records such as entries in a family Bible and other family records, including but not limited to diaries, journals, unrecorded documents of legal significance, marriage certificates and contracts, and other miscellaneous papers and records. Custody or possession is important. Are the records in possession of a member of the family and has that possession been continuous? Custody or possession adds validity to the records that possession by strangers does not inspire. A "proper custody" by a family or member of a family, is important if you are compiling a pedigree as evidence in a court proceeding, or as part of an application for membership in a hereditary society. If not, you and your client are the only persons to be satisfied.

5. Admissions (written or oral), declarations or affidavits, that the man and woman are husband and wife are important evidence. There are instances in the official records of documents in which parties have recorded (for example, an affidavit or declaration) usually under oath that they are husband and wife. Most record offices, such as a county recorder or register of deeds, maintain a "catch all" volume for this type of miscellaneous record.

6. Common or general reputation in the community where the man and woman lived is another form of evidence to establish the fact of marriage. Modernly, the only source for finding such a record is in court proceedings or in private or family records.

7. Probate court records — documents filed in probate proceedings, testimony of witnesses, wills, petitions, decrees, decrees of distribution, agreements of heirs, pedigrees filed as exhibits as evidence are some examples.

8. Civil Court Records (other than probate). There are numerous lawsuits of record which disclose marriage relationships. This is often the result of the common law marriage system in instances which require evidence in the court proceeding to establish that the parties were married. Frequently, one of the spouses is dead and neighbors and relatives testify that the man and woman represented they were husband and wife. It is easy to overlook these civil court records, due to the popularity and accessibility of probate records. These are some examples of civil actions involving the validity of marriages and also in which other genealogical data is disclosed: Actions in ejectment (Possession of land), proceedings to establish the right to dower (widow's right to one-third of husband's estate for life), curtesy (husband's right to one-third), lawsuits commenced by executors and administrators, actions to establish legitimacy of children and their right to inherit, civil actions commenced by creditors for debts alleged due, the right to military pensions, and remembering that marriage is the principle cause of divorce and annulment, do not overlook searching records for these actions.

9. Criminal Court Records. Prosecutions for bigamy, paternity, nonsupport of wife and children, incest, and some sex acts as adultery (not a crime in some states) are some examples which involve marriage or the lack of it, and often include considerable genealogical details.

10. Land Records. Marital status is important when title to property is involved. Therefore, a search of land records often discloses facts indicating a marriage relationship as well as genealogical data. Documents recorded in the registry of deeds or the county recorder's office often disclose records of deeds, mortgages, leases, agreements of various kinds, declarations of marriage, affidavits, and other documents which will describe a man and woman as husband and wife. The strict application of the rules of evidence will bar some of these documents as evidence in some jurisdictions, but if your research is not for a court proceeding, it is your prerogative to be the judge of the evidence.

11. Military records. Pension applications are an excellent source to establish the fact of marriage. This is particularly true when a widow must satisfy the pension officials she is entitled to a pension because her late husband was in military service.

12. Federal Census Records for 1850, 1860, and 1870 are a valuable source for circumstantial evidence of marriage. The man listed at the beginning of the entries for a family is presumably the head of the house. The woman listed next is *probably* his wife. This circumstantial evidence may may be confirmed as valid by reference to other record sources. Beginning in 1880, the relationship of the head of the family is stated and of course this ought to be reliable evidence of the marriage of the man and the woman. The reliability of census records will be discussed in another chapter. If you are fortunate to be engaged in research in New York State, beginning with the 1855 census the relationship of the head of the family to its members is stated.

13. Cemetery records ought to be reliable and usually are. Gravestones frequently disclose the fact that persons buried there are husband and wife, or that a deceased is survived by husband or wife. The consideration of gravestone evidence is subject to what is known as the "best evidence rule," which means that the best evidence is the gravestone. Fortunately courts admit photographs of gravestones supported by the testimony of a witness who has seen the gravestone and knows the facts. Otherwise it would be necessary to haul that block of granite or marble to the courthouse.

14. Private legislative acts or laws disclosed in legislative journals, sessions laws and statutes at large. As late as the 19th century, legislative bodies were the only source in some jurisdictions for granting divorces. Marriage was occasionally the subject matter of a private legislative act.

15. Vital Records. Birth and death certificates in which the names of parents are disclosed are at least circumstantial evidence that the parents were married. Naturally, the marriage record is direct evidence of the marriage.

16. Newspaper files or back issues are often the only sources for locating the record of marriages. Some courts would not admit this evidence in a court proceeding, because it is "hearsay," but some would, especially if the newspaper was over 30 years old and the court is convinced that the information

was admissible because it was from an "ancient document."

17. Published and unpublished genealogies, family history, county and local histories including records of marriages (please refer to the chapter on this subject for details).

18. Miscellaneous Sources: city directories, voting registers, marriage and funeral records, even inscriptions on rings or other jewelry, photographs — if a record is written on the front or back, and genealogical samplers and quilts, or other needleworks.

19. Records of abstracts of title to land, land title insurance company records, when available, and other types of insurance records.

20. Records and publications of fraternal lodges.

21. Marriage by Habit and Repute is based on the presumption that a man and woman living together are married. This type of union was difficult to prove and is not of much legal significance unless confirmed by a judgment of a court. This type of marriage in some instances could qualify as a common law marriage. A leading case on this subject is *Dunbarton v. Franklin* (1848) 19 New Hampshire 257.

ESTABLISHING FACT OF MARRIAGE MAY BE PROVEN BY DIRECT OR CIRCUMSTANTIAL EVIDENCE

The fact of marriage may be established by direct or circumstantial evidence, for example, a marriage certificate or the oral or written statement of the parties married, or the statement of persons possessing knowledge of the marriage. Official or private records which attest to the fact that the parties were married are, of course, acceptable as direct evidence.

Marriage also may be established by indirect or circumstantial evidence. Deeds, or other documents which describe a man and woman as "husband and wife," are circumstantial evidence; as these facts are an indirect indication that the man and woman were married to each other.

Identification of the parties is a problem which cannot be cast aside lightly. The beat evidence of the identity of parties to a marriage are witnesses, and at this late date they are long since gone. Therefore, it is necessary to establish identity by whatever records are available in addition to the marriage record if there is not evidence within the marriage document to establish identity. (Refer to the separate chapter on "Identity" for additional suggestions).

In spite of the fact that in many of the colonies, territories, and various states of the Union, it is often represented that informal, irregular, or common law marriages did not exist; this is a fiction and in these jurisdictions there was a period during colonial states, territorial status, or prior to admission to the Union, and during statehood that informal, irregular, and common law marriages have been and still are recognized.

Revelatory of this is the recent United States Supreme Court decision, *Mathews, Secretary of Health, Education and Welfare v. Lucas*, No. 75-58, June 29, 1976; and the provisions of the Social Security Act, Title 42, Section 416 (2)(B) which recognizes the legitimacy of a child whose parents "went through a marriage ceremony resulting in a purported marriage between them which, but for a legal impediment would have been a valid marriage." This is an indirect way of validating a defective marriage, such as an informal, irregular, or common law marriage in order to legitimate a child. Also there is a trend to recognize questionable marriages in order to protect the innocent in workmen's compensation cases. (Example: *Edgewater Coal Co., v. Yates* (1935) 261 Kentucky Reports 335, 336).

COURT PROCEEDINGS INVOLVING MARRIAGE

There are two types of divorce, *a mensa et thoro* (from bed and board), a form of legal separation whereby the husband and wife are permitted to live separately, and *divorce a vinculo*, whereby the bonds of marriage are permanently severed. Originally, civil divorce was obtained only through legislative action as a private act. Ultimately, jurisdiction for divorce was granted to the courts. Prior to court jurisdiction, divorce evidence should be in legislative records (legislative journals, sessions laws, or statutes at large). After court jurisdiction commenced, court records should be searched in the locality where the husband and wife lived — assuming they did not move. Residence is the basis for jurisdiction of the court, and wherever the husband resided was the wife's residence.

Annulment of marriage, whereby a marriage is cancelled as if it had never existed, was originally a church function. Ultimately, courts acquired jurisdiction for annulling marriages. Also legislative bodies passed private acts declaring marriages valid or invalid.

The foregoing is a statement of the general rule, and exceptions to the general rule always should be considered, for example, some early colonial courts granted divorces and dissolved marriages.

Jactitation of marriage was an action against a person falsely representing he or she was married to someone and to prevent further misrepresentation. In Scotland, the action was known as "Action of declarator of marriage" or "Declarator of putting to silence." Although these lawsuits are not known in the United States, there are forms of civil action to prevent such a false representation.

ADDITIONAL COURT RECORDS

There are many types of court proceedings involving marriages, such as inheritance, actions by creditors, legitimacy of children, validity of marriage, lawsuits involving possession to real property, ejectment, quiet title, personal property, dower rights of a widow, and curtesy rights of a widower. Appropriate sources should be searched for records. Sources where such records might be found will be court proceedings in the locality where the parties lived.

There is an additional feature regarding court records which involves common law marriages which is important. There is a general belief that if a man and woman enter into a valid common law marriage (especially if there are no witnesses present), then the man and woman, may at will, decide to abrogate their agreement and go their separate ways and marry some other person. This is a false assumption, as a common law marriage is just as valid as if the man and woman purchased a marriage license and appeared before a judge or other officer or minister and entered into a formal marriage. The only safe means of dissolving a common law marriage is by a court proceeding for an annulment of the marriage, or a divorce.

Notes and References

1. Lincoln, Anthony L.J., and McEwen, Robert Lindley (eds), *Lord Eldon's Anecdote Book*, Stevens & Sons, Ltd., London 1960, p. 110.

2. *State v. Cooper* (1890) 103 Missouri Reports, 266, 273.

3. *Meister v. Moore* (1877) 96 U.S. Supreme Court Reports 76; *Marris v. Sockey* (Court of Appeals, 10th Circuit 1948) 170 Federal 2nd 599.

4. Bouvier, John, *Bouvier's Law Dictionary*, Boston 1897.

5. Ibid.

6. Kent, James, *Commentaries on American Law*, Vol. 2, Boston 1858, 9th Edition, p. 53.

7. *Meister v. Moore*, supra.

8. Ibid.

9. Kent, James, *Commentaries on American Law*, Vol. 2, Boston, 1858, pp. 53, 54.

10. Jacob, Giles, *A New Law Dictionary*, London, 1750, Marriage col. 1.

11. An Act for the Better Preventing of Clandestine Marriages, 26 George II, c.33; 21 *Statutes at Large* 124.

12. Jowitt, Lord, *Dictionary of English Law*.

13. Ibid.

14. Holdsworth, Sir William S., *A History of English Law*, Vol. 11, London 1938, p. 609.

15. *Bissell v. Bissell* (1869, N.Y.) 55 Barbour's Reports 325, 327.

16. *Mathewson v. Phoenix* (1884) 20 Federal Reporter 281.

17. *Dalrymple v. Dalrymple* (1811) 2 Haggard's Consistory Reports 485, 489; *Askew v. Dupree* (1860) 30 Georgia Reports 173.

18. *Rose v. Clark* (N.Y. 1841) 8 Paige 574, 579.

19. *Peirce v. Peirce* (1942) 379 Illinois Reports 185, 191.

20. Van Winkle, Marshall, Common Law Marriages, *New Jersey Law Journal*, Vol. 59, p. 177.

21. Marriage Act of 1856, 19 & 20 Victoria, c. 119.

22. Swinburne, Henry, *A Treatise of Spousals or Matrimonial Contracts*. London 1686, p. 164.

23. Koegel, Otto E., *Common Law Marriage.* . ., Washington 1922, p. 112.
24. Halliwell, James Orchard, *A Dictionary of Archaic and Provincial Words*, London 1889, Vol. 1, p. 431.
25. Merriam, G. & C. Company, *Webster's New International Dictionary of the English Language.* Second edition unabridged, Springfield 1949.
26. Howard, George Elliott, *A History of Matrimonial Institutions*, London 1904, Vol. II, p. 208.
27. *The Law Times*, Vol. 107, London, May 20, 1899, p. 54.
28. *Girod v. Lewis* (Louisiana 1819) 6 Martin's Reports 559.
29. *Cabble v. Hawkins*, 186 Kentucky Reports 114.
30. *Dickerson v. Brown* (1873) 49 Mississippi Reports 357, 364.

CHAPTER 11

LEGAL STATUS OF INFORMAL
IRREGULAR AND COMMON LAW MARRIAGES

"... Murder can be proved by circumstantial evidence, and there does not seem to be any reason why a valid marriage may not be established by the same class of proof." In the matter of Hamilton's Will, 83 New York 200, 207.

CAUTION

The following summary is for research purposes only and must not be considered as legal advice relative to the validity or invalidity of marriages involving the rights or liabilities of any persons.

Alabama

The common law mode of marriage is recognized as valid in this State, and to constitute such marriage it is only necessary that there shall exist a mutual consent or agreement between the parties to be husband and wife, followed by cohabitation and living together as husband and wife. *Tartt et al. v. Negus* (1899) 127 Alabama Supreme Court Reports 301, 308.

Alaska

Common law marriages are valid prior to August 1, 1917. Prior to the above date, formalities for marriage were prescribed by statute; a marriage which did not conform to the statute, such as a common law marriage, was not invalidated. *Reed v. Hardraker* (1920) 264 Federal Reporter 834.

Arizona

Common law marriage was valid in Arizona prior to 1913. *Levy v. Blakeley* (1933) 41 Arizona 327.

Arkansas

Common law marriages are invalid according to present law. There was a period in Arkansas when informal or common law marriages were entered into, as disclosed by court decisions, for example, *Furth v. Furth* (1911) 97 Arkansas Reports 272. This is particularly true during the early history of Arkansas as a State, territory, and prior to territorial status in 1819 when Arkansas was part of Missouri Territory where common law marriages were valid. Furthermore, early statutes of Arkansas indicate that strict compliance with the statutory form of marriages was directory and not mandatory, therefore, a common law marriage although irregular would be recognized as valid. *1835 Laws Arkansas Territory*, p. 394.

California

Common law marriages were valid prior to the effective date of the Statute enacted March 26, 1895:121. *Sharon v. Sharon* (1888) 75 California Supreme Court Reports 1.

Colorado

Common law marriages were valid prior to the adoption of the Uniform Marriage Act in 1973. Title 14-2-101. Prior Case Law: *Deter v. Deter* (1971) 484 Pacific Reporter 2nd 805, 806, 807: Common law marriage adjudged valid by Colorado Supreme Court.

Connecticut

The general consensus is that common law marriages have always been invalid in Connecticut, but this opinion does not agree with early authorities. For example, Tapping Reeve in his book *The Law of Baron and Femme*, New Haven 1816, page 197, stated, ". . . I apprehend that by the provisions of the common law, marriages although celebrated by a person not qualified by law, or in the manner forbidden by law are valid. The conduct of the parties concerned, had rendered them obnoxious to the penalties of the law; but such singular conduct, is not ground for impeaching the validity of the marriage."

George Elliott Howard, Ph.D., wrote that "In New England the formalities prescribed by the statutes were doubtless usually observed. Yet there were many clandestine and other irregular marriages, and in some instances we know that these were treated as valid. . . . Moreover, at no time during the colonial and provincial periods did the statutes of Massachusetts expressly declare marriages void for disregard of the celebration or other formalities prescribed; and the same is true of the daughter-colony of Connecticut." (A History of Matrimonial Institutions, London 1904, Vol. 3, p. 173-74).

It is advisable to search all official, public, and private records for evidence of marriage. Do not limit your research to the vital records indices at the State Library. For a more complete listing of sources, refer to the *Check List of Record Sources for Establishing Evidence of Marriages* in chapter 10.

Delaware

Common law marriages have never been adopted in Delaware. *Wilmington Trust Co. v. Hendrixon* (1921) 31 Delaware 303.

The Delaware Code, Title 13, requires a license. But Section 126 of this Title states "Nothing in this chapter shall be construed to render any common-law or other marriage, otherwise lawful, invalid by reason of failure to take out a license as provided by this [Code]." This provision is construed to mean that a license is directory rather than mandatory and that a marriage which does not comply strictly with the law will be recognized.

Without a doubt there were informal, clandestine, and common law marriages in Delaware during the colonial period and following statehood.

It is advisable to search all official, public, and private records for evidence of marriage, and especially all court records, probate proceedings, civil and criminal actions. For a more complete listing refer to the *Check List of Record Sources for Establishing Evidence of Marriages.*

District of Columbia

Common law marriages have always been valid from the date of the formation of the District. *Blackburn v. Crawfords* (1865) 70 U.S. Supreme Court Reports 175; *Hoage v. Murch Bros.* (1931) 60 Appeal Cases, D.C. 218.

Prior to the formation of the District in 1800, it was part of Maryland and Virginia, therefore, for research antedating 1800, consult the marriage status of these two states infra in this chapter.

Florida

Common law marriages were valid prior to the effective date of Statute enacted 1 January 1968. Section 741.211. *Budd v. Gooch,* 167 Fla. 716.

Georgia

Common law marriages have always been valid. "Notwithstanding the statute directs a license to issue in case of marriage, and inflicts a penalty upon any minister of the gospel or magistrate who performs the ceremony without such license; yet in the absence of any positive enactment declaring that all marriages not celebrated in the forms prescribed shall be void, a marriage deliberately and intentionally entered into – *per verbi de presenti* – that is, 'I take you to be my wife,' and, 'I take you to be my husband' by parties able to contract, is to all intents and purposes a valid marriage, notwithstanding the parties have failed to comply with the statutory provisions." *Askew v. Dupree* (1860) 30 Georgia 173 (quoting syllabus).

Hawaii

Common law marriages are not recognized. However, historically common law marriages or analogous relationships were valid. *Godfrey v. Rowland,* (1905) 16 Hawaii Reports 377.

Idaho

Common law marriages have always been valid in Idaho. *Huff v. Huff* (1911) 20 Idaho Reports 450.

Illinois

Common law marriages were valid prior to the effective date of Chapter 89, Section 4, of the Illinois Revised Statutes, approved May 13, 1905.

Indiana

Common law marriages were valid in Indiana prior to the effective date of the statute enacted January 1, 1958. Burns Indiana Statutes (Annotated, Title 31-1-61.)

Iowa

Common law marriages have always been valid in Iowa. Section 595.11, 595.16 Iowa Code Annotated.

Kansas

Common law marriage has always been valid, but parties are subject to punishment for ignoring license requirement. *State v. Walker* (1887) 36 Kansas 297.

Kentucky

Common law marriages were valid prior to the adoption Act of February 14, 1866, Revised Statutes 1866, page 734. Prior Case Law: The Kentucky Court of Appeals recognized that a couple who had lived together for twenty years without benefit of evidence of a valid marriage by applying the principle that the couple enjoyed the common reputation of being husband and wife, and the surviving "widow" was allowed dower rights. *Donnelly v. Donnelly's Heirs* (1847-48) 47 Kentucky 113.

Louisiana

According to Louisiana law, common law marriages or informal marriages we not valid. This has not always been the case, as informal and common law marriages were recognized at an early date. *Patton v. Cities of Philadelphia and New Orleans* (1846) 1 Louisiana Reports Annotated 98: *Holmes v. Holmes* (1834) 6 Louisiana Reports 463.

Maine

According to existing statutes common law marriage is invalid, but this has not always been the law. However, the law applicable to Maine was that of Massachusetts prior to separation from the latter in 1820, and there are court decisions which recognize. irregular, informal, or Common law marriages. *The Case of Damon, alias Flint* (1829) 6 Maine 148; *State v. Hodgskins* (1841) 19 Maine 155.

Quaker marriages performed according to the customs of that sect are valid. Maine Revised Statutes, Chapter 166, Sections 5 to 15.

It is advisable to search all official, public, and private records for evidence of marriage. Research should not be limited to civil actions, vital, land records, and probate proceedings. For a more complete listing, refer to the *Check List of Record Sources for Establishing Evidence of Marriage.*

Maryland

If you believe the authorities, irregular, clandestine, informal, and common law marriages are invalid and never occurred in Maryland, either as a colony or state. That is not true, as verified by *Cheseldine's Lessee v. Brewer* (1739) reported in 1 Harris & McHenry's Reports 152, decided by the Maryland Court of Appeals. The Cheseldine decision was not overruled until 1871 in the case of *Denison v. Denison*, 35 Maryland 361. Without a doubt there were many marriages which were invalid according to Maryland colonial and state law as a search of the records will disclose.

It is advisable to search all official, public, and private records for evidence of marriage. Research should not be limited to available marriage licenses and other local records. For a more complete listing, refer to the *Check List of Record Sources for Establishing Evidence of Marriages.*

Massachusetts

If you believe the legal authorities, past and present, informal, irregular, clandestine, and common law marriages are now and always have been invalid. This is not the case, as Massachusetts court decisions disclose. A search of civil and criminal court records, including court decisional reports disclose that the colony and state defied the law which provided that all parties marrying should comply with the statute which required forma marriages, beginning as early as 1639.

"Moreover, at no time during the colonial and provincial periods did the statutes of Massachusetts expressly declare marriages void for disregard of the celebration or other formalities [the statute] prescribed." (George Elliott Howard, Ph.D., *A History of Matrimonial Institutions*, Vol. 3, London 1904, p. 173.)

Exception to General Rule: Marriage may be proved by evidence of an admission thereof by an adverse party, by evidence of general repute or of cohabitation of the parties as married persons, or of any other fact from which it may be inferred. Massachusetts General Laws, Annotated, Chapter 207, Sect. 47.

Michigan

Common law marriages were valid prior to January 1, 1957. Michigan Statutes Annotated, Section 25.2. Judge Cooley clearly stated in 1875 that a marriage may be valid although the provisions of the Michigan statute have been ignored:

> Whatever the form of ceremony, or even if all ceremony was dispensed with, if the parties agreed presently to take each other for husband and wife, and from that time lived together professedly in that relation, proof of these facts would be sufficient to constitute proof [of a valid marriage]. *Hutchins v. Kimmel* (1875) 31 Michigan 126, 130.

Minnesota

Common law marriages were valid on or before 26 April 1941. Minnesota Statutes Annotated, Section 517.01.

Mississippi

Common law marriages were valid prior to April 5, 1956, Mississippi Code, Title 93-1-15. *Case Law Prior to 1956:* "As marriage is a civil contract, it will be valid if entered into with all the common-law requisites [present consent, cohabitation, and reputation for marriage] though without the forms prescribed by statute." *Rundle v. Pegram* (1874) 49 Mississippi 751 (quoting syllabus).

Missouri

Common law marriages were valid prior to 31 March 1921. *Missouri Laws* 1921, page 468. *Case Law Prior to 1921:* "It is not necessary to the validity of a marriage in Missouri that any special ceremony, religious or otherwise, should be performed, nor that the marriage should be solemnized before any person belonging to any one of the classes named in the Missouri statute as authorized to perform the ceremony. Marriage in Missouri may be had by the mutual present consent of two competent persons, made in good faith and followed by cohabitation without the addition of any prescribed formalities, and may be shown by such evidence as proves that such a marriage actually exists." *Holabird v. Atlantic* (1873) 12 Federal Cases 315.

Montana

Common law marriages, by informal agreement, were valid until recent provision requiring a written declaration. For details refer to Montana Code, 40-1-311, 1978.

Nebraska

Common law marriages were valid in Nebraska prior to 26 April 1923. *Nebraska Session Laws*, 1923, Chapter 40, pages 154-155.

Nevada

Common law marriages are valid in Nevada prior to 29 March 1943. *Nevada Revised Statutes*, Chapter 122-010.

New Hampshire

According to New Hampshire law, common law marriages are not valid. However, this is not an indication that irregular, clandestine, and common law marriages did not occur. They did and not in small numbers, as court and other records have disclosed. Unfortunately marriages which were not strictly according to the statutes are not disclosed unless litigation is commenced to ascertain the legality or invalidity of the relationship. No doubt the leading case is *The Town of Londonderry v. The Town of Chester* (1820) 2 New Hampshire Reports 268. This civil action was commenced to ascertain the legal settlement of Sally (———) Aiken, a pauper. The purpose of the lawsuit was to decide which town was liable for her support. The validity of the marriage of Sally to Samuel Aiken was questioned because the state statute was not strictly complied with. There was a question whether or not the minister who performed the ceremony was authorized to do so.

The court solved the problem by deciding that the technicality of the minister's authority was not material after all, as the marriage would be valid as a common law marriage because Sally and Samuel mutually consented and agreed to marry by words stated in the present tense, the technical term of which is verba de praesenti.

Another example of a marriage disclosure which would never have been disclosed except for litigation is the case of *Dunbarton v. Franklin* (1848) 19 New Hampshire 257. It is another pauper support problem involving the two towns. Rebecca (—) Sawyer was supposed to be a resident of Franklin because of her alleged marriage to Edmund Sawyer whom it is admitted was a resident of Franklin. Before the couple lived together, they went to a magistrate and requested that he marry them. The magistrate refused because they did not have a certificate of publication. There was no evidence that the marriage was ever solemnized, either by a magistrate or a minister of the gospel, or in any other manner. Rebecca and Edmund lived together as husband and wife for about fourteen years in Franklin. Edmund died circa 1840.

Chief Justice Gilchrist in his opinion stated that "It appears from the case that the parties made a contract of marriage, lived together as husband and wife, and were reputed to be married."

The justices solved this one because the legislature had enacted a statute which provided that ". . . any persons cohabiting and acknowledging each other as husband and wife, and generally reputed to be such, for the period of three years, and until the decease of one of them, shall be deemed after such decease to have been legally married."

The marriage of Sally and Edmund was in fact a common law marriage, but because New Hampshire law did not recognize common law marriages at this time, the court applied the provisions of the statute and decided the evidence of mutual agreement to be married, cohabitation, and the reputation in the community that they were married – all of which are the elements of common law marriage.

Exception to General Rule: Persons cohabiting and acknowledging each other as husband and wife, and generally reputed to be such, for the period of three years, and until the decease of one of them, shall thereafter be deemed to have been legally married. N.H. Rev. Statutes, 457.39, 1968.

New Jersey

Common law marriage was valid in New Jersey prior to 1 December 1939. Title 37 c. 1, Section 10, *New Jersey Statutes. Case Law Prior to 1939:* In New Jersey, no more is needed to constitute a legal marriage than that the man [or the woman?] shall declare in words of the present tense that the woman is his wife and the woman agree. *Atlantic v. Elizabeth Goodin, Admx., of John H. Goodin, Dec'd,* (1898) 62 New Jersey Law Reports 394, 401.

New Mexico

Although the Supreme Court of New Mexico by a majority opinion decided in 1934 that common law marriages were not valid in New Mexico, and the consensus was that such marriages never were recognized, a strong dissenting opinion by a minority of the justices does suggest that there was a period when they were valid. It is reasonable to believe that at least prior to the time New Mexico was admitted to the Union which was on 6 January 1912, common law marriages were valid. *In re Gabaldon's Estate* (1934) 38 New Mexico 392, et seq. Dissenting opinion commences on page 397, et seq.

New York

Common law marriage was valid prior to January 1, 1902; invalid between January 1, 1902 and January 1, 1908; valid between January 1, 1908, and April 29, 1933; *and invalid on and after April 29, 1933,* 15 *New York Jurisprudence* 285, 286. Revised 1972. The Lawyers Cooperative Publishing Company, Rochester. Dom. Rel. Law Sect. 11. New York State provided the legal precedent for common law marriages because of the court decision of *Fenton v. Reed* (1810) 4 Johnson's Reports 52 et seq. This decision influenced courts in other states to recognize common law marriages.

North Carolina

The consensus is that common law marriage is unknown to North Carolina. The present law is that it is invalid. A search of the early records discloses that irregular, informal, clandestine, illegal, and what would be common law marriages in other jurisdictions, were prevalent. (*A History of Matrimonial Institutions,* by George Elliott Howard, Ph.D., London 1904, Vol. 3, p. 172)

Evidence of this fact is the case of *Felts and Wife v. Mary Foster and Thomas Williams* (1799) 1 North Carolina Reports 72; (Part 2) 1 Taylor's Reports 72: "The plaintiffs Felts and wife were entitled by the will of (——) Foster, deceased, to a considerable part of his property, in the event of his widow Mary Foster, the now defendant, marrying again." It was alleged in the pleadings that she was married to Thomas Williams, which Mary and Thomas Williams denied. In the decision on appeal the court said "There is in this case no positive proof of a marriage [between Mary Foster and Thomas Williams], but there are circumstances advancing to create a belief that a marriage has taken place: they have lived together a long time, as man and wife, have had several children, and the witnesses say that she was a woman of irreproachable character, before these things happened. If so, a presumption arises that she would not thus have cohabited with the defendant, unless a marriage had been previously solemnized. Upon such evidence, I think the jury may find a marriage. Verdict accordingly."

Obviously the court decided there was a marriage in spite of the lack of substantial evidence to prove there was.

North Dakota

Common law marriage was valid in North Dakota prior to 20 March 1890. *Statutes of 1890.*

Ohio

Common law marriages, past and present, are valid in Ohio. *Carmichael v. The State of Ohio* (1861) 12 Ohio State Reports 553; *Umbenhower v. Labus* (1912) 85 Ohio State Reports 238.

Oklahoma

Common law marriages, past and present, are valid in Oklahoma. There is a license requirement, but the purpose is to cause officials to register records of marriage when marriage is by license. The statutes requiring license are directory and not mandatory, and therefore, do not prohibit common law marriages. *In re Sanders Estate* (1917) 67 Oklahoma Reports 3.

Oregon

The consensus is that common law marriage has never been valid in Oregon. Early statutory and case law does not support that opinion. *Hills' Annotated Laws of Oregon*, 1887, Sections 2852 and 2856, enacted October 15, 1862. *Rugh vs. Ottenheimer* (1877) 6 Oregon Reports 231. The conclusion is that common law marriage was valid in Oregon, at least prior to 1877.

Pennsylvania

Common law marriages, past and present, are valid in Pennsylvania. "Marriage is a civil contract, which might be completed by any words in the present [tense] without regard to form." *Hantz, Administrator, c.t.a. of Sealy v. Sealy* (1814) 6 Binney's Reports 405, 408.

Rhode Island

Common law marriages, past and present, are valid in Rhode Island. *Mathewson v. Phoenix* (U.S. Court of Appeals, 1st Circuit, 1884) 20 Federal Reporter 281.

South Carolina

Common law marriages, past and present, were and are valid in South Carolina. "Marriage, with us, so far as the law is concerned has ever been regarded as a mere civil contract. Our law prescribes no ceremony. It requires nothing but the agreement of the parties, with an intention that that agreement shall, per se, constitute the marriage. They may express the agreement [orally], they may signify it by whatever ceremony their whim, or their taste, or their religious belief, may select: it is the agreement itself, and not the form in which it is couched which constitutes the contract. The words used, or the ceremony performed, are mere evidence of a present intention and agreement of the parties. Marriage is always an executed, never an executory contract. It is not what the parties intend to do hereafter, but they intentionally do now, that constitutes the tie and renders it indissoluble. Therefore, an engagement that the parties will marry, is not marriage: but an engagement, whereby they do take each other, in *praesenti*, for man and wife, is marriage." *Fryer v. Fryer* (1832) 1 Richardson's Equity Cases 85, 92-93.

South Dakota

Common law marriages were valid prior to 1 July 1959. Title 25-1-29, *South Dakota Compiled Laws.*

Tennessee

According to eminent legal authority, common law marriage has always been invalid in Tennessee. However, other eminent authority, namely, George Elliott Howard, Ph.D., stated in his treatise, heretofore cited, (*A History of Matrimonial Institutions*, Volume 3, page 176) that "By earlier decisions of Tennessee a strict compliance with the statute was required, the [Supreme] court even declaring in 1829 that a marriage solemnized before a justice of the peace out of his own county was 'absolutely null and void.' " This opinion was sustained by a decree of 1831; but later judgments favor [common law marriage.]

The Tennessee Code Annotated, Section 36-405 requires parties to obtain a license, followed by prescribed solemnization in order to be legally married.

Texas

Common law marriages, past and present, were and are valid, except for a short period when court decisions in 1833 and 1894 favored marriage by license and parental consent. *Grigsby v. Reib* (1913) 105 Texas Reports 597; Howard, George Elliott, *A History of Matrimonial Institutions*, London 1904, Volume 3, pages 176-177.

Utah

Common law marriage was valid in Utah prior to 1898. Utah Revised Statutes 1898, Section 1189.

Vermont

Common law marriage is invalid in Vermont. *Morrill v. Palmer* (1894) 68 Vermont Reports 1. There is no doubt that irregular, informal, clandestine and what would be common law marriages occurred. For example, Nathaniel P. Harriman and Lydia Page, citizens of Vermont, previous to 7 September 1807 went to Stanstead, Lower Canada, and entered into a common law marriage and then returned to Vermont. The Vermont Supreme Court adjudged the common law marriage of the parties valid. *The Town of Newbury v. The Town of Brunswick* (1829) 2 Vermont Supreme Court Reports 151.

Virginia

Statutory Virginia law was and is to the effect that every marriage requires a license (Virginia Code 20-13), and that common law marriages are invalid. However, there is a conflict amongst the legal authorities in regard to this subject. Howard states that "Only during the thirty-five years between 1661 and 1696 does any statute of Virginia expressly declare a marriage void if not contracted according to its provisions." (George Elliott Howard, Ph.D., *A History of Matrimonial Institutions*. Volume 3, pages 171-172.)

Or consider the U.S. Supreme Court decision in regard to an irregular marriage which did not comply with Virginia law in 1865. The court stated "By the statutes of Virginia then in force it was provided: 'Every marriage in this State shall be under a license and solemnized in the manner herein provided, but no marriage solemnized by any persons professing to solemnize the same shall be deemed or adjudged to be void, nor shall the validity thereof be in any way affected on account of any want of authority in such persons if the marriage be in all other respects lawful and be consummated with a full belief on the part of the persons so married, or either of them, that they have been lawfully joined in marriage.' " *Travers v. Reinhardt* (1907) 205 U.S. 423, 433.

Virginia court records disclose a surprising number of irregular, informal, clandestine marriages, and some of these would constitute common law marriages. Refer to the *Check List of Record Sources for Establishing Evidence of Marriage*, p. 86.

Washington

According to present law, common law marriages are invalid in Washington. This has not always been the law. For example, the 1883 *Laws of the Territory of Washington*, page 43, provide for ceremonial marriage, but the statutory provision is directory and not mandatory, therefore, a common law marriage would be valid. The 1854 *Washington Territorial Statutes*, pages 404, 405, include (in addition to directory ceremonial marriage) a provision in Section 6 that "No marriage shall be void or voidable for the want of any formality required by law, if either of the parties thereto believed it to be a legal marriage at the time."

West Virginia

Common law marriages are invalid in West Virginia. *Fout v. Hanlin* (1933) 113 West Virginia Reports 752. West Virginia prior to admission to the Union as a State was part of Virginia. Refer to Virginia for status of marriage.

Wisconsin

Common law marriage was valid in Wisconsin prior to 1917. *Prior Case Law: Becker v. Becker* (1913) 153 Wisconsin 226.

Wyoming

Common law marriages are invalid in Wyoming. Wyoming Statutes title 20-1-103(a).

Historically, common law marriage was recognized and valid, according to court decision. *Connors v. Connors* (1895) 5 Wyoming Reports 433.

CHAPTER 12

COURT RECORDS – CIVIL ACTIONS

"Civil action" includes civil proceedings; as distinguished from criminal proceedings.

Section 120 California Evidence Code and
Law Revision Commission. (1965)

I. COURT RECORDS

Imagine a scene in an English court which occurred hundreds of years ago, and try to reconstruct the dialogue at the trial as John Doe complains of the actions of Richard Roe and others. Assume that Doe's counsel has just commenced his opening statement:

"Your honor, my client John Doe was forced by the defendant Richard Roe, and others, to surrender possession of his farm without payment of any money, as described in his petition filed with the clerk of this court, and John Doe is present with his witnesses."

The judge interrupts Doe's attorney.

The Court: "Get to the point, how did this happen?"

Attorney: "Roe and his companions came to Doe's house, held a dagger at his throat, and told him that if he did not issue an indenture under seal, leave Roe in possession, and quit the premises they would kill him."

The Court: "Did Doe sign and seal the document in the presence of witnesses?"

Attorney: "He sealed it, my client does not write. Roe had witnesses present."

The Court: "You admit then that he sealed the document in the presence of witnesses and delivered possession to Roe?"

Attorney: "Yes, but he was forced to do so because his life was in danger."

The Court: "But he sealed the document, in the presence of witnesses, he delivered it to Roe, and placed Roe in possession of the land. Doe performed all the acts necessary to transfer title and possession to the land to Roe. The court cannot consider any other facts. The Common Law of England is a body of rules which are fixed and immutable authority, and which must be applied rigorously and in their entirety and cannot be modified to suit the peculiarities of a specific case such as Doe, or varied by any judicial discretion. This court and the common law has no remedy for John Doe. This case is dismissed and Doe will pay Roe his costs expended to date."

A proceeding similar to Doe v. Roe did occur, the exact date and names of the persons involved are shrouded by the passing centuries. But at some time after 1066, a litigant such as John Doe or his counsel decided there was a remedy and decided to consult the "keeper of the king's conscience," the chancellor.

The chancellor was at this time in history a member of the clergy and cognizant of natural or divine law. He realized that John Doe (or whoever he was) had been the victim of a grave injustice which the common law courts would not correct. Therefore, the chancellor cancelled the document or conveyance of the land, ordered the ouster of Roe, and put John Doe back into possession of his land.

Although the foregoing is hypothetical (and described in simple terms), it is the manner in which the court of equity or court of chancery originated. The common law courts continued to operate, and if people were unable to obtain relief there, they bypassed the common law system and went to the Court of Chancery where they were able to obtain equitable relief. Thus in England there developed two systems of justice, the common law and equity jurisprudence in the Court of Chancery, or Equity.

This brief resume of legal history is necessary for genealogists and record searchers because when the colonists came to the new world, they adapted the English legal system to what was needed in the colonies and at one time many jurisdictions or states maintained separate courts, namely, courts of law and courts of equity. But almost universally, the two courts have been merged into one and thus grant legal and equitable relief as the judges are presiding as judges of a law court and as a Chancellor in a Court of Equity. Modernly, the significance of courts of the common law and courts of equity or chancery have almost passed into oblivion, but to the genealogist and record searcher the two systems are of great historical and genealogical importance in locating and searching court records. It is necessary to search thoroughly all court records; that involves searching the plaintiffs and defendants indices of every court in existence during the periods of your search. It is necessary to understand the court system, therefore, one must study the history and jurisdiction of the courts of whatever colonies or states in which you are interested. Some of the states distinctly maintained separate courts of law and courts of equity until modern times, but there is one exception. The State of Vermont has a separate Court of Chancery and the law court is the District Court. Louisiana was never a common law court, as it adopted the civil law of France based on the Civil Law of Rome, and for that reason never organized courts of chancery or equity, as such.

To clarify the roles of the two courts, it is necessary to know the types of civil actions over which these bodies exercised jurisdiction. There is one universal rule (depending on interpretation); litigants were required to seek relief in the law courts, unless the remedy at law was inadequate. For instance, the law court did not grant specific performance of a contract if money damages was a suitable remedy. But if specific performance of a land contract was required because land is unique and the buyer wants that parcel of land, the court of equity or chancery is where relief may be granted if the buyer (plaintiff) is capable of satisfying the court that specific performance is the only remedy. Then the seller is ordered to execute and deliver the deed to the real property to the buyer and if he refuses to do so, he is in contempt of court and in the discretion of the court, consigned to the local jail to think it over until he complies.

Generally, the following is the jurisdiction of the two systems:

LAW COURTS: (Some examples of causes of action, or lawsuits and historical or legal terms which are often encountered in civil actions.)

MODERN DEFINITION

Conversion	*Action for taking personal property of another.*
Torts	*Civil wrongs, such as libel, slander, etc.*
Indebitatus assumpsit	*Debt*
Assumpsit	*Contract — debt*
Trover	*Similar to conversion*
Trespass	*Violation of personal or property rights*
Trespass vi et armis	*Trespass with force*
Trespass on the case	*Action for damages for a wrongful act not accompanied by force but secondary result occurs*
Detinue	*Recovery of personal property lawfully taken, but illegally retained*
Replevin	*Recovery of personal property illegally taken*
Covenant — Ex Contractu	*Breach of a contract under seal*
Deceit	*Similar to fraud*
Criminal conversation	*Civil action for adultery. Relief — money damages.*
Seduction	*Seduction*
De Ejectione Firmae	*Ejectment — lawsuit to recover possession of real property*
Lis Pendens	*Notice of action [lawsuit] pending, filed in land records*
Summons	*Notice of a lawsuit*
Subpoena	*Notice to appear in court as a witness*
Subpoena duces tecum	*Notice to appear in court with specific articles, e.g., records*
Depositions	*Questioning a witness in the absence of the trial court, by attorneys for both plaintiff and defendant. The questions and answers are reduced to writing and may be used as evidence.*
Affidavits	*In early records often referred to as a deposition, which is a misnomer. An affidavit is a declaration or statement signed and sealed before a notary public or other officer.*

COURT OF EQUITY OR CHAN-CERY: (Trial without a jury) (The remedy available in the law courts must be inadequate in order to obtain relief in this court.) Some causes of action or lawsuits and historical or legal terms which are often encountered in equitable court proceedings and records, and accompanying terminology.

MODERN DEFINITIONS

Bill Quia Timet	*Because he fears injury to his rights or property.*
Bill to Quiet Title	*Remove defect, or "cloud" from title to land*
Divorce (originally this was not available, the church granted annulments — maybe)	
Divorce a mensa et thoro	*Legal separation from "bed and board"*
Divorce a vinculo matrimonii	*Total divorce*
Injunctive relief — *This relief is of two types, mandatory injunctions and prohibitory injunctions.*	*To prevent someone from doing something a person believes to be wrong, dangerous, or harmful to his property or person. Originally it was necessary to prove that a property right was involved in order to obtain relief*
Equitable relief in tort	*Injunctive relief from a continuing wrong — money won't compensate, e.g., continuous trespassing.*
Uses	*Property held in trusts by a trustee for beneficiaries.*
De Ejectione Firmae (The court of equity is proper for relief if the remedy at law is inadequate)	*Recovery of possession of real property*

In the colonies, the ecclesiastical court system of England was abolished; as in the Mother Country, the church had jurisdiction over domestic matters and estates of the deceased. The colonies were not inclined to entrust churches with jurisdiction over secular affairs.

It would require volumes to describe the evidentiary sources of colonial courts. It is, however, necessary to be familiar with the courts and court records of the area in which a genealogist researches. The most complete bibliography on early courts and their jurisdiction is too lengthy for inclusion here.[1]

The colonies in establishing court systems avoided the complicated court organization in effect in England with its numerous jurisdictions. Ecclesiastical courts were eliminated and secular affairs were within the jurisdiction of the civil courts.

After the formation of the union in 1789, the colonies organized their own state court systems and the federal judiciary was organized. Because there is a tendency to overlook the fact that there is a tremendous amount of genealogical information of local concern included in federal court proceedings, these records should be thoroughly searched.

The highest court is, of course, the United States Supreme Court. In the records of the Supreme Court, it is surprising the amount of genealogical detail there is included in the files and decisions of this high court. The early original records of the court are in the custody of the National Archives. The reported decisions of the justices are published in three different published sources: the *United States Supreme Court Reports, The Supreme Court Reporter,* and the *Lawyers' Edition* (the latter two editions are privately published). These tomes are available in law libraries, but there are no adequate indices to the facts included in these reported court decisions.[2]

The intermediate tribunals are the Circuit Courts, originally three in number and presided over by Supreme Court Justices, assigned for that purpose, and a District Judge. Circuit Courts had jurisdiction in cases involving larger amounts and more serious offenses, and controversies between citizens of different states, or in instances where a federal question was involved.

The third type of federal court was the District Courts, and originally there was at least one District Court in each state. This Court's jurisdiction was limited at first to the trial of minor offenses and cases involving admiralty law.

The older records of the Circuit and District Courts, which are of tremendous genealogical value, are in the custody of the Federal Record Centers located regionally. The National Archives published a pamphlet regarding the location and services of these regional record centers and it is available without cost.

The decisions of the circuit courts and the district courts have also been published. Unfortunately, no adequate indices have ever been compiled. The lack of adequate indices is one of the handicaps involved in research in court records, as only plaintiffs and defendants are indexed. This is a handicap difficult to overcome as within the body of the court file or court reports, there are names and genealogical facts which may only be found by a page by page search. The same facts and often more facts are included in the files or records of the clerk of the trial court, but sometimes these local records are missing, and the facts in the court report are all that is available.

The high courts in the States are usually termed Supreme Courts, but the title varies from Supreme Judicial Court to Court of Appeals. Below the highest appellate courts in the States are intermediate appellate courts, and below that category are the trial courts or courts of general jurisdiction, and finally down to courts of justices of the peace, which are not courts of record. This term "Court of Record" is misleading, as all courts maintain records of their proceedings. A "court of record" is one whose decisions are perpetuated and are of importance.

The decisions of the appellate courts of the States are published in book form, and do contain, in some instances, detailed genealogical facts. However, as in the case of federal courts, there should be more facts in the files or records of the trial court in the custody of the clerk. As described above, *all* court records are inadequately indexed, as the indexing is limited to parties to the action, namely plaintiffs and defendants.

Originally court proceedings were oral, but as society became more complex, written records originated which were retained in the custody of the court or other officers of the court, such as the judges' clerks. The records were called the "rolls of the court" because they were literally in the form of rolls. The reason for rolls was because it was more practical to roll vellum or parchment than to fold it. When paper was used, the documents were folded and tied into bundles with the title of the action on the folded side of the pleadings or papers filed in the proceedings. Fortunately, by 1620 paper was in use. But, if at this late date, you go to the Public Record Office and some other record offices in England, you will be handed a roll of parchment perhaps one hundred feet long. In England, Lord Denning is Master of the Rolls (an ancient and honorable title which originated hundreds of years ago) and all of the records and rolls are constructively in his possession. That includes the original copy of the Magna Carta in the custody of the British Museum.

Courts today still cling to some of the old expressions, and even in some modern court records where flat filing has been in use for many years, there was until recent years always a flat sheet with this title printed on it in these words: "Judgment Roll," designating the place in the record file where the judgment or decree with the judge's signature is located. This is an anomaly because in the United States court records were folded, but rarely if ever formed into a roll.

CIVIL ACTION PROCEDURE AND DOCUMENTS – GENERALLY

Assuming a plaintiff decides to commence a civil action (as opposed to a probate case or other type of court proceedings), he consults counsel and the following are examples of the principal documents and procedure involved.

Originally a lawsuit was commenced with the issuance of a "Writ." (Refer to "Writs" page 206) Later, and modernly, the first documents were known as Bills, Complaints and Petitions stating facts to support the relief sought.

The clerk issues a Summons and the complaint and summons are personally (unless publication of summons is authorized) served on the defendant or defendants.

After the foregoing papers are served on the defendant(s), he or they will file an answer or reply in writing in which the facts alleged by the plaintiff are denied or admitted in whole or in part.

A second choice is to file a document known as a demurrer, alleging there is no cause of action stated in the complaint. The jurisdiction of the court may also be challenged.

There may also be depositions and affidavits filed with the clerk of court.

All documents filed with the clerk of the court should be entered in a register of actions or docket volume which constitutes a brief history of the court proceeding.

Ultimately, assume the controversy proceeds to trial, the testimony of those testifying may be recorded by a shorthand reporter. Unfortunately, the shorthand notes may never be transcribed unless there was an appeal to a higher court, in which case about the only source for information regarding the trial is a contemporary newspaper account of the proceedings.

The clerk of the court will record minutes in a record volume or ledger, a day to day account of the trial, but these are an abbreviated record of the trial, usually limited to the names of jurors, witnesses, orders of the court, and the final outcome of the trial.

A judgment or decree signed by the judge is often the last paper filed in the proceedings, unless there is an appeal to a higher court, or a return on a writ of execution of the judgment (if money is involved) or a writ of restitution if the judgment is for the return of property or the possession of real property.

In an action for divorce (whether for separation or permanent divorce), after the courts acquired jurisdiction for this type of proceeding, the information is the name of the plaintiff (e.g., wife), name of the husband (if he is the defendant, and that is usually the case), their place of residence (county), date and place of marriage, and the names and ages (perhaps the places where the children were born), and some facts regarding property of the husband and wife.

The same similar facts should be stated if the action is for annulment, except that it is possible the maiden name of the woman should be disclosed.

In an action to quiet title to land, entire families may be involved because of the possibility they claim (or allegedly claim) interests as heirs of a grandfather or other ancestor who at some time in the past owned an interest in the land. As usual in a civil action, there are plaintiffs and defendants. The cause of action is based on the allegation that the defendants claim some right or title to land, and they may not necessarily be in possession. The first document filed is a Bill to Remove Cloud on Title, or a Complaint to Quiet Title. This may not disclose much information regarding the claim, which it is alleged is not valid, the legal description of the land is included which if adequately described may be located in the county in which the lawsuit is commenced. The action to quiet title is a relatively recent form of lawsuit, simpler and more satisfactory than an ejection action, and in some jurisdictions has replaced ejectment proceedings. This is so even when someone is in possession of the plaintiff's land and claims it is his because of adverse possession, because he (the defendant) has been in open and notorious possession for a claimed number of years which would justify the defendant to claim that his adverse possession has ripened or changed into a legal title. This does not mean that his claim will be upheld as the defendant must prove continuous possession and other facts. This also being a lawsuit involving real property, the document known as a *lis pendens* or notice of action, should be recorded in the land records (modernly it must be) or notice of some type posted in a public place or published in the local newspaper. Finding evidence of any *lis pendens* is a clue to a record searcher that he or she should search the civil court records.

CHANGE OF NAME WITH AND WITHOUT COURT PROCEEDINGS

The English common law did not prevent persons from changing their names. Today in some jurisdictions, individuals are not prohibited from changing their names (given name and surname) without securing an order of court, if the change is not for the purpose of fraudulent reasons. However, for legal purposes, such as purchasing or transferring real property, they are supposed to use their legal name.

Historically in the United States anyone desiring to change his name petitioned the legislature of the jurisdiction where he resided and a private act was passed permitting the change, if the legislators cooperated. During this period, it is necessary to search the session laws or statutes at large to find the change.

Modernly, there is statutory provision authorizing changes of names (both given and surname) pursuant to court proceedings. The procedure is quite simple. A petition is prepared stating the present name, the proposed new name, and the reasons for the change. Notice of the proceedings are published for the purpose of notifying any interested persons to object to the change. There is a brief hearing (if uncontested), and the court issues an order changing the name.

Courts of general jurisdiction decide matters of change of name. The clerk of the court, e.g., county clerk, indexes all court proceedings so that it is possible to locate these petitions, supposedly available to the public. Hopefully, the clerk indexes the old name and the new name with clear cross references or there will be a real research problem.

EJECTMENT LAWSUITS

Records of ejectment actions are among the most important civil court proceedings to genealogists, not only because of the genealogical detail often disclosed, but because there was a large volume of these controversies during the colonial and post colonial period. Many of them were appealed from the local courts of general (or trial) jurisdiction to the appellate courts especially after the colonial period. During the colonial period, civil appeals to the Privy Council were limited in number.[3]

To understand the evidence available in a court file or record involving ejectment, it is necessary to know that this form of action originated in England centuries ago because it was almost impossible to regain possession of real property, such as a farm or other realty. The type of lawsuit which the English law provided was what was known as a "Real Action," the word real signifying that the restitution of the real or tangible property was sought. Unfortunately the "Real Action" procedure was cumbersome, required years to resolve, overly technical due to defense tactics, and often unsuccessful. But an action for ejectment had none of these delays and defects. As a result lawyers invented a collusive method of bypassing the "Real Action." They invented the fictitious lawsuit and utilized the simpler procedure of the action in ejectment which was originally known in the English courts as "*Ejecit Infra Terminum*," or "*Ejectione Firmae*," eventually shortened to "Action in Ejectment." This fictitious civil lawsuit was imported to the colonies along with other features of English Law. When you are searching court records and notice the title of a lawsuit with this title "Doe ex dem Thomas Smith v. John Williams" which means "Doe on the lease of Thomas Smith"; this is an action in ejectment. Doe is a fictitious person. Thomas Smith is the real plaintiff and John Williams is the defendant who has possession of the land. The lease is "phony." There is no lease. What Smith is trying to do is repossess his land which Williams is holding against Smith's will, and the only practical lawsuit is the action in ejectment. So the bill or complaint filed with the court states the following allegations:

1. Smith leased the land to Doe.
2. Doe then was in possession of the land.
3. Williams by force of arms ousted Doe.
4. Doe (really Smith) wants Williams ousted.

Assuming the court grants the relief and orders Williams ousted, then Smith (since there is no Doe) will be able to repossess his land.

In addition to the "Doe" name, other fictitious names were used in the colonies, and later the States, such as "Paul Peaceable ex dem Thomas Smith, Plaintiff, v. Thomas Williams, Defendant," "Titus Title ex dem Thomas Smith," or "Paul Friendly ex dem Thomas Smith."

The English and Colonial courts knew that the lawsuit was "phony" or collusive, but because parliament had failed or refused to enact legislation providing an adequate remedy, the courts ignored the collusive feature of the lawsuits in order to provide a just and adequate remedy.

Eventually the legislatures of the States enacted procedural laws which enabled litigants to repossess their real property without resorting to collusion, but this was many years after the formation of the Union.

These collusive lawsuits present another problem for genealogists, due to the propensity of clerks to index the plaintiff "Doe" in the "D" part of the plaintiffs' index. There is no uniformity. The index may disclose the action as "Doe ex dem Thomas Williams," but fail to index "Williams, Thomas." So when searching for Thomas Williams to locate the evidence it is advisable to search all of the "Does." Hopefully, the indexer will index the fictitious actions in full, e.g., "Doe ex dem Thomas Williams," "Doe ex dem Wyne," etc., or if he realizes the significance of the fictitious lawsuit, he will index it as "Williams, Thomas, Doe ex dem." Therefore, you must search other fictitious names in addition to Doe, such as Paul Peaceable, Titus Title, and others; but the fictitious name "Doe," is the standard name for this type of collusive lawsuit.

The titles of the documents filed in the proceeding will be similar to other civil actions, such as Bill of Complaint, Petition, Reply, Answer, Judgment, Decree, etc.

II. CRIMINAL RECORDS

In the records of criminal cases, there are occasionally some genealogical information in addition to names; there also will be relationships stated. It is not wise to ignore this source. Although the titles of the actions in criminal proceedings are "Commonwealth v. John Doe," or "State v. Doe," if the indexers are at all competent the first and surname of the individual who is charged with a crime will be indexed also. After obtaining the case number, the file should be examined.

CUSTODY OF COURT RECORDS

Civil court (and other court records) are in the custody of the clerk of court who is also the County Clerk or similar officer.

FORMS FOR ABSTRACTING FACTS OF CIVIL ACTIONS

1.   Title of Court   [e.g., Court of Common Pleas, County of.........., State of..........]

2.   Case No......... DATE ACTION COMMENCED: ....

3.   Name of Plaintiff(s)

4.   Name of Defendant(s)

5.   Basis of the Cause of Action: (For example, foreclosure of mortgage, etc.)

6.   Abstract the facts set forth in the body of the complaint, petition declaration, or whatever this first pleading or paper is entitled.

7.   Abstract the "prayer" for relief. (This usually begins with these words: "Wherefore, plaintiff prays for foreclosure, money, possession of the property, costs of the lawsuit, etc. ....")

8.   Signature of plaintiff

9.   Name and address of attorney for plaintiff

10. Name and address of attorney for defendant

Abstract subsequent proceedings of the lawsuit in a similar manner as above, include references to record volumes, register of action, or docket, minute book references, book and page of judgment, and of course all dates.

III. COURT RECORDS OF THE ESTATES OF DECEASED PERSONS

PROBATE RECORDS

WILLS AND ADMINISTRATIONS OF ESTATES

The custodian of these records is usually termed Clerk of the Probate Court, Register of Probate, County Clerk, Clerk of the Orphans' Court, and in some colonies and states, the Ordinary, and Surrogate.

In the colonies the law of wills, testaments, and estates was based on the English law, adapted to the needs of the colonies. During the post-revolutionary period and statehood, there were additional changes suitable to the conditions of the times.

Historically a "Will" referred only to a disposition of real property. A "Testament" was a disposition of personal property. During the passage of time, the term "Last Will and Testament" referred to both real or personal property.

A *codicil* is an addition to or change of a will and testament.

A *testator* is a person who signs a will. A *testatrix* is the female counterpart. If a person dies without a will, it is said that he or she died *intestate*, in which case an *administrator* (a man) or an *administratrix* (a woman) is appointed to administer the estate and oversee distribution to the heirs.

A *devisee* is a person to whom real property is devised by will. A *legatee* is a person who receives a gift of money. A *bequest* is a gift of personal property. Modernly these terms are used interchangeably and there is no legal problem if a devisee is referred to as a legatee.

Heirs are entitled to a decedent's real property if he dies intestate. Distributees or "next of kin" are entitled to personal property; however, these distinctions were abolished during the passage of time.

Descent refers to real property while *distribution* refers to personal property. In the past these words were significant because real property transferred immediately to the heirs or devisees of the deceased while personal property passed to the executor or administrator who distributed it to the legatees or distributees.

An *executor* is a person named by the testator or testatrix in his last will and testament to be in charge of the estate. If the testator or testatrix failed to name an executor or executrix in his will, the court appointed an "administrator (or administratrix) with the will annexed" (the technical term is *cum testamento annexo*, or the abbreviation c.t.a.) who administered the estate in accordance with the provision of the last will and testament.

The word "probate" (from Latin *probatus*, from the verb *probare* to prove) describes the proceeding for "proving" a will before the surrogate, judge of probate, ordinary, or other judicial officer. Witnesses testify that they were present when the testator (or testatrix) told them it was his will (publication), and signed it in their presence and in the presence of each other, and the witnesses testifying under oath also offered their opinion that the testator-testatrix was of "sound and disposing mind and memory," which of course was purely a conclusion on their part.

AGE AND CAPACITY IN REGARD TO WILLS

"Sound mind" or mental capacity and the knowledge that a testator knows significance of the will is a necessary element in wills. He or she is supposed to know the natural objects of his or her bounty, and it was and is considered unnatural to give or devise the bulk of an estate to strangers. He or she must know the nature and extent of the property owned or mental capacity will probably be questioned.

Historically, married women did not possess the right to dispose of their estate by will. The theory for this outmoded rule was that husband and wife were one person, and the husband was that person, and he controlled the wife's property. However, a widow was eligible to dispose of her estate by will or otherwise.[4]

Age as a legal disability. The age persons qualify to permit them to dispose of property by will varies according to time and place. Legal age is twenty-one, or has been in the past in most places, but it would be foolish to assume that rule is universal. In the case of *Deane v. Littlefield* decided by the Supreme Judicial Court of Massachusetts in 1822 (1 Pickering's Reports 239), the court held that an "infant" fourteen years of age possessed the legal capacity to execute a will disposing of personal property.

Age of Witnesses. This question of age poses the question as to the eligibility of witnesses to a will. At what age is a witness competent or qualified to sign and act as a witness to last wills and testaments? Again, it would be presumptuous to assume that a witness must be of legal age. There are court decisions and textbook authority that the testimony of a child five years of age was admissible evidence.[5] However, the child's ability to write a signature and understand the purpose of the will ceremony, no doubt, would be questioned. There is a case where one of the witnesses to a will was twelve years of age, and who was ajudged qualified to testify regarding the signing and execution of the will.[6]

TYPES OF WILLS

FORMAL WILLS

Formal wills must be in writing. There is no particular form which must be complied with. It should be dated. The testator or testatrix must sign it, or if unable to sign, then he must place his mark as a substitute for his personal signature and another person is required to sign his name for him. The material on which the will is written is not prescribed, but it must be of a permanent nature, such as paper, parchment, or cloth. One famous will filed for probate was written on a petticoat.

HOLOGRAPHIC WILLS

These are wills which are entirely written, dated, and signed in the handwriting of the testator or testatrix. Any other writing on that page will invalidate the will. It should not be signed by witnesses, and no will should ever be acknowledged by a notary public or other officer.

NUNCUPATIVE WILLS

These are oral wills declared or dictated in the presence of witnesses, when a person believes he is dying. After the declaration or preferably during the declaration, a witness is supposed to reduce the provisions of the nuncupative will into written form. This type of will proceeds on the assumption that the dying person is unable to sign his name or mark. Contrary to popular belief a nuncupative will is not necessarily restricted to military personnel, as validity is subject to local law.[7]

JOINT AND MUTUAL WILLS

This is one will which is signed by more than one person. These wills are rare and are often unsatisfactory to all concerned.

MYSTIC WILLS OF LOUISIANA

The testator's will is sealed in an envelope in the presence of a notary and three witnesses, and the notary and witnesses sign the envelope. Certain procedure not described must be complied with to ensure the validity of the mystic will.

THE CONTENTS OF WILLS

The following outline is what should be included in a simple will:

Title: Last Will and Testament of John Doe

Introduction: Full name, residence, occupation. (His or her opinion of soundness of mind may be superfluous, and it is self-serving.)

Payment of debts due, if any.

Marital Status: Name of wife. If a widower, the name of previous spouse or spouses.

Names of Children: Not only should the full names be stated, but if there are any deceased children, they should be named and whether or not they died with or without issue, if so, names of grandchildren. If daughters are married, husbands' full names should be stated. If there are minor children, guardians should be named, and if testamentary trusts are created for anyone, the name or names of the trustees. (The powers of the trustee should be included. It is admitted when a testamentary trust is involved, then the will is no longer a simple document.)

Disposition of Estate: The description of money and property and to whom. If married, the wife's dower right (a legal life estate in one-third of the real estate); she will also receive "moveables" such as household goods absolutely. If any of the children have received a share or all of their share of the estate prior to the death of the testator, this fact should be mentioned. (You may expect the eldest son to receive a double portion in New England. In other colonies, the law of primogeniture favored the eldest son; he was certain to receive the farm, and supposedly he was to pay some compensation to the other children. To prevent the eldest son from selling the family farm, he acquired a restricted title, known as a fee tail, or entailed estate, so that at his death the land would descend to the eldest son in the next generation and so on.)

Primogeniture was abolished in Georgia in 1777, in North Carolina in 1784, in Virginia in 1785, in Maryland in 1786, in New York in 1787, in South Carolina in 1791, and in Rhode Island in 1791. The double portion to the eldest son was abolished in New England. Restrictions on the sale or transfer of interests in land were never popular in the colonies or states.

Usually the last part of the will is the nomination of one or more executors, and states whether a bond is required. An alternate executor(s) may be provided for in the event the first named is/are unwilling or unable to act or predeceased the testator.

Date of will: (Month, day, and year)

Signature of testator:

The signature is followed by an attestation clause to the effect that the testator "published" his/her will by telling the witnesses the document is his last will and testament. Witnesses further attest to the fact that he appeared to them to be of sound and disposing mind and memory. The testator asks them to be his witnesses, and signs the will in their presence, and they sign in his presence and in the presence of each other.

Signature of the witnesses:

The number of witnesses varies from state to state, but never less than two.

PROBATE PROCEDURE

Upon death of the testator, there should be a written petition for probate of will, for letters testamentary, or if intestate, a petition for letters of administration. A case number was assigned to the proceedings. In the early days of informality, the sparcity of formal petitions suggests that the witnesses to the will appeared before the probate judge and testified and "proved" the will, and it was admitted to probate.

The judge decided if a bond was required, and if so fixed the amount, appointed appraisers to decide the value of the estate assets, and two or three overseers who acted in an advisory capacity.

Guardians were appointed for minor children, if orphaned.

The original will was filed and hand copied into a record volume for security reasons.

Notice to creditors was published in a newspaper, and before newspapers were published, the only practical means of notice was by posting written notice in a public place.

The appraisers filed their inventory and appraisement.

When the creditors, if any, were paid, the estate property was distributed in accordance with the provisions of the will.

The foregoing is a summary of the procedure unless complications arose, such as a will contest.

An intestate estate proceeded substantially the same way, except the estate was distributed according to the laws of succession in effect at that time.

If at a later date additional assets were discovered which were owned by the deceased and not distributed in the probate proceedings, a petition for letters of administration *de bonus non* are filed with the court, and the assets are distributed (less debts or liabilities) to the heirs or devisees.

INTERPRETATION OF WILLS AND ESTATE PROCEEDINGS

The problem of interpretation of wills and estate proceedings is understanding the meaning of words and phrases, and dictionary definitions are not always satisfactory. It may be surprising, but it is true that the great bulk of appeals to higher courts concerns the definitions and interpretations of words. Some of the terminology mentioned in wills and estate proceedings have been defined or discussed in this chapter. Reference to legal dictionaries and a list of words and phrases will be included in the last part of this book which will aid in the interpretation of wills, probate proceedings, and court records generally. One of the principal problems concerns relationships, as those stated in the past do not mean the same modernly.

An example of how easy it is for a researcher to go astray by careless or incorrect interpretation was contributed by the late Betty C. Lamb to *The American Genealogist*, Vol. 22, July 1945, page 58:

> An amusing example of mis-interpretation of Probate Records came to my attention recently. A correspondent wrote asking me for the marriage of Mary Morehouse, b. Nov. 27, 1727, daughter of Thomas, of Saybrook. This correspondent had been given two different names

for Mary's husband, one William Wilmot, and the other "a man named North," the latter, it was said, shown by her father's will.

In a copy that I made of the distribution of the estate of Thomas Morehouse, of Saybrook, who died, intestate, Feb. 17, 1769, land is given to "Mary, the Second Daughter," and the document reads, in part, as follows —

> Set out to Andrew Eldest Son . . . eight acres . . . East on Land set out to Mary North sixteen rods and a half on Jonathan Lays land.

Some enthusiastic reader of records, in haste to marry the daughter Mary, had given her a compass point for a husband.

There is nothing in the estate record of Thomas Morehouse, of Saybrook, which proves the marriages of his daughters, but it seems safe to say that Mary Morehouse did not marry "a man named North."

FORM FOR ABSTRACT OF PROBATE PROCEEDINGS

ESTATE OF: *DATE OF FILING*   *CASE #:*
WILL: *OR ADMINISTRATION*

1. *Name of testator or testatrix: [full names]*
2. *Place of residence: [e.g., town and county]*
3. *Occupation*
4. *Name of present, and former spouses, if any*
5. *Names and relationship of heirs, devisees, and legatees; and nature and descriptions of bequests or gifts to them*
6. *Names of any persons excluded from inheritance, and why*
7. *Special recitals [e.g., "in terrorem" clauses which if not complied with will result in disinheritance]*
8. *Names of trustees (if any) and provisions of trust and names of beneficiaries*
9. *Names of guardians of minor children (if any)*
10. *Name or names of executors or executrix or executrices*
11. *Names of Overseers*
12. *Special Provisions (if any)*
13. *Date of will*
14. *Signature (Is the will apparently signed by the testator, or by mark or cross? Is the signature legible?)*
15. *Names of witnesses who signed*
16. *Date the will was probated or proved*
17. *Abstract essential facts from bond of executor or administrator*
18. *Letters testamentary or letters of administration issued, date, and to whom*
19. *Abstract essential facts from any other documents filed in proceedings (e.g., any agreements signed by the heirs re distribution, etc.)*

117

20. *Facts disclosed in decree of distribution (if it is in the file)*

21. *Date estate closed*

22. *Caution: Do not overlook searching and abstracting information in docket volumes, minute books, record volumes; e.g., the will is supposed to be copied into will book*

23. *Recheck to be sure all references have been included in note: Case number(s) books and pages of record volumes, dates*

24. *Title of Official Custodian of records*

25. *Address and location of records in custodian's office*

26. *The date the records were searched*

GUARDIANSHIP PROCEEDINGS

The purpose of a guardianship is to protect minor children and incompetents. The power of the guardian may extend to not only guardianship of the person, but also of the estate of the ward or person subject to an order of court appointing the guardian.

The term "natural guardian" should not be confused with a guardian appointed by a court. Every parent is a "natural guardian," but this is confined entirely to the relationship and duty of parent and child.

There are two types of guardianship; the provision for guardianship at the common law and also provision by statute.

In order to appoint a legal guardian, the usual procedure is to file a "Petition for Letters of Guardianship" with a court of general jurisdiction, usually the Probate Court. After the filing of the petition, a citation (similar to a summons in a civil action) is served on the proposed ward. Citations are also served or mailed to close relatives. A hearing date is set, and at the hearing the petitioner testifies regarding the reasons why a guardian should be appointed. Anyone opposing may also testify. If in the judgment of the court, a guardian should be appointed for a minor or an incompetent person, an order appointing a guardian is signed by the judge. The guardian is required to post a bond if in control of the assets of the ward. (This proceeding should not be confused with a proceeding instituted for the purpose of confining an individual in a mental institution.) Periodically, the guardian must account for the income and expenses of the ward's estate.

Guardianship records are open to the public, although there may be exceptions. Also, because an estate is involved, guardianship proceedings are within the jurisdiction of the probate court, or another court by another title, but with similar duties.

The index to guardianship petitions is a name index which will provide the case number to a court file, and to examine it you fill out and sign a requisition form which is standard procedure for all court records.

ADOPTION RECORDS

Adoption was unknown to the English Common Law, and there was no provision there until 1926. The first adoption statute in the United States was enacted in Massachusetts in 1851. Modernly, courts of general jurisdiction hear adoption petitions and all adoptions records (whether the petition is granted or not) are confidential and sealed by the courts. Anyone who wishes to examine these records must obtain an order of the appropriate court, and judges are extremely reluctant to issue an order to permit examination of the records. Furthermore, the index to adoptions is not open to searchers.

NATURALIZATION RECORDS (FEDERAL JURISDICTION)

"To centralize the information in the naturalization records, which are among the records of more than 5,000 Federal, State, and other courts, the Works Progress Administration in the late 1930's began . . . to photograph copies of the records and to index them. Some of these copies and index are now in the National Archives."[8]

The evidence or information in these records is usually two pages of forms with spaces for some or all of the following: the petition for citizenship, the oath of allegiance to the United States, affidavits relating to U.S. residence, and a record of [previous citizenship]. Other information on the forms usually includes place and date of birth and of arrival in the United States, place of residence at the time of application, and sometimes the name of the ship on which the immigrant arrived and his occupation.

Searchers may . . . abstract naturalization records, subject to National Archives and federal regulations.

Naturalization was provided for by the U.S. Constitution Article 1, Section 8, Clause 4, and authorized Congress to provide uniform rules therefor. Pursuant to this authority, the first law on the subject was enacted on the 26th of March 1790, 1 Statutes at Large 103.

COURT RECORDS: PRO RELIABILITY

Civil Court Records

1. Court records are official records in official custody.
2. In the compilation of a large bulk of the records, this function is also officially supervised.
3. "Proper custody" preserves the integrity of this class of records.
4. Most of the records are signed and sealed under oath.
5. Officials and deputies are bonded and sworn to do their duty.

Probate Records

1. If the parties involved in the preparation, execution, and witnessing of testaments and wills are conscientious, there is a high degree of accuracy in the provisions of these documents. It would be unnatural and foolish for a testator to falsify the names of his children. It would be unusual for a testator or testatrix to forget one or more of his/her children, or other persons who should be included in the will.
2. To further ensure reliability, a close relative (e.g., spouse) may attend the initial interview with the counsel who is to prepare the will and this fact adds argument to the reliability factor.
3. Probate records are civil court records and the reasons mentioned above which encourage care, proper custody, and official status are applicable to probate records also.

COURT RECORDS: CONTRA RELIABILITY

Civil Court Records

1. All custodians of official records are not as conscientious as officially represented.

2. "Proper Custody" is ignored by some custodians of official records; and often, the older records are neither properly cared for, nor available.

3. As for the sanctity of sworn statements and oaths, this depends on the honesty and integrity of the individual. It is difficult, if not impossible (especially at this late date), to ascertain the truth.

4. Public officials are bonded, but the purpose of that is not reliability of the public or official records — bonds are for the purpose of discouraging embezzlement. An oath to perform the duty of the office again depends on the integrity of individuals.

5. The public officer, such as a county clerk, accepts for filing in the court records, any documents which comply with court rules; but this does not prevent plaintiffs or defendants from fraud, misrepresentation of facts, and outright lies.

6. All of the persons involved in the court proceedings which are of the most value to genealogists are now deceased, and the existing records are what are known as hearsay evidence as parties to the proceedings, witnesses, attorneys, judges, and clerks are deceased and there are no living persons possessing personal knowledge of the facts disclosed in the court records.

Probate Records

1. Although probate records are official records, they are subject to loss by theft, erasure, forgery, and substitution of pages in some instances.

2. Testators do forget children and sometimes on purpose — especially those born out of wedlock, or outside the marriage relation. These "skeletons in the closet" are not disclosed.

3. Genealogists must be on guard to interpret wills correctly; but in spite of all of the diligence and due care of these professionals, it is impossible to cope with vague relationships, such as "cousin," "relative," "My Brother Smith," "natural child" (may not mean illegitimate).

4. Genealogists must cope with erasures, strikeovers (this may require special photography or the use of ultra violet ray equipment to read what was originally written), interlineations of a suspicious nature, lack of initialling of changes, misspelled words, inserted or substituted pages, forgery, undue influence, duress, senility — lack of capacity to form testamentary intent, and of course, conniving immediate relatives or nonrelatives.

5. Modern interpretation has been mentioned, but the terminology of centuries past often does not mean the same today: For example, "father in law" may mean "step father," "My now wife," does not necessarily indicate a prior marriage.

6. If the will is "signed" by the cross or mark of the testator, how is it possible to be sure he knew what was in the will? In this situation, research in other sources is mandatory.

7. What if the will is not admitted to probate? This will require additional research. This is true especially if letters of administration with the will annexed are not granted. The facts in the will may be true, but additional research in other sources will be required.

8. Do not overlook the possibility of posthumous children, and the possibility that such child or children are not the issue of the testator.

9. "Adopted children" are always a problem as the testator may refer to the child as "my son John" or "my daughter Kate" and not mention "adopted."

10. Nuncupative wills are risky. It will be necessary to ascertain the length of time between the oral will and the actual reduction to writing and how many witnesses there were, and the date testator died.

11. Due care must be exercised to be certain there was not a will contest; these proceedings are not necessarily tried in the probate courts.

12. Always examine the original will if possible. It is much easier for a clerk to refer a genealogist to the "Will Book." However, the "will" in a record volume is a copy of the original, and therefore, subject to human error.

13. As explained in the discussion of civil court records, probate records are also "hearsay evidence." The testator of the will and the witnesses who attested his signature (or mark) on the will are now deceased and there is nobody alive who possesses personal knowledge regarding the execution (or signature) of the will.

14. Do not rely on printed or published wills or probate records; many of these have been published and are therefore subject to the interpretation, deciphering of the compiler and then there are bound to be mistakes in printing. Therefore, if the original records are still in existence, be safe and examine them.

Notes and References

1. Prager, Herta and Price, William W., A Bibliography of the History of the Courts of the Thirteen Original States, Maine, Ohio and Vermont, *The American Journal of Legal History*, Vol. 1, p. 336, Vol. 2, pp. 35, 148, 1957-58.

   Jeffrey, William Jr., Early New England Court Records/A Bibliography of Published Materials, *The Boston Public Library Quarterly*, Vol. 6, No. 3, July 1954, pp. 160-184.

2. Stevenson, Noel C., Genealogical Research in the Law Library, *The American Genealogist*, Vol. 18, October 1941, p. 100.

   Genealogy and the Law: Court Reports, Vol. 1, p. 428, *Genealogical Research Methods and Sources*, Milton Rubincam, editor, Jean Stephenson, associate editor, Washington, 1960.

3. Stevenson, Noel C., Research in the Privy Council Records, *National Genealogical Society Quarterly*, Vol. 46, September 1958, p. 113.

4. Stevenson, Noel C., Marital Rights in the Colonial Period, *The New England Historical and Genealogical Register*, Vol. CIX, April 1955, p.84.

5. 1 *Greenleaf on Evidence*, 12th edition, Section 367.

6. Condee, Newcomb, *Probate Court Practice*, 2nd edition, Vol. 1, Section 248, West Publishing Co., 1964, p. 157.

7. Statutes and court decisions of the state referred to.

8. Colket, Meredith B. Jr., and Bridgers, Frank E., *Guide to Genealogical Records in the National Archives*, Washington 1964, p. 142.

CHAPTER 13

LAND RECORDS

"Evidence of a statement relevant to a material matter, contained in a deed of conveyance or a will or other document purporting to affect an interest in realty or personalty, offered as tending to prove the truth of the matter stated is admissible . . . "

American Law Institute,
Model Code of Evidence, Rule 527

Included within the category of official records are documents affecting the title to land. The title of the office or officer who is the custodian of land records varies from state to state and country. In the United States, the names of the officials are Register of Deeds, County Recorder, Town Clerk, etc. In the Canadian provinces, the office is the Land Registry.

In England no system for the recordation or registration of land records was adopted until after the middle of the 19th century, and the existing system is not in effect in all of England. Furthermore, the records of land registration offices which have been established are not automatically available to the public.

For centuries, English families owning interests or estates in land simply deposited their documents of title with their solicitor or stored them in record chests or some other receptacle in the family home.

Scotland commenced the land registration system in the early 17th century.

In countries where the Roman Civil Law is the basis of their legal system, the custom is for a notary public to be the custodian of documents affecting land as well as other personal records. This official is not the same as a notary public according to the North American definition.

THE NATURE OF LAND RECORDS

Land records consisting of recorded copies of documents such as deeds, mortgages, leases, powers of attorney, notices of the filing of civil actions, decrees and judgments of court proceedings, occasional last wills and testaments, affidavits, and other miscellaneous agreements and documents are classified as official records because the Registrar of Deeds, County Recorder, or Clerk, Town Clerk, or other officer is imposed with a duty to accept custody, record the documents and retain possession, and protect the integrity of these records.

PERSONAL PROPERTY RECORDS

Documents pertaining to personal property are often recorded in the same office as land records. Chattel Mortgages and anything else which affects title to or possession of personal property which is required by law to be recorded, and some documents which do not require recordation may be found in a land record office (refer also to "Miscellaneous Records" in this chapter).

The recording system as it exists in the United States originated in Plymouth Colony in the 1620's. As the system evolved throughout the United States, original documents, such as deeds, were presented to the town clerk, county recorder, or registrar of deeds; and the original was copied verbatim into a record volume (e.g., Book 1, page 1 of Deeds). In some offices, the word "Liber" is used instead of "Book" or "Volume." After copying and comparing the original document as copied in the record volume, the original is returned to the person entitled to its possession, such as a grantee, lienee, or mortgagee.

In land record offices in the United States and prior to formation of the Union, documents were recorded according to category or title. Thus, a deed was copied into a deed book, a mortgage in a book of mortgages, leases in a lease volume, powers of attorney in a book by that name, and so on. In later years, there has been a tendency to copy any document presented for filing in the same series of volumes and these books are usually termed "Official Records"; and the volumes are numbered consecutively. In the past ten or fifteen years, a majority of record offices have changed from typewriting and photostat to microfilming of original records presented for recordation. This change has also caused the introduction of the microfiche system of record keeping for the purpose of space saving.

The key which supposedly unlocks the information included in record offices which hold the custody of records relating to real (land) and personal property is a collection of index volumes (unless the record system is of the character which provides that all documents be recorded or copied in the same series of volumes). Therefore, when searching these records there will be the following types of indexes or indices: Grantors and Grantees (sometimes on opposite pages of a volume or sometimes the Grantors index will be in one volume and the Grantees index will be in a different volume). Especially in the early records before massive recording of documents occurred, the indices will be in the front of each volume, according to the alphabet. All surnames beginning with "A" will be in one group, "B" in the next series of pages, and so on. It is unusual to find the indexes arranged in a strictly alphabetical sequence, however, there are some index volumes in larger cities which have been printed in strictly alphabetical sequence.

Don't expect to find uniformity in index systems, such as spelling of names, and don't assume the index is accurate. If a person is known by more than one name, all names should be searched. Hyphenated names, e.g., Smith-Douglas, search both names. Names such as de La Valle, search in the L's, V's, and D's.

A record office using this system will also have indices to "Mortgagors and Mortagees," "Lessors and Lessees," "Lienors and Lienees," or an index to "Mechanics' Liens." In this manner all types of records are provided with an index.

Unfortunately, these indexes or indices are not the "master index" genealogists dream they should be. Only the parties or persons directly interested in the property are included in the index. Hence, a person named in a recital in the body of the deed who is related to one of the parties will not be included in any index. To overcome this defect adequately, it would be necessary to read every page in the record office if time and money permitted this luxury.

One example recorded in the Worcester (Massachusetts) District Registry of Deeds is a record of a warranty deed signed by Tabitha Byham and Miriam Byham of Petersham, as grantors to Elijah Wilson, also of Petersham, as grantee, recorded in Book 94, Page 230 of Deeds. Because Tabitha and Miriam Byham and Elijah Wilson are the only parties to the deed, only those three names will be indexed. But in the body of the deed is a recital stating that the land deeded to Wilson was ". . . the original property of our father Abraham Byham, Deceased." There is no reason to index his name, as he was not a party to the deed.

There is a remedy available to avoid searching every page of every volume in the Registry of Deeds in a case of this type. Assuming you are (as in this case searching for the ancestors of Tabitha and Miriam Byham), you simply examine every deed word for word of every Byham who was a grantor or grantee of a deed for the period of years applicable to your problem. If this does not solve the problem, then search all other records in the same manner.

EXAMPLES OF GENEALOGICAL EVIDENCE OR INFORMATION DISCLOSED IN LAND RECORDS

The most common information disclosed is the fact of the residence of the grantor and the former residence of the grantee:

WARRANTY DEED

"This Indenture made the 20th Day of Decr in the 15th year of the Reign of Our Sovereign Lord George the third by the Grace of God . . . Anno Domini 1774. Between Jacob Bayley of Newbury in the County of Gloucester and Province of New York Esq., of the first part and Simeon Walker of Woodbury in the County of Litchfield and Colony of Connecticut of the second part. . . ." (Book 1, Pages 323-6, Proprietors Records, Town of Peacham, Vermont)

LAND RECORDS AS A SUPPLEMENT TO VITAL RECORDS

EVIDENCE OF MARRIAGE
RELATIONSHIP DISCLOSED IN DEED

This Indenture made this ninth day of September in the year of our Lord ... 1826 by and between John Walker of Peacham in Caledonia County and State of Vermont, and Charles Walker of Cabot in the County and State aforesaid ... to Simeon Walker and his wife Mary Walker (land in Cabot, Vermont) Volume 5, Page 207, Cabot Town Records)

EVIDENCE OF ERRORS IN
VITAL RECORDS DISCLOSED IN DEEDS

In an article entitled "Deeds Disprove Two Samson Birth Dates" by Robert M. Sherman, F.A.S.G., the importance of searching land records to supplement and correct vital records is disclosed. This short article should be read in order to appreciate the substantial evidence which may be discovered in land records. (*The American Genealogist*, Volume 49, January 1973, pp. 37-38)

IMPORTANCE OF "RECITALS" IN DEEDS AND OTHER DOCUMENTS

A *recital* is a statement in deeds and other documentation which is usually included because it is sometimes necessary to explain the reason for the transaction or transfer of title.

It is in recitals in various documents involving title to or rights in land that valuable genealogical information and other facts which are often clues leading to genealogical data are disclosed.

A nongenealogical recital may be that which discloses from whom the grantor acquired his title to the land he is deeding to a grantee. Assume a deed from John Doe to Richard Roe contains in the body of the deed the recital "... being the same land I [John Doe] acquired from John Smith. ... " There is no relationship stated, but it would be advisable to search the grantees index and study the deed from John Smith to John Doe to ascertain if any recitals are included in that prior deed. There is a possibility that John Smith was related to John Doe.

The following genealogical recitals in deeds will demonstrate this type of evidence:

RECITAL IN DEED DISCLOSING MAIDEN NAME
AND PATERNITY OF WIFE

To all people to whom these presents shall come Greeting – Know ye that we Timothy Walker and Sarah Walker ... of Woodbury in ye County of Fairfield & Colony of Connecticut in New England for and in consideration of nine pounds ten shillings in hand received ... Grant, Bargain and Sell unto Lemuel Sanford of Fairfield ... his heirs and assigns forever ... [legal description] ... which Right is that which ariseth on that accommodation Granted to our Honed Father John

Judson . . . (Woodbury Land Records, Volume 5, pp. 11-12). [Sarah Walker's maiden name was Judson.]

RECITAL IN DEED DISCLOSING ANCESTOR AND SIBLING RELATIONSHIP

In deeds executed in 1779 and 1780, Hannah Winthrop and Anne Mason stated they were the daughters of Hannah Fairweather, and conveyed their shares, being one third each, and in which Samuel Fairweather conveyed one-third, "derived by him by right of inheritance," but not stating from whom. (*Little v. Palister* (1826) 4 Maine Reports 181)

No doubt Samuel Fairweather is related to Hannah Winthrop, Anne Mason, and Hannah Fairweather, but it is not the type of circumstantial evidence which is acceptable. Research in other records would be necessary in order to ascertain what relationship, if any, existed.

GENEALOGICAL FACTS DISCLOSED IN AGREEMENT OR CONTRACT WHICH WAS THE SUBJECT OF LITIGATION

"Article of agreement made & concluded on this 20th Day of July Anno Domini 1773 Between Michael Low [sic] of Manchester Township, York County & State of Pennsylvania Freeholder of the one part and Casper Kerber of Paradise Township in the County & Province aforesaid of the other part . . ." (Recorded 19 September 1803, in the Office for Recording Deeds, in and for the County of York, in Book Q.Q., page 520 &c) *Lau v. Mumma (Supreme Court of Pennsylvania)* (1862) 43 Pennsylvania State Reports, 267, 269.

Because litigation resulted from this agreement, considerable genealogical data prior to 1773 was disclosed in the court proceeding regarding the Lau or Low family which is too lengthy to include herein.

GENEALOGICAL INFORMATION FROM "MISCELLANEOUS RECORDS"

The problem in this case history was to ascertain the parentage and ancestry of Benjamin Gholson Naught, born December 1844, in Schuyler County, Illinois, according to family records, but names of parents unknown. The client had written to the appropriate county official and was notified that the county did not begin registering births at that early date.

The genealogist retained to solve this problem went to the courthouse in Rushville, the county seat, for the purpose of searching all available records. Among the records searched was a volume entitled "Index to Government Lands." In this volume, it was discovered that in 1830 Benjamin Gholson and Isaac Naught purchased government land adjoining each other.

The solution was quite obvious. The genealogist walked across the hall to the County Clerk's Office and located the marriage record of John Naught and Elizabeth Gholson on 21 July 1834 which was circumstantial evidence that Benjamin Gholson Naught was their son.

PERFORMANCE BOND DISCLOSING CIRCUMSTANTIAL EVIDENCE OF PATERNITY

See copy of original bond on following page.

AFFIDAVITS FILED IN THE LAND RECORDS – MISCELLANEOUS RECORDS AND COUNTY MAP RECORDS

It is a mistake to fail to examine the most unlikely documents in the land records. The Gholson and Naught families previously mentioned moved to Oregon during the time the federal government was encouraging settlers to go there. They arrived in Oregon in the early 1850's and both families proved their claims to Donation Lands as provided by federal statute. In 1926, it was necessary to clear the title to some of the land acquired by Benjamin Gholson, long since deceased. An affidavit which was signed by one of the descendants of Benjamin Gholson and verified before a notary public was filed in the official records of Polk County, Oregon, on October 20, 1926. This affidavit exceeding two pages constitutes a brief history of the Gholsons in Oregon. (Affidavit of Thaddius Stipp, filed Oct. 20, 1926, No. 10091 by County Clerk, Polk County, Oregon)

UNRECORDED DOCUMENTS

Many land record offices have in their possession deeds and other documents mailed to them or otherwise left in their custody, and for which there was not payment or instruction for recording them. According to the July 1962 issue of *The American Genealogist*, Vol. 38, Page 191, the Salem County Historical Society, 79 Market Street, Salem, New Jersey, has a collection of 1108 original deeds, all unrecorded and dated between 1600 and 1800.

Regardless of whether or not unrecorded deeds are in the possession of an official or unofficial source, a genealogist must decide whether to accept or reject the facts in these documents.

This failure to record does not destroy the genealogical value of the documents, if they appear to be validly signed. If the document is acknowledged or verified before a notary public, validity is presumed. However, acknowledgement before a notary public in most jurisdictions causes the document to be acceptable for recordation in whatever record office it should have been presented.

If the document is signed and especially if the signer(s) have affixed their seal – even if it is not a literal seal – the chances are the document is valid. If it is not signed or sealed, it is advisable to proceed with caution. Also, it is possible the same information can be discovered in other sources – perhaps the document is a duplicate and the duplicate original was properly recorded. Therefore, the records should be searched to be certain.

LEGAL DESCRIPTION OF LAND

In every deed or conveyance or other document affecting land, a legal description should be found, which, if adequate, will enable one to find the physical location of the land.

Know all men by these Presents that we John and Charles Walker of Caledonia County and State of Vermont are holden and stand firmly bound unto Simeon Walker and his wife Mary Walker in the Town County and State aforesaid in the sum of four hundred Dollars — for the payment of which sum we bind our selves and each of us our heirs and assigns firmly by these presents — Sealed with our Seals and Signed with our hands, Dated the 9th day of September A.D. 1826 —

The condition of this obligation is Such that if the above Named John and Charles Walker or their heirs or assigns Shall at all times from the above Said well and faithfully provide for the above named Simeon Walker and his wife Mary Walker all necessary meat and drink — Clothing — Medicine and Physician if required and all and every other thing necessary in Life — in Sickness — and in health — with convenient house Room during the term of their natural lives — then this obligation to be null and void otherwise to be and remain in full force and virtue on Provided Nevertheless and it is the true intent of the parties that the above Bounden John and Charles Walker Shall have the full improvement of a certain farm on Lot No 14. the Town of Cabot of which this the Said John and Charles Walker has this day given the Said Simeon and his wife above a Life Lease of even date with this instrument — during the natural life of him and his wife So long as they the Said John and Charles Shall Support them agreeable to what is mentioned in this Bond above — the Said John and Charles to be at all the expense of the repairs on Sd farm and pay all taxes which is or may be assessed on Said farm — and pay all debts owing or due from Said Simeon Walker — to any person or persons — In witness whereof we have hereunto Set our hands and Seals this 9th day of September 1826 — in Presence of

Thos. Osgood
Ruth Osgood

John Walker (Seal)
Charles Walker (Seal)

I hereby certify that this above is a true record of the original Bond and for record Sept 9th 1826 recorded by me. Thos. Osgood Town Clerk

Cabot (Vermot Town Records) Deeds Vol. 5, p. 208.

In the Eastern states and colonies, the legal descriptions are usually metes and bounds; i.e., "Commencing at the Northeast corner of the land of Smith, thence North 89 Degrees, 7' (seven minutes) 10" (ten seconds) East [almost due East] 150 feet, to the Westerly boundary line of the land of Jones. . . . " Metes and bounds descriptions are not difficult if one is familiar with the use of a protractor and an engineer's scale, but locating the land is another problem which usually demands the services of a surveyor.

If the deed transfers title to a town lot, it may be possible to consult a map of the town, and then physically locate the property with comparative ease.

In the midwestern states and the West, the rectangular system is most generally used, which simplifies the description: E-1/2 of the SE-1/4 of the NW-1/4 of Section 9, Township 1 North, Range 5 East, Muskingum River Base Line. All of the states adopted the rectangular survey system except those on the Atlantic Seaboard, Vermont, West Virginia, Kentucky, Tennessee, parts of Ohio, and some western states.

The legal description of the land should be studied carefully because of the persons named therein, and if the land described can be located physically, it might be possible to locate old graveyards where the families involved may be buried. The real bonus is when it is possible to locate the land owned by an ancestor.

Regrettably, detailed instructions regarding legal descriptions are beyond the scope of this book.

CHECK LIST OF ADDITIONAL LAND RECORD DOCUMENTS

It is not possible to include details regarding all of the documents filed for record in Recorder's or Registrar's offices. The following is a partial listing of some documents which have not been discussed in this chapter. (For any terms not defined, consult index for Words and Phrases.)

Certificates of Residence
Declarations of Marriage
> (not in the marriage records and probably a common law marriage, which were legal in most states in the early history of the U.S. Refer to "common law marriage" in the index.)

Declarations of Relationship – in affidavit form
Map records – Name of owners often included on map. Provides means of locating land an ancestor owned.
Bills of Sale of personal property
Assignments of various types by which interests in real and personal property are transferred
Indentures – this is a misleading term. It may be an agreement, a contract, a deed, or apply to the apprenticeship of a servant.
Bargain and Sale Deed
Grant Deed
Gift Deed
Deed Poll
Quitclaim Deed
Mortgage in the form of a deed
Headright Certificates

Deed of Trust
Declaration of Trust
Uses
Partition Agreements or Proceedings
Liens
Judgments and Decrees – If you find a record in Recorder's or Register of
       Deeds, this is a clue to search court records.
Attachments
Powers of Attorney
Promissory Notes
Releases of various types, e.g., release of mortgage
Release of Dower Rights
Satisfaction of Mortgage or other obligations
Satisfaction of judgments
Marriage Contracts – Ante-nuptial agreements
Post-nuptial agreements – indication there is a divorce
Partnership agreements
Sole trader documents – wife to conduct a business
Articles of apprenticeship
Acknowledgement of Paternity
Notices of Action (*Lis Pendens*) – This is a notice that a lawsuit has been
       filed in a court proceeding and is a clue which should indicate a search
       of the court records is in order until a record of the lawsuit is found
       and the court file is examined.

"Miscellaneous Records" have been heretofore mentioned. These volumes
always have been a "catch all" in which documents are recorded which did not
(or do not) fit in any other category such as "Deeds" or "Mortgages." As a result,
some strange and interesting documents have been recorded in these volumes; it
is impossible to classify many of them, and only a few have been mentioned in the
foregoing list.

Reliability Factor of Land Records:

1.   The officer in custody of these records, in addition to his duty to protect
and preserve them, is paid to do so. Hopefully, this feature encourages the
officer to perform his duty with greater care than if he received no
compensation.

2.   Generally, the handwriting is more legible than private writings.

3.   The officer is required to copy originals accurately and except in rare
instances does so.

4.   The recording officer (except in very rare instances) has not been a party
to any fraudulent practices or forgeries in the recording process or
subsequent custody of records.

5.   Recitals in recorded documents stating family relationships are likely to
be accurate as generally there is no motive to deceive unless a controversy
has previously arisen in the family regarding the genealogical facts stated.

6. Although the primary purpose of recording documents in the land records is not for the purpose of compiling genealogy and recitals of relationship in deeds and other instruments are not necessary to the legal validity of the documents, nevertheless, persons who are parties involved are inclined to state correct relationships unless there is a motive to deceive; and that is an exception.

7. A document which is acknowledged or verified before a notary public or other officer is at least some proof of the identity of the persons executing the document, assuming of course, that the notary public does demand some identification of the person or persons involved. Some notaries public are extremely lax regarding this duty. In small towns where everyone was acquainted with each other, identity of the parties to a document wasn't a difficult problem for the notary public.

8. As it is impossible to foresee all of the problems affecting reliability of records, it is advisable in every instance to examine the records for defects or features which may affect the accuracy of every document you examine. Also, other records should be searched in order to verify or disprove the facts you have found in other record sources.

9. Historically, unless the parties affixed their seal opposite their signatures (originally there was only their seal), it was not considered valid. Wax seals were replaced with paper wafers and then the signers simply drew the outline of a seal and wrote "seal" inside the circle or outline. Be careful of seals.

10. Notaries Public and other officers were supposed to seal documents also, and doing so adds to the validity of the document.

11. The care, completeness, and appearance of documents should be be considered. Documents which include recitals explaining the reasons for transactions are not absolutely required in all instances, but the fact that genealogical or other facts are included is an indication the person who prepared the document was careful, competent, and interested in accuracy.

Contra Reliability Factors:

1. Although there is a strong presumption that genealogical information stated in land records is accurate, this is a rebuttable presumption, therefore, as in all other instances it is advisable to search other record sources for confirmation of the information.

2. The recording official has no personal knowledge of the truth or falsity of the documents he is accepting for recordation.

3. The recording official or any of the parties to the document are not available for cross examination.

4. The records are hearsay information because no person is available who possesses personal knowledge of the facts.

5. The records are copies of originals (except in rare instances there are original deeds and other documents in the possession of the recording officer, but these are, of course, hearsay also), and it is necessary to depend on the accuracy of the scrivener; and hopefully, he did not commit any mistakes in the copying process.

6. There is the possibility that the handwriting is not clear and you misread the writing.
7. The recording official is not concerned with the accuracy of the facts in documents. If documents are in proper form, and the law requires recordation, the official will accept any document presented to him for recording.
8. If a document contains genealogical facts which are stated after a controversy arose regarding those facts, the information should be scrutinized carefully.
9. Printed (publication in any form) land records are not official records as they are copies of copies. (For example, *Suffolk Deeds*, Boston 1880, are not original official records.)
10. Certified copies of land records are supposed to be copied correctly, and if microfilmed copies are authenticated as photographic copies of the official records *represented*, they are only as reliable as the originals.
11. Spelling of names has always been a problem, especially due to the lack of uniformity in previous centuries. The recorder's office cannot correct these mistakes. The searcher must consider all types of spelling and handwriting.
12. The recording officer or assistants prepare the indices and there is a woeful lack of uniformity in regard to this problem. Some indexers will index the name Devore in the "D" section. If the name is spelled with de Vore, the recorder will place it in the "V" part of the index. If spelled De Vore? Who knows? Another problem is hyphenated names such as John Wilson-Jones. The answer: search in the "W's" and the "J's."

FEDERAL LAND RECORDS

Prior to this, the subject matter has related to local land records or those in states, counties, boroughs, cities, and towns. There is a tremendous body of land records involving donation lands, lands acquired through grants (federal patents), military grants, and in accordance with the Homestead Act, etc. For information in regard to these records, land office records in the National Archives and the Federal Records Centers throughout the United States should be consulted.

Ultimately, some of these federal land records are recorded in local land records; for example, the settler who complies with the conditions of the Federal Homestead Land Act is issued a patent from the United States whereby he acquired title to the land he settled on. The settler should have filed the patent for record with the local county recorder or registry of deeds.

CHAPTER 14

CENSUS RECORDS

". . . [C]ertified census records . . . shall be competent evidence of all matters therein contained. "

Iowa Code, Section 26.5 (1971)

Census [Latin: Censere, to reckon]. An official reckoning or enumeration of the inhabitants and wealth of a county.[1]

John Bouvier

On December 23, 1801, President Jefferson in a special message to Congress transmitted another return of the census of the State of Maryland just received from the marshal of the state "which he desires may be substituted as more correct than the one first returned by him. . . ."[2]

On December 6, 1869, President Grant in his first annual message to Congress suggested the necessity of early Congressional action in order to make the 1870 census more complete and perfect than heretofore.[3]

President Jefferson's and President Grant's statements regarding census records express opinions (shared by other contemporaries) that census data should be improved and perfected — opinions which are understatements of the necessity.

In order to judge the reliability of census records, it is advisable to study the origin and history of the subject beginning with the first federal census of 1790.

CENSUS OF 1790

The marshals of the several judicial districts of the U.S. were required to compile the census . . . the marshals were empowered to appoint as many assistants within their districts as they deemed necessary, and to assign to each assistant a specific geographical area in which to record the census information, all of whom including the marshals, were required to take an oath or affirmation to perform their duty.[4]

The law also provided that every person over 16 years of age, whether the head of a family or not, to render a true account to the best of his knowledge of every person belonging to the family in which he usually resided, if requested, under penalty of forfeiting $20.[5]

Each assistant before making his return to the marshal, was further required to "cause a correct copy, signed by himself, of the schedule containing the number of inhabitants within his division to be posted at two of the most public places within his district, there to remain for the inspection of all concerned."[6]

The marshals were required to file the assistants' returns with the clerks of their respective district courts, who were, in turn, directed to receive and carefully preserve the records. Also, the judges of the district courts were required to cause the census returns of the assistants or compilers to be laid before the grand juries.[7]

There was no uniformity in the format of the census returns or records of the assistants compiling the records in the various states. All sorts and sizes and shapes of books and sheets were used. The columns and headings were ruled in ink. In some instances a printed slip stating the column headings was used following the form of the inquiries prescribed by law. It was not until the fifth census in 1830 that printed schedules of uniform size were used.[8]

The only persons mentioned by name were heads of families, which of course were men, except in the case of a widow.

The 1790 census was supposed by many to be inaccurate because of the popular notion that the people were counted for the purpose of being taxed; and, because of this, many understated to the assistant marshals the actual number of persons in their families.[9]

The method or system of census registration remained substantially the same until the census of 1850.[10]

THE SEVENTH CENSUS – 1850

Printed forms were provided for this census; and each person who was commissioned to record the information was, as usual, under oath and was to "perform the service required of him by a personal visit to each dwelling house, and to each family in the subdivision assigned to him," and to ascertain by *inquiries made of some member of each family,* if anyone can be found capable of giving the information, but if not, then the agent of such family, the name, age, place of birth, and all other particulars required concerning each member thereof. In this census, for the first time, all members of the household were listed by name, age, whether male or female, place of birth, in addition to the head of the household. The relationship to the head was not required to be stated.[11]

The census scriveners were required to file the original copy of the census returns with the clerks of their respective county courts and to forward *two copies, duly compared and corrected,* to the marshals.[12] The census takers were paid two cents for each person listed, and travel expenses were provided.[13]

Anyone charged with dereliction of duties involving the census was subject to penalties which supposedly discouraged carelessness, negligence, or failure to perform the responsibility undertaken.[14]

Beginning with the 1850 census, Mortality Schedules were compiled which included information regarding all persons who died within twelve months prior to the enumeration of the census. These schedules included full names, state of birth, date of death, age at death, and cause of death.

THE TENTH CENSUS – 1880

No substantial change was undertaken in the census until 1880. The districts were reduced in size so that they did not exceed 4000 inhabitants.[15]

The census enumerators were required to reside in their respective districts, unless no qualified or willing person could be located there.[16]

> Each enumerator was required by law "to visit personally each dwelling house in his subdivision and each family therein, and each individual living out of a family in any place of abode, and by inquiry made of the head of such family, or the member thereof deemed most credible and worthy of trust, or of such individual living out of a family, to obtain each and every item of information and all the particulars." In case no person should be found at the usual place of abode of such family or individual living out of a family competent to answer the inquiries made in compliance with the requirements of the census act, the enumerator was directed by the law "to obtain the required information, as nearly as may be practicable, from the family or families, or person or persons, living nearest to such place of abode."

> Instead of the two copies of the schedules required under the law of 1850, the enumerator was directed to forward the original schedules, duly certified, to the supervisor of his district, but before doing this, he was required, under the terms of section 6 of the Act of April 20, 1880, to make and file in the office of the clerk of the county court, or in the office of the court or board administering the affairs of the county to which his district belongs, a list of the names, with age, sex, and color, of all persons enumerated by him, which he shall certify to be true and for which he shall be paid at the rate of 10 cents for each 100 names. He was also required to give notice by written advertisement at three or more public places in his district that he would be at the court-house of said county on the fifth day after filing said list, not including Sunday from 9 o'clock ante-meridian to 6 o'clock postmeridian, and the following day, for the purpose of correcting his enumeration by striking out or adding the designation of persons improperly enumerated or omitted; and he was required at the time specified to correct, on such reliable infor-mation as he may obtain, all omissions and mistakes in such enu-meration, swearing and examining witnesses for the purpose, if necessary, and then make known to the bystanders, if any, the result of such inquiry for correction and the whole number of persons enumerated by him. In order to enable him to perform this

additional duty, the time for making his return to the supervisor was extended fifteen days.[17]

This new provision at least provided a means for persons included in the census to verify if the facts stated concerning them were true. How effective this procedure was would be difficult to ascertain now.[18]

The most important change added to the 1880 census was the requirement that the relationship of the head of the family to other members of the household be shown, such as wife, son, daughter, or the lack of relationship such as servant, boarder, etc. Also required was the civil (or conjugal) condition, such as single, married, widowed, or divorced. The information regarding place of birth was limited to State or Territory or foreign country. The profession, trade, or occupation was also listed, along with the age and whether the individual was male or female.[19]

INTERPRETING EVIDENCE IN THE CENSUS RECORDS

The major problem in deciding whether to accept or reject information or evidence disclosed in the census records is a matter of identity [refer to index for the chapter on identification].

Assume the search is for the parentage of John B. Allen who according to family records was born in Tennessee in 1837. Assume also that a John B. Allen is listed in the 1850 census, age 10 years, born in Tennessee. The head of the household is William Allen, age 28, and the next name listed is Elizabeth Allen, age 27. No competent genealogist will accept this information for the following reasons:

1. Similarity or the same name is not sufficient to accept the fact of parentage, or any other fact.

2. No relationship is stated. It may be argued that there is some circumstantial evidence of parentage, but it is not sufficient to accept.

3. The census record indicates he was born in 1840 or 1839 at the earliest, and there are two to three years difference in his age. (This age difference is not fatal, as a parent may say to the census taker "John B. is about ten," as he is not required to state a birthdate.

The competent genealogist will search other records. However, in this case, the genealogist knew that John B. Allen had two brothers by the names of James and George. The circumstantial evidence is much stronger now, but there is no direct evidence that John B., James, and George are the children of William and Elizabeth Allen. It is possible they are nephews or other relatives. The search was continued in other records and direct evidence was discovered that John B., James, and George (and other children) were the issue of William and Elizabeth Allen.

JUDGING CENSUS RECORDS FOR RELIABILITY

PRO RELIABILITY

1. There is a strong presumption that a census enumerator will perform his duty faithfully and accurately. A person in this category is supposedly acting under oath; and there are penalties which may be imposed if the

duties are not performed according to law, or if the enumerator engaged in some type of fraudulent activity.[20]

2. The census enumerators were placed under oath and subject to penalties if they failed to do their duty.

3. The census scriveners or assistants worked for supervisors, who in turn were subject to orders from federal officers.

4. Although prior to 1880 the U.S. Census did not state the relationship of members of a household to the head thereof, there is often strong circumstantial evidence to imply family relationships, subject to verification in other records.

5. The census enumerators were required to visit family homes and obtain information of a genealogical nature from someone in the home who was responsible and possessed the family knowledge.

6. The census returns were subject to inspection by officials such as county clerks, judges of U.S. District Courts, grand juries, and others. Knowing this, it should cause the enumerators compiling the censuses to try to be accurate in compiling the records.

7. When printed forms were introduced, there was less chance for an enumerator to fail to record information.

8. The penalties for failure to perform the duties prescribed for the census takers, or for fraudulent practices, tended to discourage dereliction of duty.

9. Census enumerators often lived in areas where they were acquainted with most, and in some towns, all of the residents. This would aid in compiling an accurate record. Beginning with the 1880 census, the districts assigned to enumerators were reduced to 4000 people and to personally visit each dwelling house and each family and interview the member deemed most credible and worthy of trust. To obtain accurate information was another requirement. If necessary, this information was to be obtained from someone living out of the family, if the information could be considered more accurate.

10. Beginning with the 1880 census, the enumerator was required to live in the district he was to enumerate, unless there was no person qualified to perform the duty, then an outsider was assigned. It is doubtful that residents were not available, except in few instances.

11. In 1880, the census taker was required to provide an opportunity for residents to inspect entries concerning themselves and if not correct, the census taker corrected the census entries.

CONTRA RELIABILITY

1. Considering the compilation of the 1790 census as an example, there was some problem obtaining qualified enumerators due to the low rate of compensation, which would not encourage accuracy. In some areas the compensation was so inadequate it was barely sufficient to pay living expenses, and this probably did not attract the most qualified men. The statute provided payment of $1.00 for every 300 persons recorded in cities and towns, and slightly more in country districts.[21]

2. Although federal and state census records are official records, they are hearsay evidence. In spite of the fact that census records are therefore admissible in a court proceeding if the evidence is relevant, any presumption that the census is reliable is a rebuttable presumption, and may be minimized or destroyed by opposing evidence.

3. The purpose of compiling censuses was not for the compilation of genealogies.

4. Prior to 1880 the relationship of persons within a household to the head the family was not stated. Thus, prior to the 1880 census (the 1855 New York Census is an exception) it cannot be ascertained with certainty the relationship amongst those listed within the same household. Beginning in 1880, relationships were stated, but still one cannot be sure if the person giving the information to the enumerator has correctly provided the information concerning, for example, children who may be stepchildren, formally or informally adopted; and some facts concerning the household for one reason or the other may have been withheld.

5. A Louisiana appellate court decision is opposite to the Edwards case cited in Footnote 20.

   "Additionally the inaccuracy of the census records must be considered in an effort to justly evaluate a case of this nature." [In a previous decision] this court recognized that while census exhibits are to be considered as a part of the whole picture, they are not in themselves conclusive.[22]

6. One major problem is the location of *original* census records. The original was the forms the enumerator took with him to interview the residents of the district to which he was assigned. Later two identical copies of the originals were transcribed and certified as true copies. One of these copies, which is referred to as the *Federal Copy*, was sent to Washington. The other copy was then deposited with the Secretary of State in each State and Territory. This copy was referred to as the *State Copy*. What happened to the *original copies*? These were sent immediately to the County Clerk (or similar official) in every county of the United States. Unfortunately, most of these original census records have been lost or destroyed.[23]

Therefore, original census records are not being searched unless they are found in a county courthouse. Some census records have been removed from a county courthouse and deposited in state or local archives. These facts are based on an article written by Harry Hollingsworth, C.G., of Inglewood, California, who states additionally:

> "Care was taken to avoid errors . . . [but] copies of the originals [census] I have seen show many marks or erasure and correction. I have personally found many discrepancies between the Federal and State copies themselves, and vast differences between them and the originals! Whole names have either been changed or omitted. Ages have been copied wrong. Whereas, in the originals, the surnames in each family are generally written over and over again, in the copies the word "ditto" or its abbreviation "do" appear instead. When written over and over, a surname has much less chance of being written incorrectly! In one Federal entry, I find Rebecca Gey but "Grey" in the original. In another Federal

copy, Amanda Vandyke appears, but she is Amanda A. Vanslyke in the original. Esther Hollinsworth in the original — the correct name — appears as Esther Hollenbeck in the Federal Copy!"[24]

Elizabeth Pearson White, F.A.S.G., warns researchers that occasionally pages in the census are not in sequence, and it is necessary to note the page numbers with care. In an article on this subject, she states *inter alia* "Do not depend on page numbers at the top of the page. When these have been found to be out of sequence, some kind soul has crossed out the number to make it conform with the way the pages have been put together, which often does not agree with the numbers recorded for each house and family as the census taker went down the street."[25]

CHECK LIST FOR JUDGING RELIABILITY OF CENSUS RECORDS

1. Is the handwriting careful, neat, clear, and legible?
2. Are full names recorded or initials only?
3. Examining the entire returns of the enumerator, are there indications of careful compilation, competence, and attention to details required to be entered in the census forms?
4. Are dates, when necessary, stated and consistent?
5. Does the enumerator spell given names, surnames, and place names correctly?

    Comment: For example, it seems there should be, with few exceptions, one spelling for the surname "Reynolds," yet, *A Century of Population Growth*, page 259, discloses that the enumerators spelled this surname thirty-four different ways.
6. Do you limit your search of census records to printed and microfilm copies?

    Comment: There is no objection to searching microfilm copies if the microfilm is clear and a sharp reproduction of the original — most microfilm produced by government agencies are of exceptional quality. Printed or other type of publication may be faulty due to mistakes in transcription and printers' errors. You must judge when to examine the original record.
7. Are you able to detect any other specific deficiencies in your examination of the records you are searching?

    Comment: It is necessary for you to judge the accuracy of each record on its specific merits due to the individuality of the census enumerators — some were extremely careful and some were not.

CONCLUSION

The final and most conclusive test is a search of the original census records involved in your research, if it is possible to locate them in some local courthouse, archives, or library. A comparison with the federal copy or state copy may produce surprising disclosures. In addition, all other types of records available should be searched.

If all of the questions included in the preceding check list can be answered "Yes," then the census record is an above average example. Specific problems involving census records may suggest other questions, therefore, the check list should not be relied on entirely as unique situations are bound to be encountered.

Furthermore, census records should not be accepted as final "proof," unless the evidence is so convincing and substantial that one is justified in accepting it. In all cases, additional records should be searched, such as probate and other court records (civil and criminal), land records, vital records, and any other records available in order to consider all possible facts before a final decision.

STATE CENSUS RECORDS

Many states have compiled census records in between the federal decennial censuses; one outstanding example is the State of New York which began as early as 1825. In 1855, their census stated the relationship of the members of the household to the head of the family, if the person was born in New York State, then the county of birth was included, and additional facts similar to those included in the 1850 U.S. Census were stated.

The same standards for judging reliability for state records may be applied as those for the federal census.

Notes and References

1. *Bouvier's Law Dictionary* (Rawle edition) Boston 1897.
2. *Messages and Papers of the Presidents,* Vol. 1, Washington 1896, p. 333.
3. Ibid, Vol. 7, Washington 1898, p. 42.
4. United States Congress, *The History and Growth of The United States Census,* Senate Document 194, 1st Session, 56th Congress, Washington 1900, pp. 13-14.
5. Ibid, p. 14.
6. Ibid.
7. Ibid, p. 14-15.
8. Ibid, p. 15.
9. Ibid, p. 16.
10. Ibid.
11. Ibid, p. 42.
12. Ibid.
13. Ibid, p. 43.
14. Ibid.
15. Ibid, p. 60.
16. Ibid, p. 61.
17. Ibid, pp. 61-62.
18. Ibid, p. 62.
19. Ibid.

20. *Edwards v. Edwards*, 239 South Carolina 85, 90.
21. United States, Bureau of the Census, *A Century of Population Growth . . . 1790-1900*, Washington 1909, pp. 44-46.
22. *State ex rel Schlumbrecht v. Louisiana State Board of Health*, 231 So. 2d 730.
23. Hollingsworth, Harry, C.G., "Little Known Facts About the U.S. Census," *The American Genealogist*, Vol. 53, January 1977, p. 11.
24. Ibid.
25. White, Elizabeth Pearson, C.G., F.A.S.G., "Beware the Vagaries of Census Takers!," *Illinois State Genealogical Society Quarterly*, Vol. 7, No. 3, Fall 1975, p. 122.

PART III

PRINCIPAL UNOFFICIAL RECORDS

CHAPTER 15

PRINCIPAL UNOFFICIAL OR PRIVATE RECORDS

Records of an act, condition, or event is admissible as hearsay evidence, if the record was a result of a regular course of business, at or near the time of the event, the custodian identifies the record and how it was prepared and if other relevant provisions of the hearsay rule are complied with.
Section 1271, California Evidence Code (adapted)

Unofficial records are those compiled by persons who are not appointed or elected to public office. Presumably the records of a public official are more accurate than those recorded or maintained by a nonofficial because the former are sworn to perform their official duties, paid to do so, and also must maintain the records in their custody. A nonofficial, however, is not elected, not under oath of office, and there is no official standard for his method of filing and recording documentary evidence or information. Just as in the case of officials, nonofficials may be extremely competent and concerned regarding record keeping; there is a greater possibility that a clerk of a church, secretary of a business corporation, or recorder of family records may be more careless than an official in performing his responsibilities. There is no absolute rule regarding the devotion to duty of public officials or private individuals performing their responsibilities as recorders or record keepers, therefore, each case must be judged independently.

There are numerous private records which are of value to genealogists, and because the principal problem involved in their use is obtaining permission, which if granted, the rules regarding their acceptability or rejection are governed by the rules of evidence. Discussion of most or all of these records will be included in the Rules of Evidence chapter, as the purpose of this book is not that of a guide to locating records; however, a general statement regarding the most important of these records is in order.

143

One of the problems related to some of these private records is their confidentiality. This especially involves records of physicians, lawyers, dentists, genealogists, and the clergy, all of whom must decide how much information they may disclose without the consent of their clients, patients, or parishioners, if living. If the person is deceased, each custodian of records must decide if he should assist you.

Undertakers or morticians are generally cooperative as much as possible because most of their information is in the official records anyhow. Private schools and colleges, fraternal organizations, and orphanages impose their own rules. This also applies to corporations, partnerships, and any other type of business.

Many researchers are of the opinion that the records of a notary public ought to be helpful. Usually the only records included were the names of the parties to documents, the nature of the document, and the date. In some instances, this is of assistance if the right notary public is located. When a notary public ceases to act or dies, his records are supposedly delivered to a public officer, such as a county clerk or country recorder, but this is not always done.

Title insurance corporations, abstract companies, or individual abstractors of the public records are capable of providing the history of a specific parcel (or parcels) of land; this history will include genealogical data and it may be valuable and it may not. These records, of course, are business records, and it is seldom possible to obtain the information without paying for more than you need. It could, however, be a real genealogical bonanza. A title firm who compiled an abstract of title to a tract of land, which when completed constituted four volumes and included family history of fifty families of that particular county. The fact that the source of the histories was from land, probate, civil court, and other official records searched by professionals resulted in a high standard of reliability.

Another reason custodians of private records (business and other types) are prohibited or unwilling to disclose the facts requested, is that the disclosure of information affecting living persons could constitute an invasion of the right of privacy. Therefore, the disclosure could cause the custodian of the information liable to a third party or parties for money damages if a lawsuit was instituted against them.

City and business directory companies are not subject to the same restrictions as other businesses, and there is no need to consult them if the directories are in a public library. This rule also applies to telephone directories.

Unofficial, non-official, or private records include all records which are not classified as official records. Therefore, these unofficial or private records will include all compiled genealogies, charts, family history or any type of family records, Bible records, biographies, letters, journals, diaries, etc., printed or in the form of manuscripts, typescripts, mimeographed, photocopies, or whatever subject matter of genealogical interest, regardless of format whether published and distributed to the public, libraries or other institutions, whether copyrighted or not, or unpublished and retained privately by the compiler or owner.

CHAPTER 16

PUBLISHED AND PRIVATE GENEALOGICAL AND FAMILY HISTORIES

Pedigree How Proved. Pedigree, including descent, relationship, birth, marriage, and death, may be proved either by the declarations of deceased persons related by blood or marriage, or by general repute in the family, or by genealogies, inscriptions, 'family trees,' and similar evidence.

Title 38-303
The Code of Georgia

Destiny appears to cherish and uphold a certain sacred principle, to wit — origins shall be obscure.[1]

Donald R. Richberg

Although publication of a family genealogy or history is for some reason generally considered a compilation in book form, printed and bound in a hard cover, it should not be limited to that format. A "publication" is not limited to a book, it may be a genealogy, history, or other subject in manuscript form, typescript, mimeographed, offset, photocopied, microfilmed, or a pedigree in tabular form, to offer several examples. The test is if the compilation is accessible to the public in libraries or purchase. Unpublished genealogy would be a compilation which is not accessible to the general public and possession is retained by the author or compiler and subject to inspection only with the permission of the compiler or custodian of the genealogy or family history. Insofar as reliability or authenticity of published or unpublished genealogies or those in private custody, e.g., manuscript form, are concerned, the same rules apply in judging and deciding whether to reject or accept the genealogical evidence in whole or partially.

The number of published genealogies and family histories is constantly increasing and nobody can be certain of the precise number. In 1919, the Library of Congress published the second edition of *American and English Genealogies in the Library of Congress* and listed at that time 6,965, mostly in book form. Actually there were more than that number as the Library of Congress acquires books, etc., which are sent in for copyright or are donated to the library. However, not all genealogies are copyrighted or donated to the library.

In 1972, a bibliography entitled *Genealogies in the Library of Congress*, in two volumes, was edited by Marion Kaminkow.[2] The number, according to this source, was 19,208. Some of those listed amount to only a few pages; and this figure is not represented as a correct figure, as English (and other foreign) genealogies were omitted. Only those genealogies in the collection of the Library of Congress were included, with new genealogies being added to the collection since 1972. Therefore, the precise number of published family genealogies is unknown. In regard to private genealogical records in the possession of individuals, the number would be staggering if known, but in these private records there is a tremendous amount of duplication. Many of these private records have been deposited with the Genealogical Society in Salt Lake City. Some private genealogical records are quite reliable, but some are compiled by rank amateurs. The information obtained from family sources, from parents, grandparents, and great-grandparents who pioneered in Utah in 1847 should be expected to be more accurate than usual, as these pioneers were encouraged to record family history and genealogy.

The number of unpublished genealogies is increased by collections of manuscripts and typescripts in the possession of any library maintaining a genealogy section or department.

The superior genealogical compilation is not limited to names, dates, and places, but includes in addition to such statistical data, family history, biography, interpretation and explanation of the facts presented whenever this is necessary. The inclusion of references to the source of the facts discovered during the research process is extremely important. However, references per se, do not guarantee credibility or reliability, because the source material must be correctly interpreted. The ability to correctly interpret source material from all types of records is the feature which discloses the difference between the rank amateur and the competent genealogist. Actually there are two types of competent genealogists: The competent professional genealogist who is retained by clients and is paid fees for research. The second type is the competent genealogist whose research is professional, but who does not accept retainers, is not interested in compiling genealogy for profit, and often publishes the results of research in book form or in genealogical periodicals. This type of genealogist is not an amateur.

There are many genealogists of both types active at this time. In order to avoid disclosing a preference, examples will be limited to the names of two deceased genealogists. The outstanding example of the competent professional genealogist is Donald Lines Jacobus. The second type is Walter Goodwin Davis. Examine the published genealogy of these two gentlemen and the reasons for their competence is apparent.

The quickest, easiest, and most efficient source for genealogical research is a family genealogy compiled by a competent genealogist. If your ancestry is included in one of these compilations you are fortunate, provided it is possible to verify the genealogical facts by referring to official records or other reliable sources. Even if references to book and page, or court case number are not disclosed, a competent genealogist will include sufficient facts, so that the verification process will be possible. It is safer to trust the unverified genealogical facts of a recognized competent genealogist than the references of a rank or unqualified researcher or genealogist. References in genealogies are often a snare and a delusion because the compiler did not interpret the source material correctly.

The most difficult problems in genealogical research are: *first*, locating the information you are seeking; *second*, interpreting the source material; *third*, verifying and interpreting the facts or source material; *fourth*, judging the reliability of the evidence or facts; *fifth*, deciding whether to accept or reject the evidence or information.

There are some compelling reasons for caution when the source of genealogical research is dependent on family genealogies or any printed or published sources of genealogy, and opinions of professional genealogists disclose some reasons why.

In 1928, Neal F. Mears, a professional genealogist, wrote that "There are nearly 10,000 family histories and compilations in print and probably not more than ten percent of them are worth the paper on which they are written. This is due solely to the fact that the worthless ones were compiled by persons who had no knowledge of the science of genealogy and particularly no comprehension of what constitutes proof. Anything they heard or saw from any source whatsoever, was good enough. Their work shows it. This condition is so generally recognized that the leading hereditary-patriotic societies will not accept an application-paper bearing statements from a genealogy as proof unless they can be readily [verified in authentic sources]."[3]

Mr. Mears' statement that ". . . probably not more than ten percent of them are worth the paper on which they are written," should be modified to this extent: Even in the worthless ninety percent there is bound to be some facts which are correct. The problem is the possibility of verification of the genealogical data in these books compiled by rank amateurs.

Donald Lines Jacobus offered some wise advice on this subject. "The genealogical student must be very cautious in his use of family histories, remembering the conditions under which most of them were produced. This caution applies chiefly to the earlier, let us say the first six, generations. Even the poorest genealogy contains data of value, for the compiler obtained information from family sources that is not available to us in any other way. In deciding how far back on a certain line it is advisable to trust a certain genealogy, particularly when the earlier sections do not look trustworthy, the date when the book was published must always be considered. If published fifty or sixty years ago, information was often obtained from aged descendants then living, and of course their memory went further back than would that of elderly descendants today."[4]

I. Case Histories – Unofficial Examples

Several case histories will demonstrate the lack of reliability and authenticity in published family genealogies.

SAGE FAMILY CASE HISTORY

The Genealogical Record of the Decendants [sic] of David Sage . . . Brought to Date . . . [by] Charles H. Sage, published in 1919, is a case in point. Following the title page is reproduced "The Sage Family Coat of Arms granted by William the Conqueror, A.D. 1066." Of course there is no authority for the coat of arms, therefore, ignore this mistake which is common to many family genealogies.

What is important to the researcher interested in this family is to solve the parentage of Solomon Sage, born in 1737. On page 20 of Mr. Sage's compilation is the record of the children of David Sage and Bathsheba Sage. Among them is Solomon and the date of birth is stated as 1737. (The names of his parents should not be surprising, as what would be more natural than David and Bathsheba to name one of their children Solomon, even though he would never attain the status of king.) But there was a disappointment as only the years of birth were stated for the eight children, no places of birth and only five spouses of the children. No date and place of marriage was disclosed for David and Bathsheba. Fortunately it was known that the Sage family was from Connecticut and the records at the Connecticut State Library provided additional information. The complete dates of birth of Solomon and four other children were disclosed by the Middletown records, three additional spouses of the children were also included in the Barbour Vital Records, and the fact of marriage of David Sage and Bathsheba Judd on 26 December 1728 in Middletown was disclosed.

The probate records of the Berlin Probate District were searched, and Case No. 2872 was the Estate of David Sage, his will dated 10 November 1791, probated 26 November 1798, includes the names of his eight children.

The researcher did not stop with the probate records as some additional records to search were land, civil court records, church records, as part of the Sage family project.

PHINEAS BURDICK CASE HISTORY

Problem: The parentage and ancestry of Phineas Burdick. *The Descendants of Robert Burdick of Rhode Island* was compiled by Nellie (Willard) Johnson and published in 1937. At page 48, it is stated:

> Phineas[4] Burdick of Westerly and Hopkinton, R.I., and DeRuyter, N.Y., son of (prob.) John[3] Burdick, Esq., . . . and Rebecca (Thompson) Burdick of Westerly and Hopkinton, R.I. . . . m. Hopkinton, R.I. Feb. 5, 1767 to Penelope Hall. . . ."

Solution — Verification: The pertinent issue in this case history is the statement that Phineas Burdick is "prob." meaning of course "probably" the son of John Burdick and Rebecca (Thompson) Burdick. Obviously, a thorough search of vital, land, probate, church, and other records should be undertaken. Before resorting to a search of official records, it was ascertained that the compiler, Mrs. Johnson, had deposited her research papers with the Westerly Public Library and an examination of these papers disclosed a handwritten genealogy (by an unknown compiler) which stated that Phineas *was* the son of John and Rebecca (Thompson) Burdick.

During her research, Mrs. Johnson had possession and access to this manuscript, but for some unknown reason overlooked the evidence of John's parentage. As an example of evidence, this manuscript should qualify as either an "ancient document" or a "declaration of pedigree and family history," although it might require retaining a genealogist testifying as an expert witness, if Phineas Burdick's parentage was the subject of a controversy in a court proceeding.

Circumstantial evidence additionally established that Phineas was the son of John and Rebecca because they named their first child Phineas, after his father, and their second son Thompson, which of course was Rebecca's maiden name. Although the genealogist decided the problem was solved by a preponderance of the evidence, nevertheless, the genealogist recommended that the official records and any other sources available be searched. If the last wills and testaments of John and Rebecca Burdick were discovered in the probate court records, and Phineas identified in the wills as their son, this of course would be the "best" evidence possible.

MARTIN GENEALOGY CASE HISTORY

The *Martin Genealogy* — Descendants of Lieutenant Samuel Martin of Wethersfield, Conn. — Showing Descent From Royalty . . . was compiled by Thomas Arthur Hay, circa 1911. This volume of 283 pages includes in addition to the claim of descent from Royalty, a Martin coat of arms in resplendent color in the front of the book. The claim to the coat of arms and the descent from Royalty are too ridiculous to discuss. But it is obvious after passing up the heraldic and royalty claims, the balance of the book is a valuable contribution to Martin genealogy. From an examination of the volume, it is obvious that members of the family were interviewed and others sent information to the compiler concerning their individual families. Anyone interested in this Martin family cannot rely on it in its entirety and should attempt to verify the facts stated in the book. In the copy examined (a non-library copy), there are numerous additions and amendments and obviously these were written by one or more members of the families involved.

ASHBY AND BADGER CASE HISTORY

In 1955, the *Ashby and Badger Ancestry* was published on record forms 8-1/2 x 14 inches totalling 445 pages. This family genealogy was reviewed by Donald Lines Jacobus in *The American Genealogist*, July 1956, Vol. 32, pp. 188-189. Mr. Jacobus' review is helpful to aid persons who are beginning research as his analysis of the contents of the book is a guide to what a genealogist should consider in judging the quality and validity of a genealogy or any other type of publication which includes family genealogy and history. The review will be of interested to professionals, if they have not previously read it.

> "This is an ancestral record book, lithoprinted from pedigree charts and family records on the forms put out by the Genealogical Society of Utah. The book is therefore very wide relatively to its height. Many of the families included originated in Essex County, Mass. The reviewer has not checked the lines in detail, but undoubtedly there is much of value, particularly in the recent generations obtained from family sources.

> "The most unpleasant duty of a reviewer is to call attention to defects of books received for review, but it is nevertheless a duty if genealogical standards are to be maintained. There are far too many type errors in the volume under consideration, particularly in the rendering of personal and place names. For example, on p. 224 we read Joseph Bloop (for Blood); Chesum (for Chesham), co. Bucks

England, on p. 97, and on p. 105 the same place is spelled Cheshum; and on p. 93, Ruhannah Hagar for Ruhamah. Many royal and noble lines are given, and in these unfamiliarity has led to a large number of misspellings: Saluggo for Saluzzo (p. 390 and elsewhere), Comgn for Comyn (p. 392), Verdum for Verdun (p. 393), Alphona IX for Alphonso (p. 395), Agustaine for Aquitaine (p. 395), and many others.

"Casual inspection indicates that errors of other kinds must be watched for. On p. 115, Thomas[2] Sawyer is stated to have m. (2) 21 Nov. 1672 Hannah Houghton, daughter of Ralph and Jane. But actually he m. Hannah Lewis, and on p. 225 Hannah daughter of Ralph and Jane (Stowe) Houghton is given as b. 16 Dec, 1667, which would make her five at marriage. On p. 396 the long discredited descent appears of Edmund Rice from Lady Katherine Howard by her husband Sir Rhys 'of' Griffith (so stated instead of the Welsh 'ap' meaning son of). On p. 50 a Bible descent is given back to Adam, and even this has errors in the historical section, as King David is made to descend from the patriarch Jacob through his son Joseph, although the biblical account plainly deduces his descent through Jacob's son Judah. Mythological lines are here included.

"It seems obvious that this book will have to be used with caution, and its statements carefully checked."

II. Case Histories
Official Opinions – Genealogy in Court

STRICKLER GENEALOGY

During the course of the trial of a will contest in Pennsylvania, a family genealogy entitled the *Stricklers of Pennsylvania*, published in 1942, was offered as evidence in the court proceedings in behalf of the contestants who claimed to be first cousins of the testatrix, and therefore, entitled to share in the estate of the deceased, the gross value of which was $2,000,000.

The appellate court stated that ". . . there were a number of patent errors in the book which were brought out on cross examination and to which the hearing judge made reference. Forrest H. Strickler [a witness] frankly conceded that 'There are probably lots of mistakes in that book.' " The appellate court also stated that "The burden of proof in this case was upon the contestants. There was no obligation on the part of the hearing judge to sort out those portions of this book which might be entitled to credibility and use them to establish contestants' case. Contestants' case, minus the testimony of Forrest Strickler and the Book 'Stricklers of Pennsylvania,' is weak at best."

The court continued with these words "In either event we are faced with numerous discrepancies and shortcomings in the evidence [of the contestants] and when they are considered, it became apparent [contestants] claim was properly dismissed. The burden is always upon a claimant to prove kinship to a decedent by a fair preponderance of the credible evidence."[5]

Incidentally, the family genealogy, *Stricklers of Pennsylvania*, is no mere pamphlet. It is a tome exceeding 420 pages. This was a court proceeding in which a qualified genealogist, testifying as an expert witness, would have been able to aid the court, counsel, and clients. No genealogy should be totally condemned because it contains mistakes, as it is bound to include facts which are correct.

WINTERMUTE FAMILY CASE HISTORY

In another estate contest, *The Wintermute Family History*, by J.P. Wintermute, published in 1900, was offered in evidence in a court proceeding in Hudson County, New Jersey. On appeal the court stated "The contents of the book purporting to exhibit the Wintermute 'family tree,' received in evidence by consent of counsel, is not supported by any testimony whatever. It does not disprove the respondent's contention that he is the only child of . . . the sister of the decedent . . . ."[6]

WIBIRD AND PENHALLOW FAMILIES CASE HISTORY

Oliver W. Penhallow testified to facts disclosed on a genealogical table of the Wibird and Penhallow families "now before me." The court wanted proof that this genealogical table had been exhibited (or hung up) where members of the family could see it and that it was recognized as a valid genealogy of the families involved.[7]

In regard to some of these lost causes, the result would probably have been successful if the failing litigants involved had retained the services of a competent genealogist to testify as an expert witness.

WEIGHING THE EVIDENCE – FACT OR FICTION

Judging the reliability or lack of reliability of published (or unpublished) genealogies and the decision of what facts to accept or reject is only gained by experience plus the analytical ability to separate fact from fiction. As an aid in acquiring experience, it is recommended that studying the genealogies compiled by recognized genealogists is desirable. There are many qualified genealogists currently engaged in professional research, but it would not be fair to name a few and exclude others. Therefore, the few named are deceased, except one who is not actively engaged in professional genealogical research.

Francis Bacon Trowbridge, compiler of *The Trowbridge Family . . .* , New Haven, 1908, 848 pages; and Frank Farnsworth Starr, compiler of *Various Ancestral Lines of James Goodwin and Lucy (Morgan) Goodwin of Hartford, Connecticut*, 2 volumes, New Haven 1915, are early examples of competent genealogists. They were followed later by competent and qualified genealogists such as Walter Goodwin Davis, Mary Lovering Holman, and Donald Lines Jacobus, whose books are too numerous to mention, but are listed in genealogical bibliographies and card catalogues of public libraries and genealogical society collections.

A later example of a model family genealogy which should be examined and studied for form and content is the *Descendants of Andrew Everest of York, Maine*, 1955, 488 pages by Winifred Lovering Holman, Fellow of The American Society of Genealogists. (Unfortunately, she has retired from the practice of genealogy.) In addition to studying the book, it is recommended that the book review by Donald Lines Jacobus be read:

"Mrs. Holman brought to the production of this book the wealth of her experience as a research genealogist and as a compiler of family histories, and it is one of the finest American genealogies in print. It is well arranged; it is well referenced; and Mrs. Holman carefully states what sources were covered and also (in the few places where the search was not exhaustive) what sources were not covered. The field research in certain places was done at her behest by other genealogists . . . and they are credited with the data they supplied. Original sources were used for at least the first six generations; beyond that, as is customary, records supplied by the family or found in two earlier collections of Everest data, some of them supplied from family sources many years ago, were utilized . . . . Altogether, this is a volume of which the Everest family, as well as the compiler can be proud." (*The American Genealogist*, Vol. 32, July 1956, p. 187.)

III. Printed or Published Sources
Other Than Family Genealogies

COUNTY AND OTHER LOCAL HISTORIES

There are some excellent and accurate local and county histories, but for some reason not precisely assignable, this type of publication is not as objective generally as family histories and genealogies. For example, the compiler of a county history mentioned one of the settlers of Cooperstown Township, Brown County, Illinois, unfavorably, not once but twice. In this county history it is stated that

Benoni Hewlett was the Rip Van Winkle of the settlement whose principal occupation was that of fishing and drinking whiskey. Like Rip he was always ready for a drink, and always willing not to count the last one.

In another part of the book, the compiler flayed this anti-hero again:

Benoni Hewlett was a character of the neighborhood, settling near the river, with a large family. His chief diet was catfish, which could be obtained with the least labor; and he was a man who, recognizing the debasing effects of whiskey, endeavored to remove its influence by drinking it all himself.[8]

The problem for a genealogist is whether or not bias, interest or prejudice of the compiler justify a researcher in disregarding other facts of a genealogical nature in a book which includes information of this nature. Probably not, as other parts of the book of a biographical and genealogical nature may be true. The problem is verifying the information, as local and county histories are not noted for including references to the source where the facts were obtained.

Then there is the local or county history which is not biased or prejudiced against anyone, but commits some grave errors. For instance the *History of Wallingford, Conn.* . . . states that "Maj. Thomas Miles of New Haven, married Abigail M. daughter of Thomas Mix, Sept. 7, 1709. . . . His mother Mrs. Katherine Miles, died in Wallingford, January 27, 1683 ae. 95 years. . . . The tombstone of Mrs. Catherine Miles is still in the cemetery at Wallingford. . . ."

Obviously some of the facts in this local history are not the "best evidence." If the mother of Major Thomas Miles died 27 January 1683, at the age of 95, then she was born circa 1588. According to the compiler Major Thomas Miles married on September 7, 1709, which is 121 years after his mother's birth.[9] This is a child-bearing miracle which almost equals those of the Bible.

Because of the lack of references in this type of publication, it is difficult to verify the information unless official record sources are reasonably complete. In some local and county histories, information regarding the source of information is included in the preface or introduction; and it helps to know that the compiler consulted records and interviewed older early settlers of the community. The sources the compiler states he utilized may be the only clue to the reliability of the facts in the book.

It is comforting to find a statement such as the following in a county history: "The undersigned citizens . . . have read the foregoing statements of [the compiler] and find them to be substantially true." This was followed by twenty-two names of persons who had signed the original declaration.[10]

GENEALOGICAL PERIODICALS

Beginning with The New England Historical and Genealogical Register in 1847, and subsequent publication of quality periodicals too numerous to mention, genealogists should never fail to search this source for compiled genealogies, often of book length, and articles or notes regarding amendments and corrections to previously published genealogies.

Many of these compiled genealogies include references, and so do the amendments and corrections to published genealogies. Nevertheless, an attempt should be undertaken to verify the facts in official records and any other available reliable sources.

ALL OTHER PRINTED AND PUBLISHED SOURCES

All other printed and published sources which include genealogy are subject to verification, and this includes newspaper queries and answers, souvenir histories, family publications, and especially the "mug" books published by commercial firms in which those included pay a price for the inclusion of their photograph and biography and genealogy.

Many researchers interested in research in Europe are impressed with peerage compilations and Herald's Visitations. It should be realized that these are printed volumes, and if it is not possible to verify facts on these printed pages, you cannot be certain the facts are correct. Heralds' Visitation volumes are not original records and if the College of Arms in London has the original pedigrees in its custody and you want verification, be prepared to maintain a comfortable bank balance, because these records are not available to the public and there is a charge imposed by the College of Arms for their research. Furthermore, visitation pedigrees do not establish ancestry to an absolute certainty, but only according to a preponderance or greater weight of the evidence. Also, there is evidence that some of these pedigrees were forged and fraudulent.

COMMERCIAL VENTURE GENEALOGICAL PUBLICATIONS – SOME EXAMPLES

Individuals, firms, and corporations which publish genealogy and family history lack a major feature which does not encourage accuracy, and that is because there is no professional relationship such as exists between a professional genealogist and the client. The commercial venture is strictly a money-making operation. This type of publishing includes county and other local histories, and some genealogical biographical encyclopedias or compilations. Usually these organizations are corporations and the officers, directors, and employees are not personally liable for mistakes or the financial obligations of the corporation.

One of the most successful, if sheer bulk and financial profit is an indication of success, is *The Abridged Compendium of American Genealogy/First Families of America/A Genealogical Encyclopedia of The United States*, edited by Frederick A. Virkus. Seven volumes or tomes were published between 1925 and 1942. Mr. Virkus organized The American Institute of American Genealogy and invited the public to send in their genealogies for publication, and hundreds did so. In Volume 1, on page 5, Mr. Virkus stated that "One of the principal objects of this work is to compress the lineages contained in the thousands of individual genealogies into a single volume, in order that every public library in the country may possess the very *essence* of American genealogy." [Emphasis added] On the same page he estimates that in 1920, there were 24,583,860 families in the United States with an average of 4.3 persons to a family. To "compress" as he suggests all of these families in a series of volumes and include sufficient genealogical detail was and is an impossible dream.

The principal objection to the Virkus Compendium is that it is very difficult, if not impossible, to judge what genealogies submitted for publication are reliable or unreliable. Obviously some are reliable, but due to a great lack of references to records or other sources verification of the genealogical facts is difficult and often impossible.

Another example is *Americans of Gentle Birth and Their Ancestors/A Genealogical Encyclopedia/Embracing Many Authenticated Lineages and Biographical Sketches of the Founders of the Colonies and Their Descendants Found in All Parts of the United States*, compiled by Mrs. H.D. Pittman, Editor, and Mrs. R.K. Walker, Manager, in two volumes published 1903-1907.

Again, it is difficult to separate truth from tradition. No doubt genealogies and biographies sent in for publication by those included are accurate, or reasonably accurate insofar as their personal knowledge of themselves and their immediate families are concerned, but when the compiler includes pedigrees of the subscribers or contributors to these volumes disclosing their "Royal Lineage" tracing a family's ancestry to a pre-conquest ancestor, it is ridiculous and tragic. Of course, there is a great paucity of dates, places, and references to record sources. If there were any references to sources, these are subject to a different interpretation than that of the compiler. References mean nothing unless relevant and correctly interpreted.

One of the failings of commercial genealogical organizations is that they do not undertake any original research in official records or original sources. They simply print and publish what is sent to them, or what they "lift" out of existing printed sources.

The "mug" books or biographical histories or encyclopedias either charge for inclusion of the genealogy and biography of the individual customer, or there is imposed the obligation to buy a copy of the book. But it is admitted that some of these tomes are better than nothing at all, because it is sometimes possible to verify the information, or some of it, by research in local record sources.

CONCLUSION

With some experience, it is no problem to recognize the commercial genealogical and biographical publication. But this warning must be added: Be skeptical of all of the facts — especially claims to ancient ancestry — and try to verify the facts you want to use.

SUMMARY – JUDGING THE RELIABILITY OF FAMILY GENEALOGIES AND OTHER PUBLISHED SOURCES

This category includes genealogies in any format, whether printed, manuscript, mimeographed or typescript, and included in local and county histories and other published works.

1. The Compiler: A1 — Competent recognized professional. Example, Donald Lines Jacobus. A1 — Competent recognized nonprofessional. Example, the late Walter Goodwin Davis. A2 — Competent amateur: must cite sources and INTERPRETATION of records consulted and cited must be correct. For a probable example, consult *The Descendants of Robert Burdick . . .* by Nellie Willard Johnson, 1927. A3 — Reasonably Competent Amateur: The library shelves abound with their books. B1 — Amateur: Often cites references and they may be correct citations, but the interpretation of this type of genealogist is faulty. Too many examples to mention. C — Rank Amateur: The product of this type of compiler is easily recognized.

2. Arrangement of Data: The numbering system used and format of the text should conform to recognized standards. (For example, any genealogies compiled by Mr. Jacobus are an acceptable standard). It is not implied that a genealogy which is unorthodox in form is false — it simply suggests the work of an amateur. Some of the genealogists of the previous century used some strange numbering systems and other unique arrangements of their genealogies, and often it is possible to verify the facts stated.

3. Completeness: Are full names, dates, and places stated? Examine the first five generations from the immigrant ancestor and ascertain how many descendants are included. *At least all male lines should be traced for the first six generations,* IF THEY produced issue. To do this requires intensive research in official records in the area where they lived. After six generations (depending on the date of the compilation), it may be possible to obtain information from living descendants and due to the lack of accurate vital records, family sources are often the only source of records of births, marriages, and deaths. This is particularly true upon the commencement of the movement to the West. The compiler should state names and addresses of correspondents and reference to official records and published sources. Try to find his or her papers upon which the research is based (Mrs. Johnson mentioned supra, deposited her papers in

the Westerly, R.I., Public Library). The compiler of any genealogy should do this.

4. Descent and Chronology: Examine the line of descent of one or more individuals and ascertain if it is valid. (1) Number of years between generations: Watch for "generation-skipping" and "generation merging." (2) Age of parties at time of marriage. (3) The age of parents and especially mothers when children were born — especially observe if any children were born to a mother beyond the normal child-bearing age.

5. Verification of Facts: Are the references cited correct and did the compiler accurately interpret those facts? If no references are cited, try to verify the facts in spite of this deficiency. Obviously, if a compiler states facts regarding wills and administrations of estates, places of birth, marriage and death, and residence with the requisite dates it should be possible to verify the facts if the records are in existence in some official record repository, depository, or place of custody — this is particularly true regarding probate and other court records.

6. Pre-American Ancestry: Amateur genealogists somehow "jump to conclusions" and utterly disregard proper identification of immigrant ancestors, without justification, assign royal lineage to the ancestor and appropriate and display in their books a coat of arms the family cannot legally claim.

7. Study the Entire Book or Compilation: (1) The preface or introduction should explain the method of compilation and possibly admit some deficiencies. (2) Examine the book for a listing of "errata," for corrections.[11] (3) Is the index (if any) adequate? (4) Did an editor finally finish the book? (Note: This is an indication of the amateur, but a competent editor will (or should) cure some deficiencies.) (5) Does the compiler "jump to conclusions" state "probably he was the son of . . ." and then later state "he was the son of . . . . " without the "probably"?

8. *Consult some of the leading genealogical periodicals* for reviews of the genealogy or other publication and for later corrections by the author and others.

9. *Consider the date of the publication.* It is logical to assume that a genealogy compiled in 1850 ought to be more accurate than one compiled in 1950. At least the 1850 compiler had the advantage of interviewing and corresponding with relatives possessing personal knowledge probably dating back to the 1700's.

10. Beware of the publications of commercial genealogical and biographical organizations such as Virkus' *Abridged Compendium of American Genealogy.* All facts in such books should be verified if it is possible.

CONCLUSIONS COMMENTS AND RECOMMENDATIONS

The foregoing applies to all printed and other sources compiled or written by individuals or firms. Do not believe it is possible to establish ancestry to an absolute certainty and do not base your research on any one source — search every source available. All research should be verified by consulting official records. Family record sources should also be consulted — perhaps the only source available. The results of your research can only be true and correct according to (or by) a preponderance or greater weight of the evidence. "Preponderance" or "greater weight" means Quality not Quantity. AVOID RELYING ON PRINTED OR PUBLISHED SOURCES ONLY.

Notes and References

1. Richberg, Donald R., The Rise and Fall of the Green Bag, *The Green Bag*, Vol. 18, Boston 1906, p. 465.

2. Magna Carta Book Co., Baltimore 1972.

3. Mears, Neal F., *What Is Up Your Family Tree*, 1928, pp. 13, 19, 28.

4. Jacobus, Donald Lines, *Genealogy as Pastime and Profession*, New Haven 1930, p. 72.

5. *In re Frazier Estate*, 75 Pennsylvania District and County Reports 577-584.

6. *In re Henion*, 131 New Jersey Equity Reports 293, 295.

7. *Eastman v. Martin* (1848) 19 New Hampshire Reports, 152, 154-157.

8. *History of Schuyler and Brown Counties, Illinois*, 1882, pp. 72, 320.

9. Davis, Charles Henry Stanley, *History of Wallingford, Conn.* . . ., p. 852.

10. Thompson & West, *History of San Luis Obispo County*, California, 1883, p. 300.

11. An example of the necessity of examining genealogies for errors discovered during printing and before distribution of the book, refer to *The Wentworth Genealogy*, by John Wentworth, LL.D., published in 1878. The "Additions and Corrections" for Volume 1, amounts to 52 pages, and for Volume 2, 22 pages.

CHAPTER 17

CHURCH RECORDS

A difficulty almost insuperable in this case . . . . is the omission of any entry of the baptism of the supposed Charles Crouch (the son of Thomas Crouch of Purbright) in any parochial register. . . . [1]

Sir John Romilly
The Master of the Rolls

The church records supply many of the deficiencies of the public records, and the dates of baptism often have to be learned to approximate dates of birth.[2]

Donald Lines Jacobus

Church records are admissible as evidence for the purpose of establishing genealogy if the provisions of the exceptions to the hearsay evidence rule are complied with, e.g., in regular course of church business, a record in writing, in proper custody, complying with church custom.

Section 1315, California Evidence Code (Adapted)

RECORDS OF AN ESTABLISHED CHURCH

If church records are registered or compiled by an established (meaning government or state) church, they are official records. The parish registers and records of the Church of England, for example, are in that category.[3]

Although parish registers of baptisms, marriages, and burials commenced in England in 1538, during the reign of Henry VIII, there are registers prior to that date; but these records are scarce and were not complete. Furthermore, after 1538, the standard of care and completeness varied in England. As a comparison, an examination of the parish registers of St. Giles in the Fields in London disclosed beautifully bound and well preserved written volumes for a period of over four hundred years, whereas, in some other parishes the entries commence much later, are in unreadable condition due to the ravages of time, dampness, war, or missing due to a variety of reasons. The parish was supposed to send a copy of the parish register entries to the Bishop of the Diocese periodically, but this regulation was not always obeyed. These records are known as the Bishop's Transcripts and commenced in 1597, although a few parishes antedate that year.

Canon 70 of the Church of England provided procedure for registering baptisms, marriages, and burials in the parish registers, but Lord Eldon in the leading case of *Walker v. Wingfield* (1812) wrote that ". . . there is not one [parish register] in one hundred kept according to the canons."[4]

Lord Eldon's statement is substantiated by a leading authority on parish registers, W.E. Tate, who states that baptisms, marriages, and burials were no often recorded due to the tax required to be paid for registering entries of these events in the parish registers. Other reasons for nonregistration were negligence of the registering officer, internal revolution, nonconformist status, illegitimacy, and failure to bother about baptism.[5] Marriage, burial, or baptism outside the parish would be cause of nonregistration in the resident's parish.

It should not be assumed that the registers of baptisms, marriages, and burials constitute all of the records of a parish. Other parish records which disclose valuable genealogical evidence are Churchwarden Accounts, Charity Accounts and Records, Glebe Terrier records, Tithe Records and maps, reports of "Touching for the King's Evil," Vestry Minutes and Agreements, Petty Constables' Accounts, Records of Poor-Law Administration, Records of Highway Maintenance, Records of Open Field Agriculture, Enclosure of Open Fields, Miscellaneous Records, and Church Court Records.[6]

Unless all of the available records of a parish are searched, the evidence sought probably will be missed.

NONCONFORMIST CHURCH RECORDS

It cannot be assumed all of Britain was populated with members of the Church of England. This became more obvious after the requirement that parishes of the established church register baptisms, marriages, and burials. The dissenters maintained their own records, and the existing registers are in the custody of the Public Record Office on Chancery Lane. Although these are not official records as are the records of the established church, the entries are acceptable to genealogists because they are probably as accurate as official parish registers.

CHURCH RECORDS IN THE COLONIES AND STATES

During the colonial period, some of the colonies required civil registration of births, marriages, and deaths — at early dates, especially in the New England area. Churches were at liberty to maintain church registers and records, but the quantity and quality of these records vary from place to place and from church to church.

Although these records were not official, it does not automatically decree that they are inaccurate. All records are acceptable, subject to verification, if possible. If verification is not possible, a genealogist must decide whether the records can be judged credible. One of the most important tests for credibility is custody. If the records appear to be originals or have been certified as true copies and are in the custody of the clerk of the church or some other church official, church archives, or church library, the records are acceptable as long as the facts are logical.

A *Survey of American Church Records* by E. Kay Kirkham (1958) should be used as a guide to American Church Records. Other church record sources are discussed in *The Researcher's Guide to American Genealogy* by Val D. Greenwood (1975); *A Selected Bibliography* by Milton Rubincam, F.A.S.G. (1967); and *Search and Research* by Noel C. Stevenson, F.A.S.G. (1977).

JUDGING RELIABILITY OF CHURCH RECORDS

PRO RELIABILITY

1. If the church records are those of an established church, e.g., Church of England, these are official records and are acceptable. Additional verification of the facts from other sources is advisable.
2. A pastor of a church in a foreign country testified that church records of marriages, births, and deaths had been kept according to the laws of the country; he was the proper custodian of them, and had received them from his predecessor. Extracts from these records giving the genealogy of a family sworn by him to be correct, were valid evidence in a question of identity.[7]
3. If not an official record, church records are acceptable as entries made in the regular course of business, assuming the records are in the custody of a church officer, and the records appear to be authentic. If the church records are not in the custody of a church officer, some effort should be exerted to determine their validity. Some tests for this would be the age of the paper, ink, legibility, handwriting and the source of possession, and accounting for the possession.
4. An entry made in the performance of a religious duty is certainly of no less value than one made by a clerk, messenger, an attorney or solicitor or a physician in the course of his secular occupation.[8]

CONTRA RELIABILITY

1. A baptismal record is not proof of date or place of birth.
2. A burial record is not proof of date or place of death.
3. The identity problem (refer to chapter on this subject) is always present, especially if the names of persons are common.
4. It is not reasonable to assume that the parish records are complete or correct.
5. Any pedigree which depends solely on parish registers for its authenticity is not acceptable to a competent genealogist.
6. If the church records are not those of an established church or State church (such as the Church of England), they are not official records.
7. Church records are not compiled for genealogical purposes.
8. There is a tendency for researchers to assume that the date of baptism and the date of birth are same or near the same, and that the person baptized was an infant. It is not logical to believe that dates of birth and baptism were the same day. It must be recognized that at least occasionally adults were baptized. However, there are some parish registers which disclose the date of birth as well as the date of baptism, but this is not universal. The clergy had no authority to inquire regarding the facts of birth or to enter any information in regard to that subject in the register.[9]
9. Often church records in the colonies and what is now the United States were kept by amateurs and too often they were rank amateurs. However some of the amateurs performed their duties as competently as professionals.
10. Some of the parish records of State churches were also kept by incompetents, and that includes the Church of England — each record

must be judged on its merits or demerits.

11. Unfortunately, parish registers and records have been the target of fraud, forgery, inserting false entries, and mutilation — e.g., tearing or cutting out pages or stealing entire volumes. That such practices were not rare is evidenced by two famous cases described in *A Lancashire Pedigree Case* ... by J.P. Earwaker (Warrington, England, 1887) and another book *The Principal Genealogical Specialist*; or *Regina v. Davies and The Shipway Genealogy, Being the Story of a Remarkable Pedigree Fraud*, by W.P.W. Phillimore, M.A., London, 1899.

12. Church records are hearsay evidence — if the records are of an early date and there are no persons available who possess personal knowledge of the facts.

Notes and References

1. *Crouch v. Hooper* (1852) 16 Beavan 182.

2. Jacobus, Donald Lines, *Genealogy As Pastime and Profession,* New Haven, 1930, p. 83.

3. Although the records of an established church are official records (e.g., the Church of England), the information on this subject is included with unofficial church records for the sake of convenience of readers.

4. *Walker v. Wingfield* (1812) 18 Vesey Jr., Reports 441; 34 English Reports 384, 385.

5. Tate, W.E., F.R.H.S., *The Parish Chest*, Cambridge 1946, pp. 43 et seq.

6. Ibid, various pages, refer to index.

7. *American etc., v. Rosenagle* (1875) 77 Pennsylvania Reports 507, et seq.

8. *Kennedy v. Doyle* (1865) Massachusetts, 10 Allen's Reports 161, 167.

9. *Wihen v. Law* (1821) 171 English Reports 768.

CHAPTER 18

FAMILY BIBLE RECORDS

"It is certain however, that such a registry [a family Bible record] is not, in all cases conclusive of the facts stated [therein], but its weight as evidence is subject to be weakened or strengthened by all the proof in reference to it. The party by whom the entries were made, when they were made, whether the book has been so kept as to be accessible at all times to all the members of the family, are all matters to be considered in determining the probative force of such evidence."

Weaver v. Leiman (1879) 52
Maryland Reports 708

"Entries of births, deaths, and marriages in a family Bible are competent evidence, though such a record does not contain every element in the history of each member of the family necessary to make it perfect."

In re Blythe's Estate (1890)
California 4 Coffey's Probate
Decisions 302

It would be difficult, if not impossible, to ascertain when the first family records were written in a Bible or other religious book. The custom of presenting a young married couple with a Bible no doubt influenced them to record family genealogy in a book of that character.

The entrepreneur who originated the idea to include family record forms for the entry of marriages, births, and deaths between the Old and New Testament is unknown. His (assuming that person was a male) one major mistake was the failure to include instructions to owners of the Bibles to state full names (including maiden names), complete dates, and places when and where these events occurred.

The accuracy of these records depends on the interest and care of the individual who compiled the record, the date when the entries were written, if entered by a member of the family from memory or copies from a previous record(s).

Examination of a Bible printed in Philadelphia in 1816 discloses the first entry on the family record forms was written August 25, 1747, sixty-nine years prior to publication. In the same handwriting is a marriage record dated 22 November 1787. This is one of the major problems Bible records present. The facts of birth, marriage, and death (or most of them) are written many years after the events occurred, and it cannot be ascertained when the events were recorded in many family Bible records or from what source. Were they recopied from an older record or records? Recorded by a member of the family who personally knows the facts, or did the Bible salesman or a neighbor record the information, and if so, did the recorder do so accurately?

If some place names are disclosed in the record, or if the Bible is in the possession of the family or someone who knows some clues as to the family's geographical origin, or it is possible to locate clues in printed sources or official records, there is hope for verification.

As a contrast, a record of a family began with the birth of a child on "April 16th old stile 1752," is written on the fly leaf of a printed volume entitled *Pathmos or A Commentary on the Revelation of Saint John* ... printed in London in 1629. As usual the entries were written long after the date of publication. However, the handwriting appears to be the same between the first entry in 1752 and the last one in 1792, so it is obvious that the person recording the genealogical data relied on memory, or was copying an earlier record.

Although this record was not written in a Bible, the volume concerns a Biblical subject. The question then arises, is a family record registered in a Bible (or a religious Book such as a prayer book)[1] to be judged more accurate and reliable than genealogical information written in a nonreligious book, notebook, or a sheet of plain paper? It is doubtful, although it can be argued that some people would be more careful what they recorded in a Bible record than some other source.

As an example of a nonreligious source or record, the plaintiff in a lawsuit alleged he was of legal age when he signed a document. The defendant, to prove that the plaintiff was under 21, produced an almanac in which plaintiff's father had written his date of birth as 14 February 1608, to prove the nonage of plaintiff. The Court admitted the almanac date as "strong evidence" of plaintiff's date of birth.[2]

There is no logical reason to believe that evidence written in a Bible is universally more reliable than if written in another type of book or record. Each record must be judged on its merits, and in each instance, is subject to verification by referring to other record sources.

CLASSIFICATION OF BIBLE RECORDS

Bible records should be classified into evidentiary categories, as all records of families entered in Bibles are not equally valid. Therefore, a theoretical classification of what should be the most accurate Bible record may be classed "AAA" and records which are probably less accurate classed in lower categories.

Bible Records Rated AAA are practically nonexistent because there are few, if any living persons, who possess the personal knowledge regarding the entries in the family Bible record. A record commenced in 1752 is certainly in that category. It is conceded that there are modern Bible records begun, for example, in 1900, and there are one or more living persons who are qualified to testify regarding the validity of the handwriting of some of the entries, or perhaps all of them.

Bible Records Rated AA do exist. In this classification it must be established that the book has been in the "proper custody" (that is in the possession of a member of the family), and some evidence that the book has been transferred from one generation through succeeding generations.

Example: A genealogist was tracing the ancestry of William S. Coon. From the New York State Census for 1855 for Cattaraugus County, it was ascertained he was born c. 1816 in Madison County, New York. In Madison County histories, it was disclosed that Jonathan, Luke, and Pardon Coon were early settlers in the town of De Ruyter, Madison County. A personal visit to De Ruyter and a search of town records and gravestones in the cemetery did not disclose any facts toward solution of the problem. A visit to the homes of some of the residents was of no help until one of the people remembered that a member of the Coon family living a few miles from the village knew more than anyone else concerning the Coon family history. A visit to the home of this gentleman and a few questions asked of him soon disclosed that he possessed personal knowledge regarding the family, and he also had the custody of the family Bible which he brought down from the attic. One of the entries solved the problem: "William Satteley Coon born October 22nd, 1816 . . . son of Luke Coon born August 4th 1774 and Lydia (Comstock) Coon born March the 4th 1789." Although no places of birth, marriage, or death were included in the record, some of the entries were obviously written after 1823, the date the Bible was printed. This family record would have been admissible in a court proceeding either as an ancient document (more than 30 years old and in the proper custody by a member of the family), or as a "declaration of pedigree and family history," an exception to the hearsay evidence rule, for these reasons: (1) The family record would be considered trustworthy due to possession within the family, no reason to falsify, and persons who recorded the information would be presumed to write the truth regarding family history and genealogy. Of course, there are always exceptions to the presumption to relate the truth regarding a family, but there was no indication of that in this instance. (2) This record was the only source from which the information could be obtained, so the "necessity rule" was satisfied. (3) The family information originated before any controversy had arisen, such as a lawsuit, and before the purpose for which the information was wanted at that time. Furthermore, a member of the family was available to testify regarding possession of the original record in the Bible.

Incidentally, it was possible to locate a cemetery record which stated that William S. Coon died 27 November 1870, age 54 years, 1 month, and 6 days. This record verified his date of birth as stated in the Bible record. He was buried in Portville, Cattaraugus County, New York.

Bible Records Rated A would include family Bible records in the possession of a member of the family who has no knowledge of the record except that it was among the personal effects of one of the relatives now deceased.

Bible Records Rated BB would include a family Bible in the possession of a person who married a member of the family, now deceased, and who has no knowledge of the family record except that it was among the possessions of the deceased husband or wife, or other relative.

Bible Records Rated B would include family Bible records in the possession of a distant relative (e.g., second cousin) who has no knowledge of the origin of the Bible except that the surname is one familiar to him as that of one of his reputed ancestors.

Bible Records Rated C would include family Bible records in the possession of a stranger to the family mentioned in the record forms or pages. The stranger is often a neighbor, second-hand book dealer, or a person who purchases the Bible to preserve the record, gives it to a library, or copies it and sends the record to one of the genealogical periodicals for publication.

These are some of the factors to be considered in judging Bible records:

1. Is the handwriting uniform throughout the record? If so, this is an indication that the record was written at one sitting or within a shorter period than writing which has changed. The handwriting of individuals changes during the course of a lifetime.

2. Compare the handwriting to ascertain if the entries could have been written by more than one person.

3. Has the type of ink been changed? Black to blue, or some other color? If so this is an indication that the entries were written at different dates and by different persons.

4. What is the time span of the record? If the volume was published in 1700 and the first entry was a marriage in 1701, the first birth 1702, and the birth entries continue until 1720 in handwriting which indicates that the birth records were recorded at different times (probably soon after each birth), this record would be more likely to be more accurate than a family Bible record in a volume published in 1750, and the first entry was the marriage written in the book in 1701.

5. Are the dates recorded chronologically or out of order?

6. Don't trust implicitly family records written in pencil. At least be suspicious of them as pencil records are easy to change, and there are instances a pencil was used to perpetrate a fraud and produce a false family record. It is easier to detect the age of ink than writing with a graphite pencil.

7. Erasures and substitution of names, dates, and obliterations with strokes of a pen or other instrument present a problem. Often it is possible to read what was erased or obliterated by use of ultra violet ray light or photography with special film. An amateur can detect changes with ultra violet rays, as there are short wave and long wave equipment available commercially at nominal cost; however, special film and exposure requires professional knowledge.[3]

8. Experienced genealogists agree that generally official vital records and church records are much more accurate than family Bible records. For that reason, all information from Bible records should be verified, if possible, by referring to other record sources.

9. Bible records filed with pension applications in the National Archives have been subject to scrutiny in processing claims for pensions. If the pension application has been denied, determine if the reason was some defect in the Bible record.

10. Hereditary societies receive original Bible records and these are scrutinized as part of applications for membership. Examination of these records are, of course, subject to the rules of the particular society. Again, it is important (if you obtain access to these records) to learn if the application was accepted or rejected because of the reliability or lack of reliability of the Bible record presented.

11. The general appearance of the volume and the family record should be carefully studied. In a New Jersey lawsuit in which a Bible containing a family record was introduced into evidence, the record involved a decedent by the name of Daniel F. Conklin and the trial judge's comments and judgment of the reliability of the family Bible record are excellent guides for the consideration of genealogists. The New Jersey Court of Errors and Appeals stated:
    ". . . the learned judge in the [trial] court below had the opportunity to personally inspect the book itself when offered [in evidence], and in the reasoning which led up to the ultimate finding to which the second exception under consideration applies, he uses the following language: 'The Bible bears the appearance of age. Perhaps that is hardly correct. It is mutilated and shows evidence of use for a long time, but the binding is not of a character one would expect to find in a very ancient volume. The title page being lost, it is impossible to ascertain the date of printing. The entries are certainly not contemporaneous with the facts stated. The names are written in one handwriting and apparently at one time, the same pen and ink apparently having been used. It is also apparent that the dates of the birth of the children were written at the same time, but in a different handwriting from the names, and with a different pen and ink. From the appearance of the ink and the writing, I think that the dates were appended long after the names were written. A correction has been made in one of the dates . . . . The question is, can this book, under the evidence, be regarded as a family record? I do not think there is proof in the case warranting me to so regard it. There is no evidence showing when the dates were placed in the book or by whose authority, or what information the person making the entries had. That they were not made contemporaneous with the births of the children named is apparent'."[4]
    The trial judge rejected the evidence in the family Bible record.[5]

12. If the family Bible record is in the possession of the family or a member of the family, is it accepted as the family record, or do some of the members or relatives question its validity or some part of it?

PRO RELIABILITY

1. There is a presumption that whoever recorded the facts in the family Bible possessed reliable, if not personal, knowledge of the births, marriages, and deaths, and other facts.

2. In court proceedings family Bible records are admissible, in fact the courts bend the rules to enable introduction of these records in evidence because frequently there are no other records.

3. Bible records are admissible for two reasons: First, if the record is more than 30 years old it is admissible as an "ancient document"; and second, it is a "declaration of pedigree and family history" — both exceptions to the hearsay rule. (Caution: Admissibility is not proof.)

4. A genealogist who is not compiling a genealogy for use in a court proceeding may be more lenient and ignore the strict rules of evidence, but should endeavor to verify the facts in the Bible record by referring to other sources.

5. Family records which are entered in the Bible after the date of publication are not necessarily incorrect or false. If there are mistakes, they are seldom intentional. Verification and correction may be possible in other sources.

6. Family Bible records in the possession of the family and transferred from generation to generation are probably as reliable a record as it is possible to find. This is especially true if there are no official vital records or church records available.

7. A search of U.S. or State Census records may aid in verifying the family record in a Bible.

8. Admittedly an original family Bible record is preferable to printed or hand copied records, hopefully the number of errors are few or nonexistent.

9. Original or copies which have been certified correct by a notary public in the possession of a library or archives (e.g., National Archives, in the pension files, or in the possession of the DAR genealogical library are acceptable and are a "proper custody" which would be admissible in a court proceeding, especially if the last entry was over thirty years old. If there is no question concerning the credibility of the record, it should be reliable.

10. If the Bible record is in the possession of a stranger or found in a second hand book store, it does not automatically indicate error, fraud, forgery, or unreliability. You may be sure the family Bible record is only there because the last member of the family in possession died; there were no interested members who wanted it, and it was sold with other books to the dealer or given with a lot of junk to some organization, such as the Salvation Army. A trial judge would be reluctant to rule the record admissible under these circumstances, but if it includes data which "fits" the family you are searching, it would be foolish to reject it.

11. It is reasonable to believe that anyone entering a record of births, marriages, deaths, and other genealogical facts, if at all conscientious, would not intentionally falsify a record written in a Bible. There are, of course, exceptions when carelessness, fraud, and guesswork result, but reason dictates these occurrences are minimal.

CONTRA RELIABILITY

1. Family Bible records are hearsay evidence, even in instances where the Bible is still in the possession of the family. All the individual in possession of the volume knows (unless the information is recent or that person has personal knowledge of the entries and facts) is that it has been in the family's possession and is now in his or her possession.

2.   Possession by a stranger to the family or a book dealer is not what is recognized as a "proper custody."

3.   Bible records printed in books or published in genealogical periodicals, or hand-copied Bible records are subject to misreading due to faint and careless handwriting and printer's errors. This includes those records in the possession of a library or other repository.

4.   If the Bible record is a copy and one certified as correct by a notary public or other officer authorized to issue verifications under seal, unless that officer states in the verification that he has compared the copy with the original, the reliance is still on the person who copied the record, and therefore, subject to any errors which result from the copying process.

5.   If the family Bible record commenced before the date of publication of the volume, whoever recorded the entries before that date relied on his or her memory or copied the entries from an older record. This should encourage a serious attempt to verify the facts in the record in other record sources.

6.   Printed, published, hand-copied, photographed, or photocopied family Bible records in libraries and other repositories should disclose the origin of the record and in whose possession it was at the time it was copied. If this information is not disclosed, the record discourages confidence in the record's authenticity.

7.   There is no assurance that all of the children (or facts) are entered in the Bible record. For example illegitimate children, divorces, or other facts the family considers scandalous or unfavorable may be omitted.

8.   The fact that a family record is entered in a Bible does not automatically prove that it is correct or genuine.

9.   It has been demonstrated that records of births, marriages, and deaths are more accurate in the official vital records of a town, city, county, state or other official record source than the accuracy of the same events disclosed in Bible records.

10. It has also been demonstrated that genealogical facts in church records are more reliable than family Bible records.

11. Genealogists should be suspicious of family Bible records which disclose erasures and strike-overs or obliteration of information.

12. Family Bible records written in pencil should be suspect. The age of ink can be detected, but graphite or "lead" pencil is difficult to date. There have been instances where old Bibles have been obtained with blank record forms and a record written in pencil to conceal dates of birth, marriage, and death. One reason for falsifying age was to avoid military service, and "back-dating" a birth date was one way to accomplish this.

13. Family Bible records are notorious for the omission of such vital information as the place where births, marriages, and deaths occurred, no mention of place of residence, the omission of maiden names of wives, occupations and professions are rarely mentioned, and incomplete entries such as "Grandfather was born in 1808."

14. Consider the possibility of the existence of two family Bibles with two different records. It is doubtful if this is a common occurrence, but in a court proceeding involving a family controversy, the court stated "It has been satisfactorily proved . . . that there was in the family . . . another Bible. . . . [record]" This second Bible was not produced at the trial.[6]

168

15. "Bible records are not sacrosanct either. They are sometimes falsified to make it appear that the parents were married at least nine months before the birth of the first child, or to make a woman appear younger than she really was."[7]
16. The fact that Bible records are generally admissible as evidence in court is not proof that the records are correct.

CONCLUSION

The facts disclosed in any family Bible record should be verified by searching other record sources — at least an "all out" attempt to verify should be undertaken.

Caveat: This is only a partial listing of defects in family Bible records.

Notes and References

1. *Sussex Peerage Case* (1844) The All England Law Reports 1843-1860, 55-67.
2. *Herbert v. Tuckall* (1663) 83 English Reports 46.
3. Haselden, R.B. *Scientific Aids for the Study of Manuscripts*, Printed at the Oxford University Press for The Bibliographical Society, Oxford, 1935. Mr. Haselden was Curator of Manuscripts at the Huntington Library, San Marino, California, for many years.
4. *Supreme Council v. Conklin*, 60 New Jersey Law Reports 565, 570-571.
5. Ibid.
6. *Copes v. Pearce* (1848 Maryland) 7 Gill's Reports 247-265.
7. Pitman, H. Minot, F.A.S.G., "Genealogical Proof," *The American Genealogist*, Vol. 37, October 1961, pp. 193-194.

CHAPTER 19

MONUMENTS, MEMORIALS, MEMORABILIA, AND MISCELLANEOUS

Upon questions of pedigree inscriptions on tombstones are admitted; as it must be supposed, the relations of the family would not permit an inscription without foundation to remain.

Vowles v. Young (1806) 13 Ves. 140, 144

Inscriptions on tombstones, coffin-plates, mural monuments, family portraits, engravings on rings, hatchments, charts of pedigree, and the like are [admissible in evidence if the various provisions of the hearsay evidence rule are complied with].

John Pitt Taylor, A Treatise on the Law of Evidence . . . , p. 536, Vol. 2, London, 1858.

CEMETERY AND BURIAL RECORDS

This category includes tombstones, gravestones, footstones, monuments which are simply elaborate tombstones, coffin plates, headboards, private mausoleums in private and public cemeteries, and monumental brasses common to the interiors of churches in England upon which are inscriptions regarding deceased persons.

The size, shape, and location are not as important as the inscriptions on them and especially the state of preservation of these objects. If the material is wood or sandstone, the inscriptions will be unreadable in a matter of time unless protected from the weather, termites, and vandals. Vandalism is one of the prime enemies of these records.

If the cemetery is maintained by a public agency, church, or private corporation or association, ascertain if there are burial records in the custody of a sexton, clerk, or other officer. If these records have been properly maintained, there should be a record of every individual buried there and maps or other means of locating the plot. Therefore, if the inscription is not readable, the cemetery or burial records should provide this information as well as information regarding other members of the same family. Locating cemetery records is a great time saver, otherwise, it is a matter of walking from tombstone to tombstone, reading all of them, and then ending the day with failure to find what you are seeking.

If the cemetery is abandoned or one privately maintained, the record volumes lost or never maintained, there is no choice but to read every inscription, if that is possible. If you decide to clean the stone or try to reproduce a facsimile by a rubbing, obtaining permission must be considered first. Competent photographers are able to produce a readable photograph, in instances where an amateur photographer will fail. Professional photographers utilizing scientific methods such as ultra violet ray photography (this will require darkened conditions) and special types of film may solve the problem. Even an amateur photographer taking advantage of side-lighting may be successful in reading the unreadable and often reading with side-lighting without the necessity of photography will solve the problem.

Some stonecutters caused a serious problem with their fine or delicate chiselling of names and numbers. For example, if a gravestone is old and weathered, the downstroke on the figure "4" weathers first and causes the "4" to appear as a "1." Because this affects most letters and numbers, cemetery searchers must be on constant guard to watch for these delicate and faint lines.

Determining the date of birth from the age stated on a gravestone always presents a problem — even when the age in years, months, and days is disclosed. For instance in The Hovey Book at page 165, this gravestone inscription in the old cemetery in Ipswich, Massachusetts, is disclosed:

In Memory of
Mrs. Hannah Hovey
wife of Mr. Francis Hovey
who died April 26, 1802
Aged 53

Pass on, my friend, dry up your tears
I must lie here, till Christ Appears;
Death is a debt to nature due;
I've paid the debt, and so must you.

Simple subtraction indicates she was born in 1749, but when only the age is disclosed and the date of birth is figured by subtraction, the correct age is usually one year earlier. But what is the result if it stated she died "Aged 53 years, 9 months, and 10 days." With some mathematical juggling it should be possible to determine her correct date of birth — provided, of course, the information supplied to the stonecutter was correct, and he did not commit a mistake in the cutting process. There is a problem beginners (and others) overlook and that is Hannah Hovey was born prior to the calendar change. This problem is emphasized by the erudite editor in chief of *The American Genealogist*, Dr. George E. McCracken, "If age is given on a tombstone, it has doubtless been computed by a survivor and he may be mistaken or a poor mathematician, and to compute the age at death is a task that challenges even a mathematician, especially if the life extended over the change in the calendar of 1752."[1]

The late H. Minot Pitman, a qualified professional genealogist, related an incident involving a widow who intentionally misstated the age of her deceased husband, but did not foresee the result of doing so. Her husband was two years younger than she was. To conceal this fact she caused the inscription on the tombstone to be back-dated four years, thus causing him to appear older than she was. She did not realize that the back-dating would result in stating his date of birth two years before his parents were married![2]

THE PROBLEM OF MISPLACED GRAVESTONES

There are laws to prevent vandals and thieves from damaging or stealing gravestones, monuments, or other artifacts from cemeteries. Yet on more than one occasion, genealogists report finding gravestones used for steps into buildings, rock walls, and stepping stones. Conscientious genealogists copy these inscriptions whenever possible, but the misplaced tombstone presents several problems. First of all, where did it come from? Is it possible to determine if from the immediate locality? The owner or occupier of the land where it now rests is often reluctant to talk and usually says it was there before he acquired title to the property. Another problem is the possible scattering of gravestones from family plots which destroys the actual or potential evidence of family relationships.

An illustrative case occurred to a genealogist who visited a building supply exhibit in Southern California. One prominent feature on display was a wooden headboard or graveboard with this inscription carved on it:

In memory of/Samuel Newell Terrill/
Born in Pitcher, N.Y./Sept. 22, 1825/
Died June 30, 1857/Lies Here Affec-
tionate/Friend and Father Dear.

Why was it in the exhibit? The graveboard was made of California Redwood, and the exhibitor used it to prove that his product (redwood, of course) was indestructible as the inscription was readable and the wood was well preserved although weathered by exposure to the elements. The visit to the exhibit occurred in 1938, so at that time the graveboard was obviously placed on the grave 81 years previously.

Where did it come from? It seemed reasonable to believe that the grave site was in Northern California, the location of the redwood lumbering industry. The genealogist copied the inscription and filed it with some other stray cemetery records.

In 1974 while sorting that file, the copy was noticed and a brief note was written for *The American Genealogist*. This note was published in the October 1974 issue of the magazine and the genealogist forgot about the subject again. Several months later a long distance telephone call was received and a Mrs. Newell Terrill asked if she was talking to the person who wrote the note concerning the Terrill inscription. Mr. and Mrs. Terrill had been trying to find the grave of his great-grandfather, S.N. Terrill, who came to Northern California in 1849. They learned from an obituary that S.N. Terrill was killed in an accident in Petaluma in 1857 and was buried there. When they visited Petaluma they learned that the old pioneer cemetery had been converted into a public park, and all of the Tombstones (and graveboards) were removed and certainly Samuel Newell Terrill's was distantly removed. Mrs. Terrill wrote an article regarding their search for the *Ash Tree Echo*, Vol. XI, No. 2, April 1976, published by the Fresno Genealogical Society. This article includes more than substantial evidence that the headboard was that of Mr. Terrill's great-grandfather.

Someone should organize a society for the preservation of misplaced or stolen gravestones and graveboards.

PRO RELIABILITY

The presumption is that relatives, stonecutters, sextons, and others concerned with burial records and cemeteries are careful and conscientious. There is also a presumption that if a tombstone is not correct and this knowledge is known to the family of the deceased, the error or errors would be corrected. These are disputable presumptions and each case must be subjected to careful research and interpretation of the facts.

CONTRA RELIABILITY

1.   Many genealogical researchers "swear" to the accuracy of cemetery inscriptions and burial records. The reason heretofore mentioned that the deceased's family would not permit the gravestone or other memorial to remain uncorrected, is one "sworn" by. This reasoning is faulty due to actual instances of personal knowledge. Even when some families are aware of errors on tombstones, nothing is done to correct the mistakes. Stonecutters are frequently responsible for the errors, for instance, the case of a tombstone which stated the deceased was "Born Sept. 10, 1855 — Died Sept. 14, 1842."

One authority writing on the subject of the "Admissibility of Hearsay in Questions of Pedigree," states:

"The credit of monumental inscriptions may always be impeached, and their evidence seems peculiarly open to attack, not only on account of the great facility of forgery, but also because the preparation of them is often committed to undertakers, executors, or other persons not members of the family, or because perhaps the inscription has been delayed till a period when the facts are but imperfectly remembered . . . In the epitaph upon Spencer's monument in Westminster Abbey, there is a mis-statement as to the time of his birth of no less than forty years, and as to that of his death three years." (Phillips, Samuel M., *A Treatise on the Law of Evidence*, Vol. 1, page 222, 3rd edition, New York 1849.)

2.   Published cemetery records (whether manuscript, typescript, mimeographed, or printed) are subject to the hazards of mistakes in reading, copying, and printer's errors. If possible (and at this late date, the possibility is often impossible) an attempt should be made to find the original tombstone or other inscription, or someone should be commissioned to do this for you.

3.   Identity is always a serious question to be solved in judging the reliability of cemetery records and inscriptions. There is a grave topped by an impressive monument in an Ohio cemetery which states that "Robson L. Broome" is buried there. Research disclosed that his name was not Broome, his true surname was Brewster.

4.   Researchers cannot assume similarity of name or the same name sufficient for identification either. "The mere fact that a monumental inscription is more than 50 years old and that a name inscribed thereon is the same as the one whose pedigree is [the subject matter of a lawsuit] does not, per se, make the recital on the tombstone competent evidence of the question of the pedigree."[3]

CONCLUSION

Inscriptions should be read, reread, and transcribed with care. Additional skill and care in deciphering worn or weathered inscriptions is required. CAUTION: Printed or other types of reproduced cemetery records present additional hazards: mistakes of copier, transcriber, printer, or inadequate photography. Additional records should be searched, such as the original records of the cemetery association or corporation, if in existence, all official records, and all other types of records available, for the purpose of verification of names and dates, and any additional genealogical data you discovered.

MEMORIAL RINGS AND OTHER JEWELRY

Jewelry or family silverware engraved with genealogical information, must, of necessity, be brief, and this custom has never been as popular in the United States as in England. These relics may be in the possession of members of the family, and it is a mistake not to inquire if they exist.

Anyone fortunate enough to be interested in members of any family included in a volume published by Frederick Arthur Crisp entitled *Memorial Rings/Charles the Second/To William The Fourth,* London 1908, is due for a surprise. Mr. Crisp's collection of memorial rings exceeded more than 1,000; and in addition to the name of the person or persons involved, ages and dates, genealogical and biographical information is often included, such as pedigrees, abstracts of wills, etc. One example on page 27 is a description of the memorial or mourning ring of "Mary Kirke ob: 18 May 1720 AEt 81." Following this information, she is identified as "Mary Marshall, widow of Thomas Kirke of St. Giles, Cripplegate, London, skinner," and an abstract of her will disclosing the names of her sons, daughters, and other relatives. The will was filed in the Prerogative Court of Canterbury, No. 111 Shaller.

MEMORABILIA AND MISCELLANEOUS

There is not an oversupply of genealogical samplers but this area should not be overlooked. Some samplers have even been reproduced in books.[4] Family records have also been stitched into home-made quilts or embroidered in other forms.

Valentines, letters, post cards, diaries, journals, account books, miscellaneous papers, and notes have been used to record announcements or records of birth, marriage, death, divorce, and other aspects of family genealogy, family history, and biography. The average Christmas card usually includes nothing more than a hackneyed verse and a name, but in a court proceeding in New Jersey, a Christmas card and a charge account at a store were admitted in evidence to establish a common law marriage.[5]

Photographs, tintypes, portraits (if the persons are identified) are valuable sources of genealogical information. A photographic album may be the means of obtaining the names and other facts concerning an entire family group and clues to their ancestry, if some identifying information is recorded on the front or backs of the photographs, or some writing included somewhere in the album or pages inserted in the album.

Scrapbooks are often a gold mine if newspaper cuttings concern the family in which you are interested. In the past, families deprived of the dubious benefit of modern entertainment, had the time to compile and maintain scrapbook records.

It was customary to insert newspaper clippings regarding relatives in the family Bible (Bible records are discussed in another chapter of this book).

The foregoing is not represented as a complete listing of this type of family information, therefore, a researcher should ask to examine every potential source in the possession of whoever has the custody of the records.

CONCLUSION

Insofar as reliability of records of this character is concerned, the human element must always be considered, and information discovered in a collection of family papers should be verified, if possible, through other record sources, preferably official records such as land, probate, and other court records. If the records are in the possession of a member of the family, and these records obviously have been transferred from generation to generation, this is known as a "proper custody" and adds to their authenticity tremendously.

Notes and References

1. McCracken, Dr. George E., "On Mistrusting Ages," *The American Genealogist*, Vol. 49, January 1973, p. 36.
2. Pitman, H. Minot, LL.B., "Genealogical Proof," *The American Genealogist*, Vol. 37, October 1961, pp. 193-194.
3. *Gehr v. Fisher* (1891) 143 Pennsylvania Reports 311, 322.
4. Bolton, Edith Stanwood, *American Samplers*, Boston 1921. There are other books which include samplers and other fancy work which include genealogical data.
5. *State v. Bright* (1939) 123 New Jersey Law Reports 435-437.

CHAPTER 20

GENEALOGICAL EVIDENCE IN NEWSPAPER FILES

Mrs. T. J. Murphy will celebrate her 48th birthday Sunday. She has been a resident of Springfield for 57 years.

Placer Times, Sacramento, California
August 18, 1849

Newspapers more than thirty years old are admissible in evidence as an exception to the hearsay evidence rule, as ancient documents, if in proper custody, and if other provisions of the hearsay rule such as trustworthiness are complied with.

Trustees v. Farmers,
(Ohio, 1953) 113 N.E. 2d 409

The first successful newspaper in what is now the United States was the Boston News-Letter which commenced publication April 24, 1704, followed by other newspapers in Boston, Philadelphia, New York, Annapolis, Charleston, Newport, and Williamsburg — all before 1750. By April 1775, there were thirty-seven newspapers in eleven of the colonies. The format of these early examples of the press was usually four pages with foreign news on the first page, domestic news on the second, local news on the third, and advertisements on the fourth. Any news of a genealogical nature was coincidental, such as legal notices, obituaries, and some announcements of births, marriages, and deaths.

With a war in progress after 1775, one would expect to find little, if any, genealogical news published, but there was. For example, *The Providence Gazette and Country Journal*, Saturday, July 12, 1777, included descriptions of several deserters and a legal notice.

Joseph Hambridge, about 28 years of age, Joseph Merrey, 5 feet 10 inches tall . . . and a bold looking fellow . . . about 22 years of age . . . both deserted from Capt. William Potter's Company, in Col. Angell's Regiment.

Thomas Barker, 30 years of age, about 5 feet 10 inches tall, short curled black hair, deserted from the Galley Spitfire, commanded by Capt. Joseph Crandall who offered five dollars reward and necessary secured expenses if secured in gaol or if delivered to Capt. Crandall.

Peter Burchell, "a native of Ireland, 21 years of age, 5 feet 7 inches high, blue eyes, short dark brown hair . . . deserted from Capt. John

Garzia's company, in Col. Elliott's regiment of artillery." [What apparently was the standard reward of five dollars and all necessary charges was offered.]

The legal advertisement is a notice to debtors and creditors and is similar to those presently published:

"All persons indebted to the estate of Capt. Barnard Eddy, late of Providence, deceased, are requested to make immediate payment. And all who have demands against said estate are requested to bring them in for settlement to Zachariah Eddy, Administrator."

Newspapers are often the only source in which records of births, marriages, and deaths are discovered. Obituaries vary in length and information, but that is better than nothing at all. Reports of civil and criminal court proceedings may disclose genealogical information not available elsewhere. A news account of a will contest discloses family history. The reminiscences of pioneers vary in value as do biographies or autobiographies which may be published in serial form, but not often enough.

A discussion of research in newspapers would not be complete without mentioning the *Boston Transcript* and its publication of a genealogical queries and answers department in excess of 48 years, until the newspaper ceased publication in 1941.

The Hartford Times published queries and answers beginning in 1935, however, the column is now discontinued. There are presently a number of query and answer columns published throughout the United States, and the names and addresses of these can be obtained at any genealogical library.

There are problems involved when research is undertaken in newspapers old or recent. A major handicap is the lack of adequate indexing. It is true that genealogical columns have been indexed partially (e.g., *The Boston Transcript*), and there are name indices to obituaries and other genealogical facts, but there are no complete indices. There are bibliographies which are mentioned in various textbooks and these are also available in libraries. These are a great aid, but research in newspapers, if the search is thorough, requires page by page scrutiny. About the only means of reducing the scope of the research would be to pinpoint the locality where the family or families who are the subject of the research lived and determine if a newspaper or newspapers were published for the period of the search. The availability of newspapers on microfilm saves the time and expense of traveling to distant places to conduct the page by page search.

Genealogical research books include suggestions and sources for newspaper research and it is wise to consult these books.

PRO RELIABILITY

1. Legal advertising and published notices of legal significance are usually correct, subject to printers' errors. Moreover, if a notice or advertisement has been published more than once, there is the added probability that any error, if one had occurred, will have been detected and corrected.

2. If the newspaper account indicates that the news item is based on personal knowledge of someone, this tends to establish credibility.

3.   If the newspaper is published in a small community and this is true especially during the colonial and post colonial period, the personnel of the newspaper are capable of correcting mistakes before publication. Large cities such as New York, Boston, Philadelphia, and other populated centers must be eliminated as the possibility of personal knowledge lessens as cities grow.

4.   If the newspaper is not a daily publication, and in the early days they were not, except in large cities, there is bound to be more time for writing and editing a weekly newspaper. This should result in more accurate reporting, but is no total guarantee that this is so.

5.   Newspaper reporters, editors, and newspaper personnel were not (and are not) careless enough to wilfully publish lies or libelous news, and risk legal liability.

6.   A citizen who would maliciously aid and abet the publication of false news was (and is) very much in the minority.

7.   In regard to genealogy included in queries and answers columns, many of those who contributed were (and are) competent and respected genealogists, both amateurs and professionals. Each case must be judged on its merits. Some of the contributors to these genealogical columns included references to the source where they obtained information. These references may be examined and interpreted.

CONTRA RELIABILITY

1.   Newspaper information is hearsay evidence. The reporter and editor usually did not possess personal knowledge of the facts — they depended on what they "heard said" by another person or persons.

2.   None of the persons involved are alive today to be questioned in regard to the truth or falsity of the newspaper account.

3.   Printers as well as reporters and editors committed mistakes, and typographical and other errors were and always will be with us. *The Placer Times*, Sacramento City, California, August 18, 1849, reported the death of Ambrose P. Sherwood of Charlotte, Vermont, age 21 years; in the same issue of the newspaper, he was referred to as Ambrose P. *Sherman*. Then there is the obvious mistake: "Mrs. T.J. Murphy will celebrate her 48th birthday Sunday. She has been a resident of Springfield for 57 years."

4.   There are honest mistakes too, and if the newspaper corrects or retracts them, not much space is allowed; and the type is small.

CONCLUSION

Information found in newspapers should be verified, if possible, by additional research in other records, such as Bible or family records, land, probate and other court records.

If more than one newspaper was published contemporaneously in the same or nearby locality, a comparison of the facts reported in all the newspapers is advisable.

PART IV

SIMPLIFIED RULES OF EVIDENCE

CHAPTER 21

RULES OF EVIDENCE APPLIED TO GENEALOGY

That which no sane mind would believe at all does not rise to the dignity of evidence; and a belief in something that no sane man would believe is evidence of insanity.
> *Taylor v. McClintock (Arkansas Supreme Court, 1908)*
> *87 Arkansas Reports 243, 112 S. W. Reporter 405, 414.*

Mere suspicion, of course, can not be considered as evidence, no matter how aroused.
> *Craig v. Citizens (Indiana 1940)*
> *26, N. E. 2d, 1006, 1011.*

"Evidence" means testimony, writings, material objects, or other things presented to the senses that are offered to prove the existence or nonexistence of a fact.
> *Section 140, California Evidence Code, (1965)*

The previous chapters of this book are concerned with informal rules which are satisfactory for the research of amateur and family genealogists. A professional genealogist or a nonprofessional who does not accept a fee for his research, and who is desirous of fully documenting genealogy will be concerned with compiling pedigrees which conform to the rules of evidence. If the pedigree is to be compiled as evidence in court involving heirship or probate proceedings, the genealogy must comply with the technical rules of evidence and may be prepared by either the professional, qualified non-professional, or a lawyer-genealogist. However, some genealogists compile pedigrees with the same standard of documentation even though the genealogy is not for presentation in a court proceeding. Part IV of this book is for the genealogist whether amateur, professional, or qualified nonprofessional whose research is as carefully and capably documented as if for presentation in court.

Why should genealogists be concerned with rules of evidence if not compiling genealogy for a court proceeding? It is important for a universal body of rules to be established in order for genealogists to interpret genealogical information with some uniformity. This uniformity has been lacking in the past, each genealogist applying reasons or rules for accepting or rejecting genealogical information and often without adequate reasons for deciding whether facts are reliable or unreliable. In other words every genealogist "is a law unto him or herself." With a system of rules for guidance, there is less chance of error in judging the truth or falsity of genealogical facts.

Individuals who compile genealogies which are to be documented according to the rules of evidence must realize that there are five types of pedigrees, namely:

1. *The Biological or Genetic Pedigree* which, if compiled, would constitute genealogy conclusively proved to an absolute certainty or proof of the parentage of the child or children in each generation of the pedigree. Unfortunately, such a pedigree has never been compiled and never will be. There is a limited exception in the instance of the birth of a child to a mother. If a witness is present and observed the delivery of the child, that witness possesses personal knowledge of the identity of the mother (but not the father), and if that witness testified in a court proceeding and the judge or jury believed the testimony of the witness, that is as close to "conclusive proof" as you can hope for. With the passage of years, the witness may not be able to identify the child who was born twenty or thirty years ago. The mother may or may not know of the delivery or immediate identity of the child, so technically she is not as desirable a witness as the observer. Fingerprints and footprints of babies in recent years have aided identification. The mother should know who fathered the child, but it is surprising how many court proceedings involve that issue, and how often judges and juries decide not to believe the mother. Therefore, paternity is always open to question. But genealogists are rarely concerned with the present. The skill and resourcefulness of genealogists are tested when all witnesses are unavailable due to the passage of time and records remain as the only source of information.

2. *The Legal Pedigree* or the genealogy compiled for presentation in a court proceeding. This type of pedigree is fully documented for every fact stated in a compilation and is based on a *preponderance or greater weight of the evidence.* The legal pedigree is not, however, conclusive proof and never can be in a civil lawsuit involving heirship or in probate proceedings, and before it can be considered as evidence its admissibility must be decided by the trial judge. This type of pedigree will be discussed as the main feature of the *rules of evidence.*

3. *The Historical Pedigree.* Some genealogists compile historical pedigrees with the same skill and care and with as much documentation as the legal pedigree, however, the documentation is based on printed sources rather than official records. In order for a historical pedigree to be introduced and admitted into evidence in court, a proper foundation (or reasons) for its admissibility must be presented. This may require a qualified genealogist to testify to reasons why the pedigree should be admitted as evidence for the consideration of a judge or jury. It is desirable to conform to the rules of evidence in compiling the historical pedigree, therefore, the discussion of the rules of evidence which follows will be of interest to genealogists and record searchers.

4. *The Traditional Pedigree* is a "mish-mash" of printed sources of dubious value and oral statements presumably passed from one generation to another. No doubt some of the information is true, but the documentation is faulty, inadequate or nonexistent. Unfortunately, a tradition begins with the imagination of a member of the family and like a snowball rolling down hill grows to such proportions that subsequent generations accept it as true.

5. *The Legendary Pedigree* may be written or oral, but documentation is lacking or totally inadequate. This is the bottom line of genealogy. The present facts stated in the pedigree are often true, but after a few generations, they develop into legend, and become the worst example of pedigree fiction — the pedigrees which purport to trace an individual's ancestry back to Adam and Eve. There are no records to support this type of a pedigree. If printed or published sources are cited they cannot be verified by reference to authentic records, and the interpretation of the source references are not correctly or logically interpreted. Anyone who presents such a pedigree as correct is required to prove it, and it isn't possible to meet that burden of proof.

EVIDENCE DEFINED

Evidence is information or facts. The evidence may be true or false, but it is something which the intellect must weigh and consider before deciding whether the information is reliable or unreliable and whether it should be accepted or rejected. Evidence means testimony, writings, material objects, or other things presented to the senses that are offered to prove the existence or nonexistence of a fact.

ADMISSIBILITY OF EVIDENCE

The fact that evidence is ruled by a court as "admissible" does not indicate or mean that it is true or that it is "proof." In a court proceeding the words "admissible" and "admissibility" are confusing, but the definition of these words is explained to jurors. There are some types of evidence which are prejudicial to a party to a lawsuit (such as conviction of a crime), or it may not be related to the controversy at all, or it may be repetitive or cumulative, or evidence may be of a nature which would arouse the sympathy or antipathy toward the plaintiff or the defendant in a lawsuit. Therefore, the law provides that evidence must be "screened" or decided whether it is admissible or not. Sometimes this screening process is done in the jury's absence, to prevent the possibility of prejudice or bias which might occur if improper evidence was disclosed. The trial judge decides the question of admissibility or nonadmissibility. If the trial is before a judge without a jury, the judge still decides whether evidence is admissible or not; and the judge is supposed to disregard any evidence which should not have been presented to him. Evidence which is ruled admissible, may or may not be true, that is why "admissibility" is not "proof." The jury decides whether the evidence or facts are true or false. Furthermore, what lawyers say representing clients in court is not evidence.

A genealogist should act in the capacity of an informal, one person judge and jury, and ignore the "admissibility" rule and consider all of the facts. After analyzing them, the genealogist should be able to judge whether the information is reliable or unreliable and either accept or reject the evidence, in whole or in part.

In court proceedings, the law provides for the exclusion of certain types of evidence. For example, the general rule is that "hearsay evidence" is not admissible, but there are exceptions to the "hearsay rule" which will be discussed in another chapter. Obviously there are occasions when prejudicial evidence would cause an unjust or wrong decision or verdict. Therefore, the reason for the admissibility rule is to prevent miscarriages of justice. In presenting this simplified version of the rules of evidence, such technicalities are ignored. If the research is to aid a lawyer to present genealogical evidence in a court proceeding, the interested party's lawyer will decide what he believes is or is not admissible as evidence, and quite often he will be overruled by the trial judge, but that is not a problem for the genealogist. But it is a reason why a genealogist should at least consider all of the evidence or information discovered from any and all sources. Usually a lawyer will instruct a genealogist before the research commences in regard to the admissibility problem.

PROOF DISTINGUISHED FROM EVIDENCE

The word "Proof" is not uniformly defined by genealogists. To some it means "absolute proof," or "conclusive proof." In fact, insofar as genealogical research is concerned, "absolute proof" or "conclusive proof" of ancestry is not possible. Anyone who has acted as a juror or who has attended a trial has heard the trial judge or attorneys state these or similar words ". . . there are few things in life which can be proven to an absolute certainty."

In genealogical research if a pedigree or heirship controversy is the subject of a trial, the rule that is followed is simply this: "A pedigree or ancestry is established according to a preponderance or greater weight of the evidence." That, of course, is not conclusive or absolute proof, as this is not possible. [Refer to the index for the subjects of paternity and maternity.]

The principle that genealogical facts or evidence do not require absolute or conclusive proof, but instead ancestry may be established according to a "preponderance or greater weight of the evidence," applies to civil and not criminal trials.

There is a tendency for those interested in genealogy to confuse civil controversies regarding pedigrees with criminal trials. In a criminal trial, it is necessary for the prosecution to prove the guilt of the accused "beyond a reasonable doubt," and that is much more difficult than establishing genealogical facts according to the preponderance or greater weight of the evidence.

APPLICATION OF THE PRINCIPAL OF "PREPONDERANCE
OR GREATER WEIGHT OF THE EVIDENCE"

Preponderance or greater weight of the evidence means that in order to establish facts it is necessary to produce sufficient reliable evidence which satisfies the conscience and convinces whoever is considering the evidence that the facts are believable. Absolute proof, or conclusive proof, is not required to establish a preponderance or greater weight of the evidence.

In other words, it is simply using common sense and intelligence. The evidence must also be "substantial," quality and not quantity is what counts. One witness may be more believable than ten whose testimony may create some doubt in the minds of jurors.

Substantial evidence clearly implies that such evidence must be of ponderable legal significance. Obviously, the word cannot be deemed synonymous with 'any' evidence. It must be reasonable in nature, credible, and of solid value; it must actually be 'substantial' proof of the essentials which the law requires in a particular case.[1]

". . . Inherently improbable testimony [or facts] is not substantial evidence."[2]

The greater number of books, documents, or other records do not solely establish a "preponderance or greater weight of the evidence." It is entirely possible that one family genealogy may be more valuable than a dozen other volumes — especially when it is realized that frequently more recent compilations are copied from earlier editions of the same family or subject, and continue to perpetuate the mistakes of the earlier volumes. It should always be stressed that it is quality and not quantity which is the controlling factor in judging the reliability of genealogical evidence or facts.

In determining the value and credibility of evidence, witnesses are to be weighed, not numbered, and the term 'preponderance of evidence' generally signifies that which satisfies the conscience and carries conviction to an intelligent mind. . .

While the term 'preponderance' literally means to outweigh, yet one witness whose testimony carried conviction outweighs, for judicial purposes, a dozen who tell a story which is incredible.[3]

In applying the principle of preponderance of the evidence, a genealogist will be substituting books, records, and documents instead of the testimony or statements of witnesses, unless the witnesses are living.

THE FORMS OF TYPES OF EVIDENCE

1. *The testimony of witnesses.* Unfortunately, it is often too late for testimonial evidence to establish facts relating to pedigrees. However, there is an exception to this, as it is sometimes necessary and possible for an expert witness such as a qualified genealogist to testify as to the reliability or unreliability of a family genealogy, county or local history, the genealogical significance of documents and other writings. The genealogist's testimony would be admissible as "opinion evidence."

2. *Documents and various types of writing.* These may be official records, also known as public records, or they may be private records. This category would also include gravestones and other monumental inscriptions. Also included in this group of records are some books (e.g., family genealogies, county and local histories), manuscripts and typescripts in private possession or in public and private libraries and in federal, state, and local archives.

3. *Personal Inspection.* A genealogist does this all of the time, but what is intended here is personal inspection of the original records and objects. Under supervision of the court or one of its officers, juries are escorted to various sites for personal inspection of evidence which is not possible to bring to court. If a pedigree is involved, the court may send or take the jury to the cemetery to read or inspect a tombstone or monument which is impractical to bring to the courthouse. A photographic copy or other reproduction of a gravestone is usually acceptable, but it is necessary (unless by agreement of the adverse party) for the photographer to testify that it is a true and correct photograph of the object.

4. *Real Evidence.* This applies to tangible objects which are offered in evidence for the consideration of the jury, such as documents, books, photographs, and records, motion pictures, all of which may or may not be the originals.

5. *Judicial Notice.* This notice is the knowledge of facts which the law judicially recognizes. Historical facts are an example of this type. A trial judge, if it was relevant, would take judicial notice of the fact that George Washington was a president of the United States without any extraneous proof.

PRIMARY EVIDENCE – THE BEST EVIDENCE RULE

What the law contemplates as "primary evidence" or "best evidence" is the original object – the original letter, the original last will and testament, the original of any type of evidence. Unfortunately, many genealogists and historians do not always understand just what is primary evidence. If a genealogist or historian goes to the register and examines a book of deeds or mortgages, the deeds, mortgages, or other documents recorded in these books are not primary evidence; they are copies of the originals which have been returned to the grantee or mortgagee. If the same person goes to the register of probate for the purpose of searching the probate records and he consults the record volume of "Wills," that is not an original record. If the file of the estate is still available, the original will is supposed to be in that file or bundle of documents. If it is, supposedly it is the original and that would be insofar as the law is concerned, "primary evidence."

There is a major problem which fortunately the law, in its wisdom, provides a remedy. All of the foregoing records are "hearsay evidence," because the testator is dead, because the will was probated in 1739, the witnesses to the will are dead, and the lawyer who prepared the will – assuming the testator or testatrix possessed the good sense to consult a lawyer – is dead also. Therefore, these records are not the best primary evidence, but they are admissible in court proceedings. If it is not feasible to cart the record volumes or probate files to the courtroom, the judge will rule that certified copies are admissible, unless counsel for the opposing litigant demands the actual files and record volumes be brought over by the clerk or recorder. This usually does not happen, as there is an agreement between attorneys that certified copies will be admissible.

The reason for "Primary Evidence and Best Evidence Rule" is that experience throughout the centuries has demonstrated that there is less chance of fraud, forgery, mistake, and dishonesty if original records are produced.

SECONDARY EVIDENCE

Secondary evidence is a substitute for the production of the original and is only permitted when it is impossible to produce the original or extremely inconvenient or impractical for the custodian of the original records to present them in court. Frequently in court proceedings, counsel for the plaintiff and defendant agree or stipulate the copies of secondary evidence may be substituted as evidence for the originals.

THE MODERN VERSION OF PRIMARY EVIDENCE – BEST EVIDENCE

Originally, the only type of evidence included in the interpretation of primary evidence or best evidence was original documents. Over the years, this rule has been modified and includes not only documents, but various kinds of records, as well as chattels, such as jewelry and other objects. An original genealogical record in a family Bible would be considered primary evidence and would satisfy the "Best Evidence Rule," but it would be necessary for a witness to testify that it was the family Bible and the record in it was that of the family, and that it had been continually in the custody of the family or one of its members. If it was not in possession of the family, a genealogist and no doubt a lawyer would claim that it was an ancient document, if it was over thirty years old and in a "proper custody." Proper custody indicates a member of the family.

There are numerous family Bible records in the military pension files and service records in the National Archives, and there is no doubt that this is a proper custody, as these files are official records, and the Bible records sent in by a family member are part of that official file.

If a family deposited family records (especially Bible records) which were compiled over thirty years ago, in a library, it should be possible to successfully argue that the library was a proper custody.

Genealogists who haunt second-hand book stores searching for and buying old Bibles which include family records, may find it difficult to convince a lawyer, judge, or jury that a bookstore is a place of proper custody. I know of a genealogist who has been successful in accomplishing this. In more than one instance, the names of the persons recorded in the family Bible record have also been included in family genealogies. Under certain rules of evidence, some family genealogies are admissible in contested court proceedings and by connecting the entries in the family Bible with the published family genealogy, the result is primary evidence which satisfies the best evidence rule.

The practical course of conduct for a genealogist is to obtain legal possession of the Bible record and worry about the authenticity of the records and the technicalities later.

"BEST EVIDENCE" AS A VERNACULAR TERM

Modernly, the use of the term "best evidence" often does not refer to the Best Evidence Rule at all. On these occasions, what is meant is that the best evidence that can be produced is the testimony of a witness (which does not apply to the original rule) or some other form of evidence – as long as it is not an unverified statement copied from Virkus' *Compendium of American Genealogy* or similar printed volume.

EVIDENCE MUST BE RELEVANT

Logical relevancy is that there must be a relationship between the evidence and the facts to be proved. If the problem is establishing the ancestry of Richard Roe, it would be irrelevant to present or consider facts concerning the John Doe family unless facts regarding John Doe would cause it to be possible to establish the ancestry of Richard Roe.

Legal relevancy means that the proposed evidence must be of probative value to justify admitting it into evidence. If Richard Roe was born in New York in 1750, it would be of no probative value to consider evidence that there was a Richard Roe born in 1640 and try to convince anyone that because of the same name that the Richard born in 1850 was a descendant of the Richard born in 1640. The evidence is too remote and certainly of no probative value.

EVIDENCE MUST BE MATERIAL

Material evidence is that which will prove facts which are proper and material to the problem which requires solving. It is immaterial evidence and not admissible if of a character or nature which has nothing to do with facts which must be established. If you were attempting to establish the parentage of George Washington, it would be immaterial to discuss or consider evidence of the parentage of George III.

COMPETENCY OF EVIDENCE

This term is another with a double meaning. Originally it meant the competency of a witness to testify. In centuries past, a party to a lawsuit (plaintiff or defendant) was not a competent witness to testify in his own behalf. The term also applies to mental competency. Modernly, because of custom and usage, the term is descriptive of the character, value, or admissibility of the evidence offered.

DIRECT AND CIRCUMSTANTIAL EVIDENCE

Evidence may be either direct or circumstantial. *Direct evidence* acts on the mind in a clear and direct manner. A hypothetical example of direct evidence is a provision in the last will and testament of John Doe which states: "I give to my son John Doe, Jr., the sum of $5,000. . . ." There is nothing indirect about that gift. The mind is not required to spend any time figuring the meaning of that sentence.

Circumstantial or indirect evidence requires the mind to juggle the facts to ascertain their meaning. For example if you visited the cemetery in Cheshire, Massachusetts, there is (or was some years ago) the gravestone of Preserved Fish. Assume his grave is located in what appears to be a family plot surrounded by a fence, and there are a number of other persons buried there by the name of Fish. This is circumstantial or indirect evidence that this is the Fish family burial site, and they are related. Because there is no direct evidence which states a relationship, it will be necessary to search vital, probate, and land records for the direct evidence which will disclose the relationship of the Fish buried in that cemetery.

"Evidence is none the less effective because it is circumstantial, if it be consistent, connected and conclusive."[4]

". . . The law makes no distinction between direct evidence of a fact and evidence of circumstances from which the existence of the fact may be inferred."[5]

AUTHENTICATION OF DOCUMENTS

1. *The Ancient Document Rule.* An "ancient document" is a paper, map, book, document, or other writing over thirty years of age. Some examples are legal documents, such as wills, leases, deeds — including recitals in deeds or other documents, family Bible records, diaries, letters, or a genealogical sampler. (Family genealogies are discussed elsewhere in this book.)

In order for ancient documents to be admissible as evidence, they must be authenticated by complying with the following requirements: a) Age. b) Unsuspicious appearance, such as lack of erasures or other features which would arouse suspicion. c) The nature of the contents of the document must be logical, material, and relevant to the controversy or problem. d) The custody or possession of the document or other record through the years must be explained, and it must be a "natural" or "proper" custody, such as in the possession of a member of the family, family law firm, or other authorized person or corporation. If it is a record in a family Bible, the natural or proper custody would be possession by a member of the family. An exception to this would be if the family record was filed as evidence in official records, such as pension or military service records, or in a court proceeding — this would be a "proper custody." e) Signatures and handwriting are subject to scrutiny and the services of a document examiner may be required to offer an opinion as to the authenticity of the paper (such as age and substance), contents, signature and handwriting, printing or modernly typewriting. f) If a seal is affixed to the document, this is subject to expert opinion evidence.

All of the foregoing conditions must be satisfied before the document is admitted into evidence and then its truth or credibility will be judged by the judge or jury — or by a genealogist as part of the compiling of a genealogy.

There are some courts which admit ancient documents according to more liberal rules — this is true especially in an uncontested trial. However, in a contested proceeding if the trial judge rules an ancient document with little or no proof that it is authentic and few or none of the six procedural features mentioned have not been observed, there is a duty to conduct a rigorous cross examination of the party offering the ancient document, as cross examination by skilled counsel is one of the most effective tests for truth.

A genealogist should abide by the six procedural rules above mentioned, and this is possible for an experienced genealogist to accomplish, except for qualifying as a document examiner.

2. *Authentication — By Notary Public or Officials.* Original documents, the execution or signature of which have been acknowledged by a notary public or other qualified officer, do not require further authentication inasmuch as the official acknowledgement (or verification if the document is under oath) is proof of its authenticity. Therefore, such documents (less than thirty years old) are admissible without any preliminary proof, but are subject to scrutiny by the adverse party (plaintiff or defendant) and cross examination of the party offering the document which could be a deed, lease, will, power of attorney, contract, etc. Also, it is in order for a document examiner to inspect the document(s) prior to trial testing for age, forgery, or other signs of defects, using scientific instruments such as microscopes, ultra violet ray light, special photographic film, and then testify as an expert witness stating his opinion regarding the validity or

authenticity of the document(s).

3. *Authentication of Documents* --- Certified Copies. A certified, exemplified copy of a document is usually admitted into evidence with nothing more than inspection of the certificate of the officer, such as county clerk, clerk of a court, or recorder of deeds. However, if the document is from a foreign country or from another state, some jurisdictions require an additional certificate from an additional officer, such as the secretary of state, certifying that the officer issuing the certified copy is the duly qualified and acting officer he represents to be.

A certified copy is not always the "best evidence." There is no completely reliable substitute for the personal examination of an original will or other document. While the possibility of the issuance of a fraudulent or forged certified copy is not likely, it has happened. When an original is personally examined, often many features are disclosed which might not appear clearly on a photocopy or a print made from a photographic negative. Obtaining a print from a photographic negative is superior to modern photocopying methods — especially if special film and appropriate filters are utilized which may disclose faint writing, erasures, or crossed out lines or words. Thus, modern photographic techniques may even disclose original document material covered by more recent writings.

In the past, when certified copies were handwritten or typed, there was a greater chance of error due to mistakes of copiers. The photocopying process does eliminate that; unfortunately, photocopies are not always entirely readable.

There is one technical rule which affects not only documentary evidence, but also any other types of evidence which involve ancestry, pedigrees, heirship, or any similar subject relating to genealogy, and that is that to be admissible, the evidence must have existed before any controversy arose.

Notes and References

1. *Lee v. Helmco* (1962) 199 C.A.2d 820, 833.
2. *Cucuk v. Payne* (1956) 140 California Appellate 2nd 881, 883.
3. *Foulke v. Thalmessinger* (New York 1894) 8 Miscellaneous Reports 445, 447.
4. *State v. Samuels*, 6 Pennewill's Delaware Reports 36, 39.
5. *Lancaster v. State*, 204 Arkansas Reports 176, 178.

CHAPTER 22

HEARSAY EVIDENCE

"The attestation of the witness must be to what he knows and not that only which he hath heard, for a mere hearsay is no Evidence, for 'tis his knowledge that must direct the Court and Jury in the Judgment of the Fact and not his mere credulity which is very uncertain in several persons. . . ."[1]

Baron Gilbert, 1754

"Types of Evidence and their value — (3) Hearsay, that which one has been told, or family tradition, is not evidence and cannot be accepted. While it may furnish clues for the genealogical researcher, and so be helpful to the person preparing the lineage paper originally, it is not to be considered in any way by the verifier."[2]

Is That Lineage Right? 1958

If the above mentioned quotations were true, it would not be possible for genealogists to compile or verify any pedigrees or family histories whatsoever, because the records and publications they search are hearsay evidence sources.[3]

Some examples of hearsay evidence or information are: family records (including family Bible records); church records; vital records of births, marriages, and deaths; deeds, last wills and testaments; court records, census records, pension files, military service records, and other official records; all manuscripts, local and county histories, all family genealogies whether published in book form or printed, mimeographed, typewritten, or published in the photocopied format. Any other record or published source you can think of,

189

including oral statements of family members are examples of hearsay information, *unless those persons possess personal knowledge of the genealogical facts concerning the family.*[4] How many people are living today who possess personal knowledge regarding facts relating to their family which occurred in 1700?

Fortunately, those quotations of 1754 and 1958 are not true or correct.[5] Also, there are exceptions to the hearsay evidence rule which permits information from Bible records and all of the other sources mentioned above to be genealogically and legally acceptable by compliance with several specific conditions which will be discussed.

It is extremely important to genealogists to understand the scope and limitation of hearsay evidence in their daily research, whether in or out of court. An adequate definition will be of assistance.

HEARSAY EVIDENCE DEFINED

> *"The term* hearsay *is used with reference to that which is* written, as well as to that which is *spoken*; and, in its legal sense, it denotes that kind of evidence, which does not derive its value solely from the credit to be given to the witness himself, but rests also, in part, on the veracity and competency of some other person."*[6] [Emphasis added]

The key word in the above definition is "written" rather than "spoken," as it is written or published records and books and official or public records which are the major sources genealogists must search rather than oral statements. Anyone who is alive and speaks of his genealogy has no personal knowledge of his ancestry. He is repeating what he has been told and that is hearsay evidence. But patience will be rewarded, as there is a remedy to cure the defects of hearsay statements or evidence whether written or oral.

THE REASON FOR OBJECTIONS TO HEARSAY EVIDENCE

The general rule is that hearsay evidence is not reliable or trustworthy because of the lack of personal knowledge regarding spoken or written records. For example, the witnesses to a will, the testator who signed it, the lawyer who prepared it for his client in 1723, have all passed on to what they believed would be a better life. None of them are here to testify regarding the signing or execution of the will. The clerk who filed the will and the judge who admitted it to probate have also gone to their reward.

In the register of probate, a will is examined which purports to be the last will and testament of a remote ancestor whom the records disclosed died in 1723, but there is no person alive to authenticate the will or tell you anything about that document at this late date. There is nobody to testify under oath, and there is no opportunity to cross-examine the witnesses to the will or the attorney who prepared it. There is no opportunity for confrontation, therefore, it is not possible to observe the demeanor or appearance of the witnesses, attorney, or testator. It is not possible to know if the testator read the will. If he (or she) "signed by mark" or a cross or "X" mark, it is possible someone read the will to the testator or testatrix. Then all of this causes the genealogist to wonder if the "maker" of that will was mentally competent and realized what provisions were included therein.

But as intimated, the law has provided a remedy for this dilemma to the advantage and benefit of genealogists, historians, lawyers, and litigants.[7]

THE REMEDY: EXCEPTIONS TO THE HEARSAY EVIDENCE RULE

The law is not as stupid as Dickens' character Sgt. Bumble said. The principle objection to hearsay evidence being that it is not trustworthy. If that objection can be diminished or overcome, why shouldn't the courts (and genealogists) rule that it is admissible, remembering that admissibility is not proof of truth, but the opportunity for genealogists, judges, and juries to consider the evidence and decide if it is reliable or unreliable? That is how exceptions to the hearsay rule developed over the centuries.

Because facts or evidence of ancestry cannot be established without resorting to hearsay evidence, the following rules or conditions were adopted which would permit hearsay evidence to be considered and a decision could be made to accept or reject the facts.

1. If there is a special guarantee of trustworthiness that the evidence or facts are true.
2. If there is no other means of obtaining the information required to establish facts — then what is generally referred to as the "necessity principle" is satisfied . . . e.g., all of the witnesses are dead.
3. If the evidence or information originated before any controversy arose (the technical term for this is *"ante litem motam"* — very useful to know if delivering a speech) or if the evidence or facts existed prior to the time it is presently needed . . . then hearsay evidence or information is admissible and may be considered subject to cross-examination, the test for credibility or believability, and if the evidence survives this, it is possible for a judge, jury, or genealogist to decide that the facts are established according to a preponderance or greater weight of the evidence.

SPECIFIC EXCEPTIONS TO THE HEARSAY EVIDENCE RULE (NOT LISTED IN ORDER OF IMPORTANCE)

1. *Official Records, Official Statements, Also Referred to As Public Records*

Trustworthiness Principle: Records in this category or exception are considered trustworthy because public officers acting under oath, bonded, are duty bound to retain proper custody of the records, maintain them, and protect them. They cannot vouch for the truth of the contents of the documents or records, but there is a presumption (which may be rebutted) that generally people who file or record documents concerning their business or personal affairs do not falsify or forge them. The human element must always be considered and in criminal proceedings and civil litigation, it would be foolish to believe that litigants and their witnesses are always truthful.

Necessity Principle: If it is the only source of information and that is usually the situation (e.g., the last will and testament), then the necessity is obvious.

Origination of the Evidence: It must be before litigation or some other controversy arose.

Official or Public Records includes *Land Records* (deeds, mortgages, leases, notices of action or the fancy term *"lis pendens,"* copies of judgments or decrees of court, decrees of distribution of estates, and miscellaneous records. Vital records — births, marriages and deaths are included. *Court records:* Included are civil court records such as probate and civil litigation, and criminal proceedings in federal, state, county and local jurisdictions. State census records are an additional official source.

In addition to the foregoing, a special category should be considered as part of the federal record system and the principal official records (in addition to the court records) are the various census, military, pension, naturalization, and administrative records of various government departments.

The above listing is not represented to be complete, but is offered merely for the purpose of providing some common examples of official records.

2. *Dying Declarations*

Trustworthiness: A person who is dying ordinarily would not resort to falsehood, presumably because of the fear of divine punishment, if a religious person, and if not, it is a solemn occasion when the most disreputable person would be inclined to be truthful. If the person does not die at that time, then it is not a dying declaration.

Necessity: He is dead; the necessity is obvious. This is assuming that the deceased was the only source of the information he imparted.

Origination of the Evidence: If the dying declaration was uttered concerning facts related to a controversy, the declaration to be considered must have occurred before the dispute or litigation arose.

An example: Assume a man is seriously ill and appears to be dying. He says in the presence of one or more witnesses: "I am dying. My name is John Doe. My wife Mary Doe lives in Woodbury (in the state where he is dying). I am the father of two children, David Doe and Joseph Doe." John Doe dies immediately. The witnesses (or at least one of them) notes the date, time, and place, and what the deceased said. Hopefully he writes these facts in some form as soon as possible. That would qualify as a "dying declaration" in some jurisdictions, but there are some states which refuse to consider dying declarations except in criminal cases. A genealogist would not be bound by this strict application of the rule unless a court proceeding was involved. A written record of a dying declaration may be discovered in court records or other sources in the form of testimony, deposition, affidavit, or in a newspaper report.

3. *General Reputation*

To consider the general reputation in a community as evidence in a court proceeding or in solving genealogical problems may seem like resorting to gossip, but the "general reputation" that is admissible is not in the nature of scandal.

There are a number of occasions when it is necessary to introduce evidence of the general reputation of persons in court proceedings. Some examples of these occasions are to establish birth, death, marriage, identity of a person (such as the individual's name, place of residence), or perhaps the legitimacy or illegitimacy of children. Often unusual results derive from this type of evidence with court proceedings revealing facts previously not known or discovered; and it is surprising to learn how often general reputation, which of course is hearsay, becomes an important issue in litigation.

Lord Kenyon said that "Evidence of reputation, upon general points, is receivable, because all mankind being interested therein, it is natural to suppose that they may be conversant with the subjects, and that they should discourse together about them, having all the same means of information."[8]

There are no doubt more lawsuits involving general reputation to establish the fact of marriage than any other reason for introducing evidence of this specific exception to the hearsay rule. Due to the lack of marriage records in many states and especially the recognition of common law marriage which did not require records, general reputation in the community that a man and woman were husband and wife was the only means of establishing the fact of their marriage.[9]

General reputation for land ownership and boundaries is another facet of this subject which results in lawsuits and because family rights are involved, there are often genealogical facts disclosed in the court records. This is especially the situation if the land has been in the possession of the family for more than one generation.

Trustworthiness: The principle of law involved in regard to whether or not "general reputation" is trustworthy, is based on the proposition that observation and discussion of the people of the community regarding the fact that is the cause of the controversy, is recognized and accepted as a fact. The example of marriage is probably the most reliable. A man and woman living together, raising a family, perhaps attending church as a family, children attending school as part of a family, and as the years pass, the marriage is deemed a fact. Of course, in contested lawsuits there is cross-examination of witnesses; and that is a protection to prevent error. There are some jurisdictions in which reputation in regard to genealogical facts, such as pedigrees, are not admissible by nonfamily members. Reputation for marriage is recognized everywhere as admissible.

Necessity: The lack of marriage records cause general reputation evidence to be necessary as there is no other means of establishing the fact of marriage, other than the statement of the man and woman. There are occasions when the putative husband and wife are deceased and the children are forced into court to establish their right to inherit the family estate. It may be difficult to justify establishing facts relating to pedigree or ancestry by general reputation. A strict interpretation would require that only members of the family involved are competent witnesses.[10]

Origin of the Evidence: As usual, the fact sought to be established must have originated before any controversy arose.

4. *Declarations Against Interest*

A declaration within this categorical exception to the hearsay evidence rule is one of the rarer type in genealogical importance. It is not often that anyone says anything of importance which would be harmful to that individual's interest or rights. The declaration may be oral or written, and is admissible in a court proceeding subject to these conditions:

a. The person who wrote or said the declaration must be dead, out of the court's jurisdiction, otherwise unavailable such as insane, or some other reason incapable of communicating.

b. The declaration must be against or adverse to his monetary or property interests.

c. That the person possessed competent or correct knowledge of the fact or facts of his declaration or statement.

d. That the declarant in stating what he said or wrote was not motivated for any probable reason to falsify the facts.

Trustworthiness: The natural conduct of a person is not to say or write anything against his monetary or property interests. If he does so to his prejudice, it is presumably true.

Necessity: Death causes the necessity for admissibility of the declaration and the written statement or the testimony of the person who heard the declaration are admissible. Although death is usually the reason for necessity of the evidence, unavailability of a witness is another reason.

Origin of the Declaration: It would be unusual for a person to declare against his interest if he was due to gain by remaining silent. However, someone else may benefit by the declaration against interest, and in that case, it should be written or spoken before a controversy arose.

Example of a Declaration Against Interest: "I borrowed $5,000 from my grandfather Richard Roe. He didn't ask me to sign anything. If I don't repay him, I won't demand anything from his estate after he dies." (signed) Woe Roe. Assume he writes this in a letter to someone, or states it orally, and now is dead. His administrator or executor tries to claim Woe's share of Richard Roe's estate. It would be a miracle if any sum is recovered.

This is another instance of the value of court records as that is probably the only source this information will be disclosed, unless a newspaper account of the court proceedings was available.

5. *Business Entries and Records*

The types of records are the business records of corporations, partnerships, sole proprietorships and other small businesses. If a family business is involved, there is a better chance of genealogical data in the records. Church records also come in this category and registers of baptisms, marriages, burials, and other church records should provide valuable genealogical data.

Trustworthiness: Due to practical reasons, the records are supposedly correct. In earlier periods it is possible that the clergy, rather than a clerk, wrote the entries himself. If a commercial business was operated by a sole proprietor or a family, there shouldn't be any motive to falsify records of genealogical significance. Modernly it is alleged that some businesses maintain two sets of books because of tax liability. If there is truth to this statement, both sets of books should be examined, but it would be unusual to find more than one set anciently or modernly. There are several conditions which must be complied with before the records are admissible in court proceedings. These conditions will aid a genealogist or record searcher in judging the reliability of the records whether there is a court proceeding involved or not.

a. The person who recorded the entries in the records must testify regarding them, unless deceased or unavailable.

b. The entries in the records must have been written in the ordinary course of business — including church business and at or soon after the time of the transaction or event described in the records.

c. If the person responsible for the records did not write the entry or entries personally, then personal knowledge or observation of the transaction or event (for example a baptism, marriage, or burial) is required. This may be difficult to establish, but fortunately records over thirty years old may qualify as admissible as "ancient document" under the rule by that name.

d. The records produced must be the original entries or a reason must be advanced for copies of the records as secondary evidence.

Necessity: Frequently records in this category are the only source from which the required information may be found. This is particularly true of church registers, entries of baptisms (birth records, if also included), marriages, deaths, and burials, because of the failure of governmental agencies to maintain vital records.

Origin of the Records: The records must be entries which existed before any controversy, if any, arose.

6. *Spontaneous Exclamations* (also erroneously referred to as "Res Gestae" or "things done")

This exception to the hearsay evidence rule is an oral statement or declaration which is uttered because of an occurrence which is shocking or something occurring which is unexpected. Because it is oral, it is not important genealogically unless somehow the exclamation is disclosed in older court proceedings, letters, diaries, or some other written record, such as a newspaper account of a trial or other event.

Trustworthiness: This is due to surprise and individuals are believed to be more likely to speak the truth because of a sudden confrontation, and speak at once without time to consider the effect of the spontaneity of their exclamation or declaration.

Necessity: The exclaimer or declarant is dead or otherwise unavailable.

Origin of the Evidence: The statement or exclamation must have been uttered spontaneously, and therefore, before there was time to falsify or misrepresent any facts, and before a controversy, if any, arose.

Example: A prodigal son returns home after an absence of several years. When he arrives at the family home, he learns that his father is dying. When he is ushered into the bedroom, the father recognizes him in spite of his shabby clothes and starved physique and says: "Welcome home, Joshua, my son," in the presence of witnesses.

All that is needed to aid a genealogist is for one of the witnesses to write an account of this event and what the father said. It would help if a newspaper account of this event was published and that was found, if a letter or other record was not found.

7. *Declarations of Pedigree and Family History*

This exception to the hearsay evidence rule includes evidence regarding birth, marriage, death, and pedigree or ancestry. The technical rule provides that the declaration must be spoken or written by a member of the family. Some jurisdictions will not permit declarations to be admitted if from a neighbor, friend, or an in-law. Another technical rule is that before the evidence or declaration will be admitted in evidence, it is necessary to establish the blood relationship to the declarant. Some jurisdictions or states relaxed this rule so that it was relationship by "blood or marriage." The practical application of this exception insofar as a genealogist is concerned is to accept for consideration declarations of friends, neighbors, business associations, and even strangers, if the facts they know appear credible. Certainly a genealogist who is a stranger to the family often knows more in regard to the ancestry and family history than members of that group.

As usual, when hearsay evidence is involved, the usual conditions must be present:

Trustworthiness: Lord Eldon explained why declarations by a family member are trustworthy in a decision he wrote in 1807:

"Declarations in the family, descriptions in wills, descriptions upon monuments, descriptions in Bibles and registry books, all are admitted upon the principle that they are the natural effusions of a party who must know the truth [regarding family ancestry], and who speaks upon an occasion when his mind stands in an even position, without any temptation to exceed or fall short of the truth.[11]

An early decision by Justice Pearson of North Carolina is representative of the American viewpoint in regard to the trustworthiness of these declarations or statements:

[Pedigree] is a matter about which [the members of a family] are presumed to be particularly interested to ascertain and declare the truth. Everyone from a feeling of nature endeavors to know who his relations are and will seldom declare those to be his kinsmen who are not.[12]

It would be a great experience if it were possible to turn back the "time machine" and listen to an ancestral declaration. Suppose at a family reunion, those attending began to talk regarding family history and genealogy. It would be natural for a family patriarch to say: "My grandfather was Hezekiah Winslow. He was born in 1730, and he married his second cousin Silence Winslow in 1750. They built their house on one of the old town lots and never moved. They had eleven children. My father Obadiah and . . ." This is what Lord Eldon termed "natural effusions," because for what possible reason would this elderly ancestor utter a falsehood? Obviously no motive whatsoever. Assume that after this patriarch dies, one of the Winslows who occupies the house on the old town lot, must remove a defect in the title to the lot he now claims to own, and a lawsuit is the result, and he must establish his pedigree in order to successfully defend his title to the house and lot. Before his ancestry or relationship to Hezekiah Winslow is established, it will be necessary to satisfy all of the requirements of the "declaration of pedigree and family history," orally stated by this ancestor.

Is the Declaration Trustworthy? Yes, according to Lord Eldon and Justice Pearson, and modern statutory and case or court law of the various states.

Is the Declaration Necessary Evidence? Yes, because the old patriarch is dead.

Did the Declaration Antedate the Controversy? Yes.

Judge, jury, lawyers, and the genealogist agree that the declaration is admissible. Of course, it is much preferred if someone immediately or soon after the declaration was spoken, picked up a quill and inkpot and recorded what that ancestor said. If not, someone (one or more) will be able to establish their relationship to the declarant, that person will testify, and the right and title of the descendant to the old town lot and house will be established.

Of all of the exceptions to the hearsay evidence rule, declarations of pedigree and family history are the most important to genealogists, except perhaps the massive number of lawsuits which have involved establishing the fact of marriages. There have been thousands of controversies involving ancestry, legitimacy, and marriage in the courts since 1620, and it has been necessary to establish the facts by introducing declarations of pedigree and family history as evidence in some form. As indicated, the most effective evidence is the declaration in writing.

There is some overlapping for the forms or types of evidence, as a declaration of pedigree and family history may also be classified as an ancient document in some instances; it may be included in other records in addition to official records or private records. It is impossible to list all of the examples; however, family Bible records, letters, diaries, journals, samplers, or other embroidered material, a written manuscript or printed genealogy of the family, if compiled by a member of the family, who obtains the genealogy and family history from other members of the family may be classified as an ancient document.

Genealogies compiled by a researcher for a family do present more than a simple problem as the general rule in court, if the genealogist is not related to the family. A genealogist should ignore these technical rules and do all possible to verify the facts in any family record or published or unpublished genealogy. For some practical rules or information for judging genealogies, refer to the chapter on this subject.

8. *County and Local Histories, and other published records.*

Compilations which include historical and genealogical data are admissible (for consideration) when compiled by disinterested persons. "Disinterested" in this instance means the compiler has no monetary motive or personal interest which would affect the compiler's judgment to favor either side to a controversy, and the book or publication must have been compiled before a controversy, if any, arose. This same type of publication may also qualify as an "Ancient Document."[13]

Published decisions of court proceedings or court reports, legislative journals, session laws, statutes at large, and other official statements or records which are published and printed in book form are hearsay evidence, but are admissible as evidence because they are presumed to be correct copies of the original records. This presumption is rebuttable. However, the original records of all of the foregoing are hearsay evidence also, but the original records or documents are not subject to the hazard of printers errors.[14] With the advent of photoduplication science, such as microfilming and other photographic reproduction, chance of error is greatly lessened; and microfilms are admissible in court proceedings if authenticated as true and correct copies of the original records or documents.[15]

9. *Oral Genealogy* (When admissible, it is as a Declaration of Pedigree and Family History.)

An individual is permitted to relate genealogy regarding his family as a declaration of pedigree and family history as previously discussed; it is admissible as hearsay evidence and then subject to believability. There is no provable record in regard to how many previous generations of ancestry a human being is capable of memorizing, especially if a detailed record of names, relationships, dates and places of births, marriages and deaths are disclosed.

The human memory is not as dependable as a person's written record, and the more time that elapses between the event or fact and the time of an oral recitation, the greater the possibility of error.

Justice Joseph Henry Lumpkin of the Georgia Supreme Court wrote his opinion in regard to human memory in one of his court decisions:

How frail and fallible is memory! History records a few examples, of men of whom it may be said, that whatever knowledge they acquired, either sensible or intellectual, remained as indelibly fixed upon their minds, as if it was engraved on a rock.

Seneca reports of Hortensius, that he could repeat at night, the prices and purchases of every article sold at auction throughout the day; and of himself, that he repeated two thousand names in the same order in which they were spoken to him; and it is told of Cyrus, that he could salute all the soldiers in his vast army by their names, respectively; and of an Englishman, that he recited verbatim, one of Voltaire's great poems, having heard it read once by its author to Frederick of Prussia.

But these are rare instances. Usually, the impressions made on the memory resemble much more the traceless track of the arrow through the air, than the enduring hieroglyphics upon the pyramids and obelisks of ancient Egypt. *Many memories are mere sieves. And I would sooner trust the smallest slip of paper for truth, than the strongest and most retentive memory ever bestowed on mortal man.* I once preferred a claim in behalf of one of the frontier settlers of middle Georgia, for revolutionary services, rendered as a guide to the American army in its retreat before Cornwallis. He was a preacher of the gospel, and one of the best men I ever knew, and so reported and esteemed among all his acquaintances; but it was pretty well ascertained, that he was at the time several miles distant from the theatre of his fancied achievement. Things are told to persons, till they verily believe that they witnessed them; and we repeat events until we are ready to swear in the utmost sincerity, that we are spectators of their occurrence.[16] [Emphasis added]

10. *Declaration as to Physical and Mental Condition*

This exception to the hearsay evidence rule is not directly applicable to genealogy.

OPINION EVIDENCE – EXPERT WITNESSES

Opinion evidence is a form of testimonial evidence. The general rule is that witnesses must testify only to the facts which they know of their own personal knowledge. An opinion is a *conclusion* which is a result of the intellect. As a general rule, *opinion evidence* is not admissible in a court proceeding, however, the testimony of an expert witness is admissible under specified conditions. Before a genealogist would be allowed to testify as an expert witness offering his opinion in regard to genealogical evidence or facts, it would be necessary to establish that he is qualified as an expert genealogist. The method of qualifying him to testify and state an opinion regarding the reliability or lack of reliability of genealogical information or records, is answering questions regarding his education, training, experience, and accomplishments as a professional genealogist or as a qualified nonprofessional.

A genealogist in everyday research is applying "opinion evidence" by forming conclusions regarding the reliability and authenticity of genealogical evidence or information in books and records. It is necessary to form a conclusion in the decision of whether to accept or reject the results of research. Hopefully, this is done in an expert manner.

Notes and References

1. Gilbert, Baron, *The Law of Evidence. . .*, Dublin 1754, p. 107.

2. National Society of the Daughters of the American Revolution, *Is That Lineage Right?*, Washington, D.C. 1958, p. 15.

3. Greenleaf, Simon, LL.D., *A Treatise on the Law of Evidence*, 12th Edition revised by Isaac F. Redfield, Volume 1, Boston 1866, pp. 114 et seq.

4. Ibid, note 3, pp. 114, 119 et seq.

5. Ibid, note 3, pp. 114 et seq.

6. Ibid, note 3, pp. 165 et seq.

7. Refer to the subject "Declarations of Pedigree and Family History" p. 196.

8. *Morewood v. Wood*, 14 East's Reports 327, 329.

9. Stevenson, Noel C., "Marriage Records Disclosed in Court Proceedings," *National Genealogical Society Quarterly*, September 1977, Vol. 65, p. 169 et seq.

10. Ibid. Note 7.

11. *Whitelocke v. Baker* (1807) 13 Ves.Jr. 514; 33 English Reports 385.

12. *Doe on the Demise of John Moffitt v. Joshua Witherspoon* (1849) 10 Iredell's Reports 192; 32 North Carolina Reports 145.

13. *California Evidence Code*, Section 1341.

14. Ibid, Sections 644, 645.

15. Ibid, Section 1550.

16. *Miller v. Cotten* (1848) 5 Georgia Reports 341, 348, 349.

PART V

GENEALOGICAL — LEGAL TERMINOLOGY

CHAPTER 23

DEFINITIONS OF WORDS, PHRASES, AND ABBREVIATIONS

"Most of the disputes in the world arise from words."
Lord Mansfield, C.J.
Morgan v. Jones (1773)
98 English Reports 587, 596

Many of the words and phrases of genealogical-legal significance are defined in the text of this book. In instances where words or phrases are not included in the following list, the index of this book should be consulted for the proper definition. If it is not included in the index, then legal dictionaries, such as *Black's Law Dictionary*, which has been published since 1891 by the West Publishing Company, should be consulted. The second edition, published in 1910, is suitable; and it should be possible to purchase a second-hand edition at a reasonable price from a dealer. Other law dictionaries available are just as helpful. One which may be of assistance to a non-lawyer is the *Law Dictionary of Practical Definitions*, by Edward J. Bander, LL.B., published in 1966 by Oceana Publications, Inc., Dobbs Ferry, New York. It is a short version for a law dictionary.

Also, many of the same words are included in standard unabridged dictionaries; for example, the G&C Merriam, second edition unabridged, published in 1949, is an extremely helpful source and is preferable to the newer and "jazzy" unabridged dictionaries published in recent years.

As it is impossible to compile a complete list of terms encountered in genealogical research, it is necessary to resort to the above described selective methods.

Ab esse absent.

Ab initio from the beginning.

Ab initio mundi from the beginning of the world.

Abstract a summary of the essential facts included in a document.

Abstract of title shortened versions of the documents affecting the title to land.

Action a lawsuit.

Action in personam a court proceeding commenced against a person rather than against property.

Action in rem a lawsuit the purpose of which is to determine the legal status of property.

Administration, Letters of a document issued by the court authorizing the administration of the estate of a deceased person in instances when an executor is not nominated in a will; or if named in the will, the executor or executrix fails, refuses, is deceased, or is unable to act or perform the duties of an executor. An administrator will be appointed by the court if there is no will or if the will is defective.

Administrator (male), Administratrix (female). (Refer to Administration, Letters of, and Administrator c.t.a.) Usually the administrator is a close relative of the deceased.

Administrator c.t.a. an abbreviation of Administrator cum testamento annexo, or with the will annexed.

Administrator cum testamento annexo an administrator with the will annexed appointed by the probate court in instances where there is a defective will, an executor is not nominated in a will, or if the person named as executor in will refuses or is unable to act.

Administrator d.b.n. refer to Administrator de bonis non, infra

Administrator de bonis non an administrator appointed by the court to distribute property discovered after the probate of an estate has been completed.

Advowson an ecclesiastical right or benefit.

Affiant a person who signs an affidavit.

Ancillary In probate proceedings, if the decedent owned property in more than one place, for example, more than one state, ancillary proceedings would be commenced for probate in the other state.

Appurtenant an "accessory" incidental to land in which a person owns an estate. Such as an easement or right of way across the land of another.

Assumpsit an agreement to perform an obligation, which if not performed may result in a lawsuit known as an "Action in assumpsit."

Attornment the act of accepting or recognizing a new landlord.

A vinculo refer to divorce.

Baron et feme husband and wife.

Bequest historically a gift of personal property by a testament. Modernly, the distinction between a testament and a will has been abolished.

Bill of Sale a document the purpose of which is to transfer title to personal property.

Bona fide good faith.

Capitation tax refer to poll tax, infra.

Caption the title, first lines or "heading" of a document, including court records.

Cause of Action the basis or reason for commencing a lawsuit.

Caveat a warning, a precautionary notice.

Caveat emptor literally, let the buyer beware.

Cestui Latin for "He."

Cestui que trust a beneficiary of property held by a trustee in trust. Refer to "trust" and "use" infra.

Cestui que use a person whose property was transferred for the benefit of another person. Refer to trusts, infra.

Cestui que vie a life estate transferred to a person.

Change of venue transfer of a court proceeding to a different court.

Chattels personal property.

Collateral relationship an indirect or distant relationship.

Common law unwritten law based on custom, usage and precedent which originated in England, as distinguished from the Civil Law of Rome.

Conservator similar to a guardian of a person and/or the person's estate.

Constructive notice the opposite to actual notice. It is notice with which a person is charged because of documents filed in the public or official records.

Contingent rights dependent to accrue on the happening of a future event.

Corporeal hereditaments right to inheritance of tangible property, e.g., an estate in land.

Corporeal rights tangible rights in property, such as an estate in land as opposed to "incorporeal rights," infra.

Croft a small parcel of land.

c.t.a., refer to Administrator cum testamento annexo, supra.

Curtesy the life estate of a widower in the lands of his deceased spouse, if he sired issue by her which were or was born alive.

d.b.n., *de bonis non*, refer to Administrator d.b.n., supra.

Declaration of Trust refer to trust, infra.

Deed a document in writing if signed and acknowledged by which an estate or interest in land is transferred from a grantor to a grantee; donor to donee — if a gift deed.

Deed Poll a deed executed or signed by one person only, even though other grantors were involved, and in some instances the names of the grantees were added later.

Demise a lease, transferring from a lessor to a lessee a leasehold estate for a term of years, for life, or "at the will" of the landlord.

Deponent a person who testifies before an officer (e.g., notary public) at a deposition hearing.

Deposition refer to deponent, supra – often confused with affidavits

Devise pertains to gifts of an interest in real property by means of a will.

Disseisin the ouster or removal of a person from possession of real property.

Divorce
   mensa et thoro (from bed and board) a type of legal separation, and
   divorce a vinculo absolute divorce.

Dower the interest of a widow in the freehold lands of her deceased husband, owned by him in fee simple, or fee tail during marriage. After the death of the husband, his widow is entitled to a one-third interest in his lands for the rest of her life.

Easement, right of way, a right or interest over or in lands of another person—a right of use but not the right of possession.

Eleemosynary relates to charitable purposes.

Eminent Domain the right and power of a government to condemn private property for public use if just compensation is paid the property owner.

Emptor a buyer.

Enfeoff to transfer to a person title in fee simple in lands. The act of feoffment.

Enjoin refer to injunction.

Entirety, Tenancy by, whereby the persons owning an interest in land both (or all) own the whole of the land. Similar to joint tenancy.

Equitable title one who owns an equitable title to property, possesses the right upon complying with certain conditions (e.g., payment of a mortgage or deed of trust) to require the transfer to him of the legal title to the property.

Equity of Redemption the right a mortgagor (debtor) to redeem after an action to foreclose a mortgage (or other evidence of debt) has commenced.

Escheat the reversion of property or money to the crown or government under some circumstances—e.g., unknown heirs to the property of an estate of a decedent.

Estate, Estates the interest which a person possesses or owns in lands or any other type of property. There are several types of estates, and may be absolute or conditional, the terminology of which will be disclosed in various types of records. Briefly these estates are:

Freehold estates (for a definition of freehold, refer infra.)

Fee simple absolute estates (not a conditional estate) q.v. infra.

Fee tail, or estates tail an estate of inheritance given to a man and the heirs of his body, or limited to certain classes of heirs.

Life estate an estate the duration of which is limited to the life of the person to whom it is transferred, or for the life of another or "pur autre vie." Dower, q.v. and curtesy, q.v., are what are known as legal life estates as they are created by operation of the law.

Less Than Freehold Estates: Refer to Estates for years.

Estate for years this is an estate created by a lease and often referred to as a "leasehold interest." Some leases are for lengthly periods of time. For example in England there are leases for hundreds of years. In the United States the term or length of leases are restricted to shorter periods.

Periodic tenancy a month to month tenancy is an example. The tenancy may be terminated by a month's written notice.

Tenancy at Will the tenancy continues so long as the landlord or the tenant wish to continue it. It may be terminated "at the will" of the landlord or the tenant upon notice.

ex dem upon the demise or lease of; Indication of a fictitious lawsuit for circumventing the laws regarding gaining possession of real property, or clearing title to it. Refer to Ejectment, Action for, in index this book.

ex rel upon the relation of e.g., Doe ex rel *John Smith vs. Jones*

Fee Simple absolute an estate or interest in lands without any limitation.

Feme Covert a woman who is married.

Feme sole a woman who is unmarried.

Filius nullius an illegitimate person.

Filius populi a child of the people—illegitimate child.

Freehold an estate or interest in land which may be transferred to heirs or others. A fee simple estate.

Habendum clause (habendum et tenedum) "To have and to hold to the grantee (buyer or donee) his heirs and assigns." The habendum clause is required to be included in some jurisdictions.

Headright Certificate provides for a head of a family to obtain a grant of land. Analogous to homestead grants.

Hypothecate similar to mortgaging.

Idem Sonans the doctrine of identical sounds due to variations in spelling. Example: Reynolds and Renols or Reynols would be considered the same name when this doctrine is applied.

Indenture a document, such as a deed by which two or more persons are involved (such as a seller and a buyer, or grantor and grantee). The word indenture is cutting of the two documents in half so that each copy will match if placed together at a future date.

In esse in being, i.e., alive.

Infra (Latin) Below.

Injunction power of a court to prohibit or require a person to do or not to do or perform a specific act by means of a mandatory injunction or prohibitory injunction or restraining order.

In propria persona an individual acting for himself or herself without an attorney.

In Terrorem Clause a provision in a will to warn legatees, beneficiaries or a specific heir to do or not do a certain act, such as marrying or be subject to the punishment of disinheritance. Such clauses are usually disregarded by the courts as against public policy.

Intestate a person who died without executing (signing) a will.

Intra Quatuor Maria within the four seas.

Jurat a certificate of a notary public or other authorized officer.

Laches an inexcusable delay in asserting a right.

Legatee a person who receives personal property as a result of a will or testament.

Life estates refer to Estates.

Lineal a descendant in the direct blood line.

Livery of seisin a delivery of the feudal possession or ownership of lands, now superseded by modern conveyancing by a written deed.

Mensa et thoro refer to divorce.

Mistery a trade or occupation. A master was required to teach an apprentice the "misteries" of whatever trade, or craft known to the master, e.g., printing, weaving, etc.

Mystery refer to mistery.

Nunc pro tunc—now for then—a nunc pro tunc order of a court is the means of correcting errors or omissions after the event.

Obiter dicta last words.

O.E.D. - Oxford English Dictionary.

Patent a type of deed or conveyance of government land to an individual.

Per stirpes the right of heirs to inherit according to blood relationship or ascent or descent of pedigree.

Per verba futuro words uttered in the future tense.

Per verba praesenti words uttered in the present tense.

Pleadings documents filed in court proceedings.

Poll Tax a tax levied on each head or person.

Pretermit to omit an heir from a will.

Primogeniture the superior or exclusive right possessed by the eldest son to succeed to the estate of his ancestor, but now obsolete.

Pur autre vie for the period of the life of another.

q.v. (Latin: quod vide) which see.

Restraining Order refer to Injunction.

Seisin refer to Livery of Seisin, supra.

Settlor a grantor or donor of property, a trustor.

Sic [Sic] So, thus to indicate an error, such as appearing in a record or other source the author does not correct.

Supra (Latin) Above.

Tenure in the modern sense tenure means the occupying or title to land and thus the right to rents and profits accruing from the land and improvements.

Testate decedent executed a will.

Testator a male who executed a will.

Testatrix female died leaving a will.

Testimonium clause at the conclusion of documents, "In witness whereof. . ."

Trust, an equitable or beneficial right or title to land or other property, held for the benefit of a person(s) known as the beneficiary.

Trust Deed, Deed of Trust similar to a mortgage, except there are three parties involved, a trustor (mortgagor if it was a mortgage) 2nd. a trustee, who holds the legal title during the existence of the trust, and a beneficiary, who is analogous to a mortgagee. Refer also to "trusts."

Trustee one who holds legal title to land or other property for the benefit of another person known as a beneficiary.

Tort a civil wrong other than a wrong involving contracts.

Use a trust, q.v.

Vendee buyer.

Vendor seller.

Venue involves the jurisdiction of a court.

Warrant, Warranty a guarantee e.g., a warranty deed.

Writ, Writs, historically a document (copied from a register of writs) delivered to a defendant notifying him to appear and defend a civil action or lawsuit commenced against him by a plaintiff. There were various types of writs. An example of a writ pertaining to a civil lawsuit was a "Writ of Ejectment," the purpose of which was for the recovery of the possession of lands. (Refer to "Ejectment," in Index.)

TABLE OF CASES

TABLE OF CASES

CHART OF RELATIONSHIPS *

Through a Common Ancestor

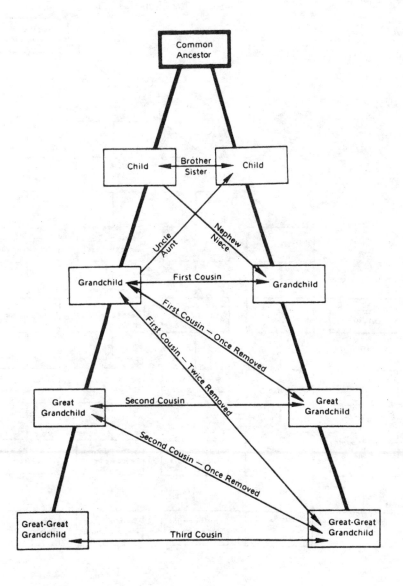

213

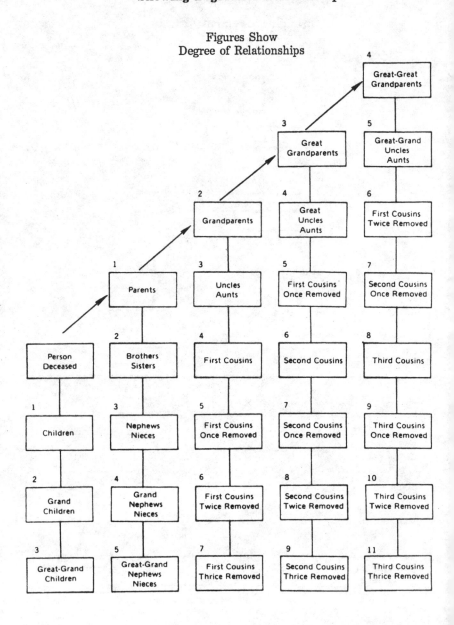

GENERAL RULES FOR JUDGING
RELIABILITY OF GENEALOGICAL SOURCES

Class	Source of Evidence	Type of Evidence	Rating of Evidence
1st	Testimony of Witnesses: Evidence from a witness who has personal knowledge of the facts sought to be proven. An "eye-witness."	Testimonial: Personal knowledge	Excellent—depending on the competency and credibility of the witness.
2nd	Official Records, such as vial, land, probate and other court records.	Hearsay	Excellent, but still hearsay. Nevertheless, apt to be correct in most cases.
3rd	Testimony of Witnesses: Evidence from a witness who does not know the facts from his own personal knowledge. (Testimonial family declarations.)	Testimonial: Hearsay	Generally reliable, but still hearsay. In isolated cases more reliable than Class 2.
4th	Private records, such as church, corporation and other business records.	Hearsay	Reliability varies greatly but generally dependable.
5th	Family records: Diaries, journals, letters, Bible records, and any other records compiles by a member of a family. (Documentary Family Declarations.)	Hearsay	Reliability varies from poor to reliable. If it is a contemporary record made by one having personal knowledge, rate it excellent.

Class	Source of Evidence	Type of Evidence	Rating of Evidence
6th	Newspaper files: Contemporary accounts of births, marriages, and deaths.	Hearsay.	Generally reliable. The hazard here is the informant and printers' errors.
7th	Family genealogies: Printed and manuscript works.	Hearsay	Poor to reliable. The test is who compiled the work and when, and from what sources.
8th	General printed works: County and other local histories. Newspaper accounts: Obituaries, biographies, genealogies which are not contemporary accounts.	Hearsay	Fair. Often unreliable, but there are some excellent local histories. Judge each on its merits.
9th	Traditions: Stories or information presumably passed from one generation to another.	Hearsay	Unreliable. It is necessary to search additional sources.
10th	Folklore: Legends, stories and other information not originating in the family.	Hearsay	Very unreliable.

Byham, Abraham, 125
    Miriam, 125
    Tabitha, 125

Camden, William, 43, 44, 52
Cases, Court records of, Refer to index: Table of Cases
Cattaraugus County, New York, 164
Cemetery records, 170-175
Census records, 134-141
    Interpretation of, 137
    Reliability of discussed, 137-141
    New York State Census, 141, 164
Centenarians, reputed, problem of, 19-20
Certified copies, risk of reliance on, 53, 188
Champlin, John D. Jr., 57, 58, 59
Chancery Courts, 106
Change of names, 22, 24, 109, 110
Charge account records as evidence, 174
Charlemagne, mania to establish descent from prevalent, 30
Charles II, issue of, 5, 40
Chetwode family, 30
Child bearing period and maternity, 7, 8
Children, illegitimate, status of, 3-7
    spacing of time between births in family, 7, 8
Christmas cards including genealogical data, evidence of, 174
Church affiliation and identity, 25
Church of England, parish registers, 158, 159
Church Records, 73, 158-161
    Non-conformist, 159
    Discussed and distinguished from official records, 158
    Reliability of, discussed, 158-161
City Official Records, summary of, 64
Civil actions, lawsuits, 103 et seq.
Civil Court actions, types of, 105-113
Coat of Arms (refer also to index: Heraldry) 30, 56-59
    Legality of, 56-59
    When included in family genealogies, legality questioned, 30
Coddington, John I, 16
Cokayne, G.E., 31, 40
Coke, Lord, 43, 81
Coldham, Peter Wilson, 28
Colket, Meredith B., 122
College of Arms, London, 153
Colonial Families of the United States of America, accuracy questioned, 18
Commercial genealogical publications, discussed and accuracy questioned,
    153, 154, 155
Common law marriage defined and discussed, 75 et seq.

Common Law Marriage in the Colonies and in the States after the
Formation of the Union.

Alabama, 93
Alaska, 93
Arizona, 93
Arkansas, 93
California, 94
Colorado, 94
Connecticut, 94
Delaware, 94
District of Columbia, 95
Florida, 95
Georgia, 95
Hawaii, 95
Idaho, 95
Illinois, 95
Indiana, 95
Iowa, 95
Kansas, 95
Kentucky, 96
Louisiana, 96
Maine, 96
Maryland, 96
Massachusetts, 96-97
Michigan, 97
Minnesota, 97
Mississippi, 97
Missouri, 97

Montana, 97
Nebraska, 98
Nevada, 98
New Hampshire, 98-99
New Jersey, 99
New Mexico, 99
New York, 99
North Carolina, 99, 100
North Dakota, 100
Ohio, 100
Oregon, 100
Oklahoma, 100
Pennsylvania, 100
Rhode Island, 100
South Carolina, 100-101
South Dakota, 101
Tennessee, 101
Texas, 101
Utah, 101
Vermont, 101-102
Virginia, 102
Washington, 102
West Virginia, 102
Wisconsin, 102
Wyoming, 102

Compendium of American Genealogy, Frederick A. Virkus, editor, 18,
154, 156, 185
Comstock, Lydia (married William Satteley Coon), 164
Condee, Newcomb, Judge, 122
Connecticut State Library, record collections, 66, 148
Connecticut Vital Records, 66, 73, 148
Convict immigrants, 24
Coon family, 164
Correspondence, family, as evidence, 174
Cotgreave family, 51, 52
Sir John, 52
Council of Trent (1563), 80
County and Local Histories, as evidence, 152, 153, 198
County records, summary of, 63, 64
Courts and Court Records, 103-122
Crandall, Capt. Joseph, 176
Credibility of evidence, 182-183
Crisp, Frederick Arthur, 174

Daly, Judge, (New York), 43
Daughters of the American Revolution, National Society of the, 200

Laborers, bound, 24
Lamb, Betty C., 116
Land Records, 123-133
    Check list to, 130-133
    Reliability of land records, 131-133
Lau family, 127
Lawsuits, civil examples of, 103-113
Law Times, The, 92
Leach, W. Barton, age and male fertility, 2
Legal pedigrees discussed, 180
Legendary pedigrees, 181
Legitimacy, 2-9, 90
Legitimacy, problem, twins with two different fathers identified, 10
Letters, family as evidence, 174
Library of Congress, 145, 146
Lie detector tests (polygraph) for identification, 27
Link family of Pennsylvania, 13
Link, John, 13
Lis Pendens, (notice of civil action pending), 109, 131
Local histories as evidence, 152, 153
Local official records, summary of, 63, 64
Longevity and identity, 19-20
Lord Eldon, 196, 197
Lord Kenyon, 193
Lord Mansfield, 46
Low family of Pennsylvania, 127
Low, Michael, 127
Lumpkin, Justice Joseph Henry, 198, 199

Mackenzie, George Norbury, 18
Macmillan Publishing Co., Inc., 69
McCracken, Dr. George E., 171, 175
Madison County, N.Y., 164
Magna Carta, 108
Magna Carta Barons, 30, 32
Magna Carta Book Co., 157
Mansfield, Lord, 46
Marriage, Marriages, 75-92
    Affinity and validity of marriage discussed, 77-78
    Age, marriageable, 76, 77
    American Indian marriages, 86
    Annulment of marriage, 90
    Bogus marriages, 84
    Capacity to marry, 76
    Ceremonial marriage, 77, 78
    Check List of marriage record sources, 86-89
    Circumstantial evidence, marriage established by, 89
    Common law marriage, 78-102

White, Elizabeth Pearson, 140
Wibird family, 151
William the Conqueror, 1, 30, 33, 36-40, 50, 147
Wilmot, Mary, 117
Wilmot, William, 117
Wills, and administration of estates, 112-121
Wills, Abstracting wills and probate records, 117, 118
Wills, Age and capacity and execution of, 113-114
Wills, Contents and text of, 114, 115
Wills, Types of wills, 114
Wills, Witnesses to, age and capacity, 113, 114
Wilson, Elijah, 125
Wintermute, family genealogy, 151
Wintermute, J.P., 151
Winthrop, Hannah, 127
Witnesses, age and capacity, 113, 114
Witnesses, expert and opinion evidence, 199
Witnesses, number of discussed, 183
Woodhull family, 30-33
Writ de Ventre Inspiciendo, 4